RENEGOTIATING CULTURAL *DIVERSITY* IN AMERICAN SCHOOLS

Edited by
PATRICIA PHELAN
ANN LOCKE DAVIDSON

Teachers College
Columbia University
New York and London

Published by Teachers College Press, 1234 Amsterdam Avenue
New York, NY 10027

Library of Congress Cataloging-in-Publication Data
Renegotiating cultural diversity in American schools / edited by
    Patricia Phelan, Ann Locke Davidson.
        p.   cm.
    Includes bibliographical references (p.) and index.
    ISBN 0-8077-3288-5. − ISBN 0-8077-3287-7 (pbk.)
    1. Multicultural education−United States−Congresses.
    2. Educational anthropology−United States−Congresses.
    3. Education−Social aspects−United States−Congresses.
    I. Phelan, Patricia.   II. Davidson, Ann Locke.
    LC1099.3.R46 1993
    370.19'6'0973−dc20   93-22720

ISBN 0-8077-3288-5
ISBN 0-8077-3287-7 (pbk.)
Printed on acid-free paper

Manufactured in the United States of America

98 97 96 95 94 93   8 7 6 5 4 3 2 1

For George and Louise Spindler, who have unfailingly mentored, nurtured, and supported us.

CONTENTS

PREFACE

The chapters in this volume grew out of papers commissioned by Stanford's Center for Research on the Context of Secondary School Teaching for presentation at a working conference, "Cultural Diversity: Implications for Education," held in October 1991. The Center was established in the fall of 1987, through funding by the Office of Educational Research and Improvement (OERI), U.S. Department of Education (Grant No. G0087C0234), with the goal of advancing knowledge of contextual factors that affect secondary-school teachers and teaching. The analyses and conclusions presented in this book do not necessarily reflect the views or policies of OERI.

With changing student demography and cultural diversity a foremost concern for many of the teachers interviewed by Center researchers, this conference grew naturally out of the Center's mission. Each of the scholars attending offered work that deepened our understanding of diversity as a lived experience in schools and classrooms, whereas the professional educators invited to discuss, critique, and comment on the implications of this work asked questions and offered analyses often forgotten or ignored by those engaged in educational research. The voices and ideas of students and parents, prominent in some chapters, generated a wealth of ideas for discussion among conference participants; descriptions of the meaningful ways in which teachers and school personnel have approached cultural, ethnic, and linguistic diversity as a resource provided new insights into ways that the understandings generated from research can be applied.

We hope that our readers will find, as we have, that the work provided here offers new insights and understandings into renegotiating cultural diversity in American schools.

Acknowledgments

Both the Stanford University conference on Cultural Diversity in October 1991 and this book would not have been possible without the support and encouragement of Milbrey W. McLaughlin, Director, Center for Research on the Context of Secondary School Teaching; Joan Talbert, Associate Director; Hanh Cao Yu, Research Assistant; and, Juliann Cummer, Project Administrator. We would also like to thank George and Louise Spindler and Henry T. Trueba who provided invaluable assistance in planning the conference, and Harry Handler for his skill, patience, and humor in facilitating the conference proceedings. Overall, we have found it a great pleasure and privilege to work with all of the contributors to this book.

INTRODUCTION

CULTURAL DIVERSITY AND ITS IMPLICATIONS FOR SCHOOLING: A CONTINUING AMERICAN DIALOGUE

Ann Locke Davidson and Patricia Phelan

It could be said that cultural diversity is the topic of the 1990s. While politicians, policymakers, authors, and educators raise issues and grapple with questions surrounding an increasingly diverse population, contemporary media (films, television, newspapers, and magazines) remind us daily that we live in a country where diversity prevails. We are told, for example, that "the 'browning of America' will alter everything in society, from politics and education to industry, values and culture" ("Beyond the Melting Pot," 1990, p. 28). Likewise, newspapers evidence daily the public's growing interest and concern: "Why Latinos Drop Out," "Ethnic Clash in Central Valley: An Immigration Lab for U.S.," "Melting Pot May Come to Boil," and "The Culture Question" are just a few of the headlines that San Francisco Bay Area residents woke up to in 1991. Further, the commercial successes of *Boyz in the Hood*, *Do the Right Thing*, and *Mississippi Masala*, as well as the visibility of such disparate personalities as Jesse Jackson and David Duke, remind us that issues emanating from diversity and social stratification are taken seriously by people across the political spectrum. And indeed, demographic figures indicate that they should be. Today, children of color are the majority in 25 of the largest school districts in the country, and by the year 2000 one-third of the total U.S. school population will be children and youth currently referred to as "minorities" ("Here They Come," 1986).

The growing attention to our nation's changing demography makes it easy to forget that interest and concern about matters of diversity have been reoccurrent in American history. While it is often assumed that the

1

children of southern and eastern European immigrants coming to America in the late 1800s willingly and easily assimilated to America's Anglo-centered culture (Montero-Sieburth & LaCelle-Peterson, 1991), we know that among immigrant children there was a high rate of "educational retardation" in the early twentieth century. In fact, relatively few of these children completed high school (Ravitch, 1983). Moreover, although many immigrant parents welcomed the opportunity that the common school gave their children to learn American ways, historian Carl Kaestle (1983) reminds us that "American immigrants' confrontation with the dominant culture involved a mixture of accommodation and resistance, of assimilation and cultural maintenance, of cooperation and conflict"[1] (p. 161). These themes remain prominent today.

This book, the outcome of a 1991 conference on cultural diversity at Stanford University, is a part of the continuing American dialogue on the meaning and implications of cultural diversity for American schools. The Stanford conference, sponsored by the Center for Research on the Context of Secondary School Teaching,[2] brought together educational researchers and professional educators to explore the applicability of current research to schools and learning. The ideas generated at the conference and included in this volume are intended primarily for two audiences—first, those who face daily the complexities of building optimal learning environments for diverse student populations (professional educators) and second, those concerned with generating new ideas and articulating clearer understandings of the intersection of culture, ethnicity, and learning (educational researchers).

Our own experiences as researchers working in urban high schools for three years have heightened our awareness of how much we have to learn from being in the field. At the same time, educators tell us repeatedly that they are hungry for ideas and information that will help them to reflect on their work and enable them to better serve their student populations. Because we were increasingly convinced that bridges must be built to enable researchers and professional educators to join forces in efforts to optimize learning environments for *all* students, we embarked on planning the Stanford conference. Our goal was to provide a forum where scholars and practitioners could come together to explore the applicability and relevance to schools and learning of a variety of models, frames of reference, ideas, and theories grounded in empirical work. We were particularly motivated by our knowledge that connections between research, policy, and practice are frequently weak.

The issues explored at the conference were diverse, though many were relevant to circumstances we had encountered during our time in the schools: the differences in attitude, and often achievement, of immigrant and domestic minority youth; the consequences of tracking; the psychosocial costs to students of having to adjust to new and different cultural circumstances; the dynamics and consequences of second language acquisition; the implications of home, school, and community relationships; and the overall circumstances in the society that impact people's lives in schools. This volume represents the consolidation of ideas generated around these issues and provides a compendium of some of the recent scholarly thinking relevant to culturally diverse school populations.

CONCEPTIONS OF DIVERSITY FROM THE FIELD

It is not unlikely that schools, more than any other arena, are the stage on which issues of cultural diversity are being played out in the society. Our own experience in urban, desegregated high schools in California reminds us that schools, as microcosms of society, mirror many of society's issues. We find that cultural diversity, perhaps more than any other topic, is a matter of concern to teachers and students. Questions about cultural and linguistic differences, debates about transportation programs, worries about gangs, assumptions about tracking, frustrations with culturally diverse parents, and a variety of other problems cross-cut almost every aspect of peoples' lives and thoughts as they navigate the multicultural environments in which they find themselves. Here we briefly describe dynamics and circumstances we found during our time in school settings that prompted us to initiate the Stanford conference.

Teachers

A Science Teacher: Let me go back to the first day I walked into this classroom and I looked out, and [saw] blonde hair and blue eyes. I mean all Caucasian. I think we were 98 percent Caucasian. And I'd come from a school that was 65 percent Latino. And so it was different. It was just different. And it was pleasant from the standpoint that it was quiet and everybody was polite and didn't bother one another and so on. But it also, after a few years, became a little bit boring? And I would hear racial comments from the predominantly white students—not picking on students who were ethnically different, I didn't see a lot of that here—but just because everybody here was white, why not tell an ethnic joke? And do those sorts of things. And it would bother me. It

would bother me to some degree and I found myself ignoring it. I
would ignore it because it was easier to ignore and so I was happy
when we started bringing some diversity in. (RA057ST1:1160–
1189)[3]

A Principal: The faculty feel "We had a perfectly good school, look
what they've done to us." [referring to desegregation]. . . . The
faculty frustration level has risen by leaps and bounds. . . .
Teachers who've been here for years and now have different
kids . . . a lot are old and have no capacity to change.
(ES06801:257–261, 164–175)

For teachers, conceptions of diversity frequently stem from the challenges they face in working with students they perceive as dramatically
different from students in years past. Almost all agree that the pedagogical demands associated with diverse student populations are greater and
more complex than ever before. At the same time, as McLaughlin (1992)
so aptly points out, ". . . teachers' interpretations of students' behavior and
performance, their construction of 'student,' varies profoundly" (p. 11).
For some teachers, diverse student populations provide a catalyst for further training, the development of relevant curricula, and an opportunity
to expand their teaching repertoires. Many of these teachers express genu-
ine concern for individual students' needs and make special efforts to
understand and respond to the unique features of the cultural backgrounds from which their students come. Although frequently referring
to problems they associate with increased immigration or youth from low-
income backgrounds—a higher turnover rate, lower skill levels, more
absenteeism, transportation issues—many are determined to tailor their
pedagogical methods to the distinctive characteristics of the students with
whom they work. In fact, some become advocates for a curriculum that
will empower, rather than impoverish, the chances for *all* youth to succeed.
    For other teachers, diversity is viewed as a problem that dominates
their thoughts and actions and provides a rationale for their inability to
relate to, or positively impact, their clientele. What they teach, how they
teach, and the environments they create are the same as in years past when
their students possessed cultural characteristics similar to their own. For
these teachers, conceptions of cultural diversity are found in their descriptions of the inability of students to fit in and act as they "should" and in
their pejorative comments about students' parents, home lives, neighborhoods, and cultural backgrounds. Many of these teachers believe that a
good number of their students are not capable of succeeding and, as a
consequence, abdicate any responsibility for helping them to do so.

Students

Students, like teachers, have questions and concerns about the increasing diversity of the student population. Students' interactions with peers and relationships with teachers, and the ways in which schools are currently structured are just a few of the factors that impact students' conceptions of their own ethnicity and that of others. Classrooms, teachers, peer groups, and schools can all powerfully affect the ways in which students view and interpret their circumstances. For example, in one school in which we worked, tension and hostility between ethnic groups permeates the air (Phelan, Davidson, & Cao, 1992). In this particular setting, minority youth speak frequently of the discrimination they experience, whereas European-American, mainstream students describe their fear and misunderstanding of those different from themselves.

> *Filipina-American female:* I don't know, I guess they are not willing to integrate or they don't really want to. Sometimes I'm fine. But like walking with a friend, there are these two [European-American] guys and they're like saying, "New York City, here comes de' pogam" [reference to these students' status as transported students]. I hate that, it's like "oh my God," and I try to ignore them but. . . . (OR09STA:113–128)

> *African-American male:* I don't mess with the Hispanic kids because most of them are—I can't talk to them—most of them seem pretty cool. But it's stupid to mess with them, because you don't know what kind of people they are, like, they could hurt you actually if you don't know them. You don't know what they're about, so [it's] best not to mess with them. (ES51STA:315–324)

Comments such as these contrast dramatically with those from youth in other schools where boundaries are fluid and students navigate cultural borders with relative ease.

> *European-American female:* The whites hang out with everyone, and the blacks and the Mexicans and there's the Chinese—everyone hangs out together. Everyone gets along . . . I have lot of good friends that live in northeast [area from which students are transported] . . . everyone hangs out together. (OR06STA:449–461)

Although almost all students agree that the quality of peer interactions—particularly among culturally diverse groups—has a significant effect

on their feelings about school, they also speak intensely about the importance of adults. Negative messages embedded in teacher-adolescent relationships are particularly troubling and influence students' conceptions
of their diverse environments. In one school, for example, we watched as
the enthusiasm and hope of newly arrived immigrants (described by scholars such as the Suarez-Oroscos in this volume) gave way to a sober and
skeptical view of their circumstances. As students encounter stereotypes
about their abilities, assignments to low-track classes, and adults who seem
to have little time and even less inclination to assist them, their desire to
succeed is tempered. "Marbella," a 16-year-old, high achieving female,
Mexican immigrant, is an example:

> I think my teachers should learn another method of teaching,
> because the one they use is not very effective. I also would like
> them to realize we are intelligent, that we can do things, would
> like them not to discriminate against us, to treat us like civilized
> persons, not like some sort of objects. (ES50STC: written protocol)

As a freshman, Marbella spoke eagerly of her desire to learn English
and attend an American college. Channeled into basic math like most
recently arrived immigrants in her school, Marbella fought for access to
higher level courses. Yet, by the end of her sophomore year, encounters
with American-born peers who taunted her about her immigrant language
and status, her feelings of academic and cultural marginalization, and the
lack of positive recognition she received from the adults in her environment left her feeling increasingly powerless and reluctant to interact with
others.

> In the [one] class where I have contact with Americans, well, I
> simply don't speak to them . . . I apply myself to my homework
> and don't pay attention to them. They think that they are better
> than us. They think that because we are in their country, we are
> underneath them. That makes us afraid to talk to them in English
> because we think they will laugh at us. (ES50STD:939–971)

Well aware of this dynamic, the school's English as a Second Language
(ESL) resource teacher comments: ". . . the students that come here tend
to be just arriving from Mexico, and they still have a lot of high expectations that you can build on. When students have been here a few years,
that rubs off. And they kind of lose their enthusiasm, and their spirit,
and their hope" (ES090ST1:438–446).

Although Marbella has been able to maintain her high academic achievement, two years in this American high school have tempered her hopes and transformed the outgoing and enthusiastic student we first encountered into a far more cautious youth. We watched sadly as Marbella's initial openness and excitement about being in a new school and country gave way to a fearful and defensive stance.

Finally, for many students, conceptions of diversity stem from their encounters with school structures. Of particular significance are the meanings students attach to their experiences of stratification—characterized most frequently by academic tracking. Although it is no surprise that almost all youth are aware that some ethnic groups are clustered in low-track classes, these divisions are a powerful means of shaping students' views.

> *Wendy, European-American female:* My accelerated classes . . . most of the people that are in there are white. Or Oriental, now—it used to be just white—'cause they're certainly smart, and hard workers. (ES47STEN:1863–1887)
>
> *Joey, African-American male:* 'Cause mostly the advanced kids are the real smart students and most of the people here, they ain't.
>
> *Interviewer:* And who are the real smart students?
>
> *Joey:* Mostly Vietnamese, boys and girls, most of them. And girls. Mostly Vietnamese and girls. There's some guys I guess.
>
> *Interviewer:* Are there any black students in the advanced track here?
>
> *Joey:* I think there might be one. Not in my grade level that I know of. (ES51STD: 432–450)

Although some educators make attempts to integrate academically diverse youth, for the most part we find that advanced level classes are dominated by European-American and Asian-American students. For the few youth of color from underrepresented groups who do attend these classes, the circumstances they encounter are not always positive.

> *Patricia, Latina female:* Well, the only problem I can see in the advanced classes is that there's a majority of . . . white kids. And sometimes we have—like first semester we used to have—class discussions with our student teacher. . . . And they [the white students] used to like sort of put, you know, the other races down. And it used to, you know, sometimes I wanted to blow my top. . . .
>
> *Interviewer:* Did you say anything?

Patricia: I don't remember, but I don't think I did. I was just—I couldn't because I knew if I started I wasn't going to stop, I wasn't. It just got me mad. I just held it in. (VA17STD:1112–1140, 1181–1190)

Only one European-American middle-class female in our study expressed regret that there are few Latino youth in her advanced level courses. For this student, academic stratification hinders her expressed desire to develop friendships with culturally diverse youth. Although some mainstream students comment little on the effects of stratification, for others tracking serves to solidify their stereotypes and add to their disdain for students whose backgrounds are different than their own. From the perspective of these students, conceptions of diversity are bound in negative messages that reinforce their belief that social divisions are justified.

Working and going to school with people of varying backgrounds is a salient feature in both the substance and process of what happens in educational settings. For teachers, as well as for students, issues emanating from participation in culturally diverse environments abound—affecting their lives, shaping their conceptions, altering their views.

CONCEPTIONS OF DIVERSITY: AN HISTORICAL PERSPECTIVE

The ideas presented in this book grow out of a long history of scholarly writing and research that seeks to understand the implications of cultural diversity for the U.S. As knowledge has been produced, it has also been used to shape educational policies and influence people's orientations toward both immigrant and domestic minority groups. Interestingly, many of today's concerns are little different than those in years past. For example, as early as the mid-1800s, American scholars and educators, as well as the general public, expressed dismay and apprehension at the arrival of large numbers of impoverished Irish Catholics, Germans, and Scandinavians (the "old immigration"). As thousands of Southern and Eastern Europeans arrived steadily through the mid-1920s, people's concerns turned into demands for immigration restrictions on incoming groups. Summarizing the situation at the turn of the century, historian Lawrence Cremin (1964) writes:

> For settlement workers laboring in the ghetto-slums of the cities, the fundamental problems remained wealth, corruption, and the unwillingness of

the privileged to share their knowledge and ideals with the poor. For others equally dedicated to reform, however, the problems lay more directly with the unfortunates themselves. Social Gospel ministers denounced the high rates of crime and immorality among the immigrants, speaking vaguely in the language of racial origins; unionists blamed the newcomers for unemployment and declining wage rates; while municipal leaders voiced alarm over the boss-ridden immigrant vote. A growing chorus of voices began to demand restrictionist laws as the most rapid and painless way of combating the corruption, the squalor and the injustice of urban industrialism. (p. 67)

Even those groups that had relatively high rates of academic success were criticized. In 1936, for example, the editors of *Fortune* magazine devoted their entire February issue to "Jews in America," commenting:

Can this universal stranger be absorbed in the country which has absorbed every other European stock? The other immigrant groups accept the culture of the country into which they come . . . the Jews for centuries have refused to accept it and are now, in many cases, unable to accept it when they would. The habit of pride . . . is too strong in them. (Quoted in Silberman, 1985, p. 56)

In a move similar to that of today, universities adopted quotas designed to insure that children of immigrants were not too prominently represented in U.S. colleges. At Harvard, for example, the number of non-Anglo students was limited to 15% (Silberman, 1985, p. 54).

Conceptions of American cultural diversity stem historically from three primary philosophical positions (Gordon, 1964):

1. Assimilation/Anglo conformity is based on the conviction that newcomers to this country must adapt the values, beliefs, behaviors, and lifestyle of mainstream Anglo citizens;
2. Amalgamation (the "melting pot"), takes the view that the society is and should be a composite or blend resulting from the mixture of diverse peoples;
3. Proponents of cultural pluralism argue that it is possible and desirable for people to retain their native culture and, at the same time, to acquire the competencies necessary for functioning in America.

In the following section, we briefly describe these positions and discuss their influence on public education policies in the U.S. In addition, we locate this book philosophically in the context of cultural pluralism, summarizing the contributions in this volume and identifying the princi-

pal beliefs, ideals, and assumptions that underlie the ideas and convictions of the authors in this book.

Assimilation/Anglo Conformity and "Melting Pot" Ideals

Both assimilation/Anglo conformity and "melting pot" ideals stem
from functionalist theories of ethnicity that see ethnic solidarity as contradictory to the unity necessary in a modernized society (Shamai,
1987). An assimilation/conformity ideal assumes the desirability of maintaining English institutions, the English language, and English-oriented
cultural patterns as the standard for American life (Gordon, 1964). Both
historically and today, positions within this general framework vary widely—
from those who view the rapidly changing demography as a threat to the
"pure" America they envision (that is, purely of Northern European
descent) to those who tolerate the arrival of culturally and ethnically different individuals as long as they adopt Anglo, mainstream cultural patterns. A letter written by John Quincy Adams in 1818, when he was Secretary of State, sums up the latter position well:

> They come to a life of independence, but to a life of labor—and if they cannot
> accommodate themselves to the character, moral, political and physical, of
> this country with all its compensating balances of good and evil, the Atlan-
> tic is always open to them to return to the land of their nativity and their
> fathers. To one thing, they must make up their minds, or they will be dis-
> appointed in every expectation of happiness as Americans. They must cast
> off the European skin, never to resume it. (Quoted in Gordon, 1964, p. 94)

Today, these beliefs are played out in language policies (e.g., English-only
legislation), in programs and practices predicated on the assumption that
culturally different children are either genetically or culturally inferior to
their mainstream counterparts (i.e., training parents to socialize their
children "correctly"), and in comments made in day-to-day conversations
(ethnic Americans are merely "guests"). In the latter case, "guest" implies
politeness, deferential behavior towards the host, and the implicit expectation that one must not stay forever (Silberman, 1985).

In contrast, the "melting pot" or amalgamation ideal assumes that
an evolving American society is not, and should not be, a modified
England, but rather a totally new blend, a "melting pot" in which the contributions of various cultures have and can continue to play a prominent
role (Gordon, 1964). The early conceptual underpinnings for this position were laid by Frederick Jackson Turner (1920), who in 1983 argued
that "the frontier promoted the formation of a composite nationality for
the American people. . . . In the crucible of the frontier the immigrants

were Americanized, liberated and fused into a mixed race, English in neither nationality or characteristics" (pp. 22-23). Turner's ideas were popularized in *The Melting Pot*, a drama by Israel Zangwill (1909):

> America is God's crucible, the great Melting Pot where all the races of Europe are melting and re-forming! Here you stand, good folk, think I, when I see them at Ellis Island, here you stand in your fifty groups, with your fifty languages and histories, and your fifty blood hatreds and rivalries. But you won't be long like that, brothers, for these are the fires of God you've come to—there are the fires of God. A fig for your feuds and vendettas! Germans and Frenchmen, Irishmen and Englishmen, Jews and Russians—into the Crucible with you all! God is making the American. (p. 37)

Proponents of the amalgamation position see immigrant and domestic minorities as "melting" into the mainstream. They believe that in the process society will be transformed into something different than before. The melting pot ideal has and continues to be embedded in both the rhetoric and the textbooks of America. Yet its accuracy for what has actually taken place within the U.S. is highly questionable, both with regard to Southern and Eastern Europeans and indigenous ethnic minority groups. As Herberg (1955) points out, although "Our American cuisine includes antipasto and spaghetti, frankfurters and pumpernickel, filet mignon and french fried potatoes . . . it would be a mistake to infer from this that the American's image of himself is a composite or synthesis of the ethnic elements that have gone into the making of the American." For a substantial proportion of our nation, an American ideal centers around "the Anglo-American ideal as it was at the beginning of our independent existence. The 'national' type as ideal has always been, and remains, pretty well fixed. It is the Mayflower, John Smith, Davy Crockett, George Washington and Abraham Lincoln" (Herberg, quoted in Gordon, 1964, p. 128).

Regardless of whether individuals espouse an assimilation or melting pot ideal, in practice the dominant ideology shaping American public school policy through much of our history has been that of assimilation. At the turn of the century, for example, with public high school enrollments skyrocketing, urbanization and industrialization increasing, and waves of new immigrants arriving, educational leaders sought to make education more relevant to changing social conditions. The progressive educational movement (1890-1950), stressing diversity, unity of school and community, and child-centered instruction, was born out of this desire for reform. Progressive ideology demanded a curriculum sensitive to the needs of the families and communities of all students. At the same time, influenced by the application of Darwin's theory of evolution to social and cultural systems, many educators assumed that Southern and Eastern European immigrants were genetically or culturally inferior to their Northern European counterparts (Tyack, 1974).[4] Ellwood P. Cubberly (1909), one of the most influential leaders in school administration at the time, voiced a commonly held assumption:

> These southern and eastern Europeans are of a very different type from the north Europeans who preceded them. Illiterate, docile, lacking in self-reliance and initiative, and not possessing the Anglo-Teutonic conceptions of law, order and government, their coming has served to dilute tremendously our national stock, and to corrupt our civic life. . . . Our task is to break up these groups or settlements, to assimilate and amalgamate these people as a part of our American race, and to implant in their children, so far as can be done, the Anglo-Saxon conception of righteousness, law and order, and popular government, and to awaken in them a reverence for our democratic institutions and for those things in our national life which we as a people hold to be of abiding worth. (p. 90)

Based on a conviction about the need for relevant education and negative assumptions about immigrant cultures, instruction about manners and cleanliness were introduced into school lessons in an effort to transform immigrants into Americans (Cremin, 1964, p. 72). Moreover, using intelligence and scholastic achievement testing as an ostensibly unbiased means to measure students' intelligence, public educators shuttled immigrants, particularly prone to low intelligence scores on these tests (Cohen, 1970), directly into vocational classes.[5] As some scholars have pointed out, rather than meeting the needs of immigrants, educators by and large met the needs of both the state and the economy by assigning immigrant students to educational tracks that would teach them to be obedient citizens and dutiful workers (Bowles & Gintis, 1976).

The adoption of restrictive immigration legislation beginning in 1921 temporarily stemmed the public outcry for the Americanization of culturally different youth. However, when African Americans left the rural areas of the South for urban areas in record numbers during the decade following World War II, concerns again arose. As urban slums grew and civil rights activism brought into focus the high unemployment rates, lack of education, and inadequate schooling and housing of African Americans, fear of racial disorder grew. In the early sixties, James Conant (1961), then president of Harvard University, expressed a widely shared sense of foreboding:

> When one considers the total situation that has been developing in the Negro city slums since World War II, one has reason to worry about the

future. The building up of a mass of unemployed and frustrated Negro youth in congested areas of the city is a social phenomenon that may be compared to the piling up of flammable material in an empty building in a city block. (pp. 24–25)

Out of a concern for the decline of urban education and dissatisfaction with the common belief that African-American children and children from low-income families did poorly in school because of genetic inferiority, educational scholars turned their attention to exploring the environmental determinants of learning. Much of this research focused on the effects of poverty on the African-American child's learning process, portraying these children's home environments as cognitively unstimulating places. For example, these scholars argued that poor parents had less time to read to, talk to, and interact with their children, and concluded from this that their children's acquisition of language skills is dampened. Compared to the middle-class home, the poor were said to have few books, toys, and games—items considered necessary precursors to educational success. In contrast, these researchers noted that the middle-class child was rewarded for paying attention and learning to learn, taught to defer gratification for future goals, and taught to look to adults for information and approval (cf. Bereiter & Engelmann, 1966; Deutsch, 1967; Hess & Shipman, 1965).

Cultural Pluralism Ideals

Discontent with both assimilation and melting pot theories was being voiced as early as 1915, but criticisms came to a head in the mid-1960s when the debate over racial issues expanded. The call for black power was followed by the demands of Chicanos, Native Americans, and other ethnic groups for an end to the assimilationist ideal, the legitimation of their ethnic differences, and equal access to educational and economic opportunity. At the public school level, scholars and activists pointed out the "ethnic distortions, stereotypes, omissions and misinformation" in textbooks (Gay, 1983, p. 561), and argued that their children were educationally damaged by being forced to deny their native culture in the classroom.[6]

Anthropologists and some sociolinguists were very much a part of this national trend, as they devoted their efforts to pointing out the cultural biases in previous portraits of culturally diverse children. While aware that minority children's upbringings are often different from those of middle-class European-American children, such scholars pointed out that it is a significant leap from these observations to conclude that the academic failure of some minority children stems from the fact that they have not learned how to learn. These criticisms brought into question the assumptions and methodology that had informed earlier research. As sociolinguist William Labov (1969) pointed out:

> In the literature we find very little direct observation of verbal interaction in the Negro home; most typically, the investigators ask the child if he has dinner with his parents, and if he engages in dinner-table conversation with them. He is also asked whether his family takes him on trips to museums and other cultural activities. This slender thread of evidence is used to explain and interpret the large body of tests carried out in the laboratory and school. (p. 183)

Beginning in the 1960s, a series of ethnographic and sociolinguistic studies demonstrated that students of color and poor children are not, in fact, deprived of stimulating learning environments. Labov (1969), for example, provided detailed descriptions of the conversations of urban African-American youth to support his argument and concluded that:

> In fact, Negro children in the urban ghettoes receive a great deal of verbal stimulation, hear more well-formed sentences than middle-class children, and participate fully in a highly verbal culture; they have the same basic vocabulary, possess the same capacity for conceptual learning, and use the same logic as anyone else who learns to speak and understand English. (p. 179)

Ethnographies of Native Hawaiians (Gallimore, Boggs, & Jordan, 1974) and various Native American communities (cf. Cazden & John, 1971; John, 1972; Philips, 1972, 1982) provided further evidence of the rich learning environments that can characterize culturally different homes.

Critiques concerning the cultural biases embedded in the policy and research oriented toward culturally diverse children are rooted in ideals of cultural pluralism, an ideal first enunciated by Horace Kallen (1915), a Harvard philosopher. Cultural pluralism rejects both assimilation and melting pot theories, arguing that these are neither correct models for what has transpired in American society nor appropriate ideals for a democracy (Gordon, 1964). The continuing prevalence of Greek, Italian, Polish, and Jewish neighborhoods on the East Coast and the existence of churches, clubs, and social organizations catering to ethnic group members indicate that even for those groups considered to be assimilated, *acculturated* might be a more appropriate term. Indeed, as Portes and Rumbaut (1990) point out, the descendants of late 19th- and early 20th-century immigrants, particularly those from Mediterranean and non-European countries, tend to remain in their original areas of settlement.

Cultural pluralism is predicated on three basic assumptions (Gordon, 1964). First, there is no necessary contradiction between parts of one's cultural heritage and modernization; one can retain one's subculture while acquiring the cultural, educational, and economic competencies to operate within other cultural systems. This is an important point in that pluralism is often confused with separatism. Whereas separatist movements desire to establish their own governmental and economic systems, pluralism assumes membership in a common body politic and some interaction between groups. It also assumes that one can remain committed to one's home language and culture while remaining loyal to the nation as a whole. There are numerous examples of this among ethnic groups in the U.S. For example, although Miami's Cuban Americans are sometimes criticized for their public use of Spanish and for settling in ethnic communities, they are in fact active politically and highly verbal in their support of American democratic processes. And, as Portes and Rumbaut (1990) point out, "perhaps the most telling case against nativist fears is that of Mexican Americans in the Southwest. Despite the large size of this minority, its proximity to the home country, and the fact that these territories were once Mexico's, secessionist movements within the Mexican American population have been insignificant" (p. 55).

A second assumption underlying cultural pluralism is that nations derive positive value from diversity, both directly as ethnic groups contribute elements from their cultural heritages to the total national culture, and indirectly as the end product of the competition, interaction, and creative relationships that derive from the interaction between various groups. Diversity can and often does imply conflict; however, such conflict is not necessarily negative. Indeed, it is consistent with our nation's democratic system and with our system of checks and balances.

Third, for cultural pluralist ideals to be achieved there must be relative parity and equality between and among groups. Given that this is not the case in contemporary America, pluralists tend to be concerned with matters of social stratification as well as diversity.

As in the case of those who argue for assimilation, cultural pluralists differ, both with respect to specific goals and to educational approaches. In classical cultural pluralism, for example, the emphasis is on maintaining the integrity and viability of the cultural group. Education, for the most part, is under the control of the social group and is designed for the enculturation and socialization of children to its cultural norms (Appleton, 1983). In contemporary American society, the cases of the

Amish and Hasidic Jews, as well as some of the recent efforts to establish schools for African-American males, stand out as examples.

Modified cultural pluralism places a much greater emphasis on interactions between members of different groups. Groups with a common cultural heritage maintain a degree of distinctiveness but also see themselves as belonging and contributing to mainstream American culture and society in a significant way (Appleton, 1983). Modified cultural pluralism allows for change in groups over time, as well as for the ability of individuals to develop bicultural abilities. Education ideally develops respect for and understanding and tolerance of cultural diversity (Appleton, 1983). In addition, because lack of respect and intolerance are related to economic and political stratification, we believe that education for modified cultural pluralism should also provide youth with an understanding of the sources and means to act against political, economic, and racial discrimination.

Finally, some have argued for a new pluralism, whose key thrust is to provide individuals the right and opportunity to make of their cultural heritage and identity what they desire. Within this philosophical framework, evolution is implied; ideally, individuals can develop bicultural or blended identities. As such, in addition to providing the understandings associated with modified cultural pluralism, education ideally also provides individuals with the opportunity to become consciously aware of the values, beliefs, feelings, and behaviors they grow up with and take for granted, as well as the critical skills to evaluate these values and beliefs (Appleton, 1983).

The authors in this volume write primarily from the second and third perspectives. Fueled by the desire for a community that acknowledges differences but realizes the necessity of intergroup cooperation, these authors envision America as becoming what we might term a state of united and evolving cultures. Their contributions are anticipated in the following section.

CONTRIBUTIONS TO THIS VOLUME

The authors of the chapters in this book derive their frames of reference primarily from anthropology and sociolinguistic theory. Although they recognize the educational challenges associated with cultural diversity, the authors see these difficulties as stemming from cultural differences, a group's history with economic and political stratification, and practices institutionalized in the culture of schooling. They are concerned both with the way that differences between groups of people become valorized and in understanding the ways in which individuals perceive and react to these meanings.

The first two chapters of this volume deal primarily with understanding the implications of culture—as embedded in the values, beliefs, expectations, sanctions, and behaviors that characterize social settings—for educational processes. There is considerable evidence to indicate that cultural differences can generate interactional difficulties in the classroom. Studies of African-American (Heath, 1982), Mexican-American (Delgado-Gaitan, 1987), Native-Hawaiian (Au, 1980; Au & Jordan, 1981) and Native-American (Erickson & Mohatt, 1982; Philips, 1972, 1982) communities have documented differences between school children's interaction styles at home and in the classroom, and demonstrated how such verbal and nonverbal communication styles can lead to different and often conflicting expectations within the classroom. George and Louise Spindler build upon this idea in Chapter 1, "The Processes of Culture and Person: Cultural Therapy and Culturally Diverse Schools." The Spindlers describe and discuss various models they have generated over 40 years to understand how human beings adapt to changing cultural circumstances. Using a number of examples from their own fieldwork—in a German village, in a rural Wisconsin school, among the Menominee and the Blood Indians, and in a Bay Area California school—the Spindlers illustrate how they have learned about the diverse cultural assumptions that guide behavior. The Spindler's work has led them to advocate the use of "cultural therapy" as a viable means first, to assist teachers and students in bringing their cultural assumptions to a level of awareness that permits them to perceive those assumptions as a potential bias in social interactions, and second, to understand and examine the adaptations they make across culturally different settings. Further, they suggest that "cultural therapy" can be effectively used to help resolve conflict that stems from inaccurate cultural perceptions of the "other." The Spindlers also describe and explain the concepts of enduring, situated, and endangered selves, and the importance of understanding these concepts as educators attempt to work with ethnically diverse children in school settings.

In Chapter 2, "Students' Multiple Worlds: Navigating the Borders of Family, Peer, and School Cultures," Phelan, Davidson, and Yu present a model of the interrelationships between students' family, peer, and school worlds, focusing in particular on how meanings and understandings derived from these worlds combine to affect students' engagement with schools and learning. Pointing out that differences between family, peer, and school worlds do not necessarily lead to educational difficulties, the authors identify types of borders that can exist between students' worlds that impede their engagement in school. For example, they point out that psychosocial, sociocultural, socioeconomic, gender, and structural borders can all block students from connecting positively with learning environments. Using a typology and individual case materials, the authors illustrate four transition or adaptation patterns found among 54 ethnically diverse students in four desegregated high schools to illustrate the ways in which students move across settings. The typology includes descriptions of students who exhibit the following patterns: (1) Congruent Worlds/ Smooth Transitions; (2) Different Worlds/Border Crossings Managed; (3) Different Worlds/Border Crossings Difficult; (4) Different Worlds/ Borders Impenetrable. This chapter emphasizes students' perceptions of their circumstances and the factors that they believe affect their involvement in schools and learning. The authors conclude by discussing the educational implications for students who exhibit various patterns.

Chapters 3 and 4 move beyond the day-to-day experiences of youth to consider the larger forces associated with youths' language and immigrant status. In Chapter 3, "Perspectives on Language Maintenance and Shift in Mexican-origin Students," Lucinda Pease-Alvarez and Kenji Hakuta present a strong argument for the advantages of bilingual competency. However, they point out that their data and that of others suggests that the native language of many immigrant students will not be passed on to their children. The authors inquire into the process of language shift by describing two studies that examine patterns of language choice, attitudes, and proficiency among high school and elementary school children of Mexican descent. They conclude that language shift is not a cognitive necessity, but one that is powerfully conditioned by social attitudes and beliefs. It is possible, they argue, to combat shift and promote the perpetuation of native language. Evidence to support this view is illustrated by the authors' descriptions of two school-based efforts to combat shift. They point out that these programs are not founded on cognitive principles, but rather, build on the social and community base of the language. They believe that in the absence of such social engagement, language proficiency, no matter how aggressively and elaborately developed, will not translate into sustained language maintenance.

In Chapter 4, "Hispanic Cultural Psychology: Implications for Education Theory and Research," Carola and Marcelo Suarez-Orozco dispel conceptions of the Hispanic condition as a monolithic phenomenon by exploring varying themes in the cultural psychology of Mexican immigrants, Mexican Americans, Cuban Americans, and mainland Puerto Ricans. Their chapter is particularly important in that during the past decade, scholars looking to explain the variance in academic success of children from different minority groups have argued that the particular history of a minority group within a given country may effect its members' orientation toward schooling (Gibson, 1987; Ogbu, 1987; Suarez-Orozco, 1987, 1989).

In particular, these scholars point out that "immigrant minorities"--peoples who moved more or less voluntarily to the U.S. because they believed it would bring them greater economic well-being, better overall opportunities, and greater political freedom—often perceive America as a land of opportunity and believe that school achievement will insure their success. Academic excellence is therefore seen as additive learning and cultural differences as barriers to be overcome. In contrast, "involuntary minorities"—peoples who were originally incorporated into the U.S. through slavery, conquest, or colonization—are more likely to believe that opportunities for gainful employment are limited because of oppression and racism. Doing well in school therefore seems pointless.

The Suarez-Orozcos discuss this issue as they consider differences between first- and second-generation American individuals and families, noting that the children of immigrants indeed evaluate their experiences in a new country differently than their parents. By reviewing previous research, the authors focus attention on identity development, cultural marginality, and barrio gang formation as critical issues facing the children of Hispanic immigrants. Turning to their own psychocultural study of Central-American youth recently arrived in the U.S., the authors elaborate on the results of the Thematic Apperception Test, which provides psychological profiles of the motivational dynamics of these Central-American refugees. Of particular importance is their finding that the achievement concerns of these immigrants are quite different than those reported for majority Americans. The authors emphasize the importance of recognizing the basic cross-cultural limitations of theoretical achievement motivation models derived from an Anglo-American research bias.

In Chapters 5 and 6 issues of school-level practices are raised in discussions about tracking and family-school relationships. In "Research and Policy in Reconceptualizing Family-School Relationships," Concha Delgado-Gaitan critically examines the assumptions that underlie past and current approaches to parental involvement and calls for an alternative approach. Drawing on theories advanced by Paolo Freire and data from a 6–year study of parental involvement in Carpinteria, a largely Latino Southern Californian community, Delgado-Gaitan argues for an empowerment approach to parental involvement. Delgado-Gaitan demonstrates how one school district has benefited from a collaborative home-school partnership. In Carpinteria, Latino parents share their educational needs and concerns with one another and school officials and work together to find solutions appropriate to the history and current conditions of the local community. Pointing out that such an approach differs from that often promulgated by policy makers, Delgado-Gaitan calls on educators and policy makers to negotiate parental involvement and collaboration in a manner that respects and takes into account the needs and strengths of local communities.

Also focusing on school-level policies that affect the ability of diverse youth to succeed in school, Reba Page examines how schools use curricular differentiation as a means to respond to diverse students. Curricular differentiation, or tracking, is "one of those taken for granted school practices" (Oakes, 1985, p. 6). Despite the fact that numerous research studies have shown that no group of students benefits consistently from being in a homogenous group, such situations continue to exist. Because poor, African-American and Latino youth are disproportionately represented in low-track classes (Persell, 1977), and because some studies have shown that the learning of average or "slow" students can actually be harmed by track placement (Esposito, 1973; Goodlad, 1960; Oakes, 1985), tracking has come to the fore of academic debate. Reba Page contributes to this discussion by enlightening us about what tracking looks like day-to-day. Her analysis of the lower-track knowledge that two veteran history teachers in two respected high schools provide for "different," academically unsuccessful students documents the strength and subtlety of ordinary school lessons. In "For Teachers: Some Sketches of Curriculum," Page tells us that people learn about their places as they learn their lessons. She argues, however, that these processes are complicated, and related to local contexts. In this respect, the chapter contrasts with many other analyses of tracking, multicultural education, and national curriculum standards which, in the main, "ignore, confound, or radically simplify" the relationship between curricular and social differentiation to render school knowledge capable of making all the difference or none at all. Because the chapter presents a systematic account of the school knowledge some teachers and students encounter, it increases our ability to discuss issues of curricular differentiation from an informed point of view.

In Chapter 7, "Cultural Diversity and Conflict: The Role of Educational Anthropology in Healing America," Henry Trueba provides an overview of the challenges associated with cultural diversity and summarizes various anthropological approaches to grappling with this issue. Drawing on census data and Jonathan Kozol's study of the conditions facing some of America's inner-city schools, Trueba reminds us of the serious social inequities and problems found in many of America's communities of color, including unemployment, lack of basic public services, poorly funded schools, and crime. But Trueba also points out that societal problems are compounded by the fact that teachers and students often do not understand the causes and consequences of their own or others' actions. He calls on educators to consider how they might begin to approach and attack societal problems by enabling themselves to understand the effects of cultural and societal dynamics on students' self-concepts. Trueba draws strongly on the model of cultural therapy explicated by George and Louise Spindler in their chapter in this volume.

The final chapter in the volume, "The Voices of Professional Educators," offers insight into the connections between the research presented in this volume and the lives of professional educators. For us, bridging the worlds of research and practice for a period of time has been an important opportunity. At the same time, our work has brought into sharp focus some of the significant differences between researchers and those who tend the daily lives of youth. For example, when classroom observations left us frazzled by the tumult and commotion of everyday life in large urban high schools, we could retreat to the university and the quiet though tedious chore of coding our interviews and analyzing our data. Exhausted from the intensity of interactions with myriad adolescent youth, we were well aware that we could escape, at will, by simply choosing to schedule interviews at a later time. Even the need to regain our equilibrium during a day of field work could be managed by taking a break in the teachers' lounge or retreating briefly for a quiet cup of coffee at a nearby restaurant. As researchers we were able to enter and exit at will, and to arrange a schedule, for the most part, to suit our needs—a luxury hardly afforded those in schools. While we recouped, the day-to-day responsibilities of operating large, diverse and inherently complex educational institutions remained for someone else to carry out. On many occasions we asked ourselves if what we were doing would be valuable in the long run to those who educate youth. Sometimes it seemed as if an hour's conversation with an adolescent or the opportunity we provided to teachers to discuss their frustrations was more worthwhile than the hours we spent coding interviews. Would the work we were doing ultimately contribute in any meaningful way to the lives of those in schools?

In Chapter 8, five professionals from different parts of the educational system offer their perspectives on the relevance of the ideas discussed in the preceding chapters, as well as the utility of working in a conference format. Harry Handler, former superintendent, Los Angeles Unified School District; Don Hill, a social studies teacher for 27 years and currently Director of the Professional Development Center of the Stanford/Schools Collaborative; Richard P. Mesa, Superintendent, Oakland Unified School District; Laurie Olsen, Executive Director, California Tomorrow; and Arlando Smith, Principal, Gunderson High School, San Jose, California, speak for themselves.

CONCLUSION

We believe that in the U.S., ethnic and cultural diversity must become a strength—a source of richness rather than an excuse for separatistic intentions. More than any other arena, schools are the stage upon which issues of diversity will continue to be played out in the society. We are beyond the time when the functionaries of education can hope that America's youth will come to them mirroring the homogeneity of students in years past.

The authors in this volume are committed to programs of research or work in schools oriented toward creating bridges of understanding and environments of equality for children and youth. All are concerned, not with the impossibility of communication, but with the very necessity of it. It is our hope that this book will make a contribution in the building of educational environments predicated on the belief that a truly pluralistic society is far superior to one in which any cultural group succeeds in submerging the rich cultural variety with which we are blessed.

NOTES

1. For example, in Wisconsin, a state that did not want to foster the development of nonpublic alternatives to its then new public schools, some districts provided public school instruction in languages other than English (Kaestle, 1983, pp. 164–165). In 1915 over 20,000 students in Milwaukee were studying German, and a few thousand studying Polish or Italian (Superintendent's Monthly Enrollment Summary, 1915, p. 434).

2. The Center's core research aims to specify ways in which the contexts of secondary school teaching shape different kinds and degrees of student and teacher engagement. The various strands of the center's work are organized to describe how diverse contexts interact to affect teachers' professional roles and dispositions and students' orientations toward school environments and learning.

3. Here and elsewhere in this chapter, quotations are identified by interview file code (e.g., RA057ST1) and line numbers. These interviews are part of a public-use file that will eventually be made available to interested researchers through the Center for Research on the Context of Secondary School Teaching at Stanford Unviersity.

4. There were dissenters to these assumptions, and their ranks grew over the years. In the early part of this century, Franz Boas (1917) was urging his fellow anthropologists to consider a societal rather than genetic explanation of the generally low economic achievement of minorities. Educational philosopher John Dewey also criticized the assimilationist ideal and the use of intelligence

tests, pointing out first, that these tests are crude measures at best, and second, that whatever they measure is very uncertain. (Powell, Farrar, & Cohen, 1985).

5. While a few scholars (cf. Jensen, 1969) were continuing to argue that such tests are indicative of genetic differences in mental ability as late as 1969, there is no convincing evidence that a relationship between racial background and native intelligence exists (Gould, 1981). Many researchers have pointed out the racial and cultural biases embedded in the questions and activities used to generate these ostensibly objective measures of intelligence (cf. Chung, 1988; Cole, 1975; Davis & Eells, 1951; Persell, 1977; Reibeiro, 1980).

6. One end result of this political action was the Bilingual Education Act of 1968 (Title VII), which provides money to local districts to develop and carry out new programs for non–English-speaking children. Today, such concerns continue to be manifested in debates over multicultural curriculum at both the collegiate and public school levels.

REFERENCES

Appleton, N. (1983). *Cultural pluralism in education: Theoretical foundations*. New York: Longman Press.

Au, K. H. (1980). Participant structures in a reading lesson with Hawaiian children: Analysis of a culturally appropriate instructional event. *Anthropology and Education Quarterly, 11*(2), 91–115.

Au, K. H., & Jordan, C. (1981). Teaching reading to Hawaiian children: Finding a culturally appropriate solution. In H. T. Trueba, G. P. Guthrie, & K. H. Au (Eds.), *Culture and the bilingual classroom: Studies in classroom ethnography* (pp. 139–152). Rowley, MA: Newbury House.

Bereiter, C., & Engelmann, S. (1966). *Teaching disadvantaged children in the preschool*. Englewood Cliffs, NJ: Prentice Hall.

Beyond the Melting Pot. (1990, April). *Time*, pp. 28–31.

Boas, F. (1917). Modern populations of America. *Proceedings of the 19th International Congress of Americanists*, Washington D.C., (pp. 569–575).

Bowles, S., & Gintis, H. (1976). *Schooling in Capitalist America*. New York: Basic Books.

Cazden, C., & John, V. P. (1971). Learning in American Indian children. In M. L. Wax, S. Diamond, & F. O. Gearing (Eds.), *Anthropological perspectives on education* (pp. 252–271). New York: Basic Books.

Chung, C. H. (1988). The language situation of Vietnamese Americans. In S. L. McKay & S. L. Wong (Eds.), *Language diversity: Problem or resource?* (pp. 276–292). New York: Newbury House.

Cohen, D. (1970). Immigrants and the schools. *Review of Educational Research, 40*(1), 13–27.

Cole, M. (1975). Culture, cognition and IQ testing. *National Elementary Principal, 54*, 49–52.

Conant, J. B. (1961). *Slums and suburbs*. New York: McGraw-Hill.

Cremin, L. (1964). *The transformation of the school: Progressivism in American education 1876-1957.* New York: Random House.

Cubberly, E. P. (1909). *Changing conceptions of American education.* Boston: Houghton Mifflin.

Davis, A., & Eells, K. (1951). *Intelligence and cultural differences.* Chicago: University of Chicago Press.

Delgado-Gaitan, C. (1987). Traditions and transition in the learning process of Mexican children: An ethnographic view. In G. D. Spindler & L. Spindler (Eds.), *Interpretive ethnography of education: At home and abroad* (pp. 333-359). Prospect Heights, IL: Waveland Press.

Deutsch, M. (1967). *The disadvantaged child: Selected papers of Martin Deutsch and associates.* New York: Basic Books.

Erickson, F. D. (1987). Transformation and school success: The politics and culture of educational achievement. *Anthropology and Education Quarterly, 18*(4), 335-355.

Erickson, F. D., & Mohatt, G. (1982). Cultural organization of participation structures in two classrooms of Indian students. In G. D. Spindler (Ed.), *Doing the ethnography of schooling: Educational anthropology in action* (pp. 132-175). New York: Holt, Rinehart & Winston.

Esposito, D. (1973). Homogeneous and heterogeneous ability grouping: Principal findings and implications for designing more effective educational environments. *Review of Educational Research, 43,* 163-179.

Fordham, S., & Ogbu, J. U. (1986). Black students' school success: Coping with the 'burden of acting white.' *Urban Review, 18*(3), 176-206.

Gallimore, R., Boggs, J., & Jordan, C. (1974). *Culture, behavior and education: A study of Hawaiian Americans.* Beverly Hills, CA: Sage.

Gay, G. (1983). Multiethnic education: Historical developments and future prospects. *Phi Delta Kappan, 64,* 560-563.

Gibson, M. A. (1987). Punjabi immigrants in an American high school. In G. D. Spindler & L. Spindler (Eds.), *Interpretive ethnography of education: At home and abroad* (pp. 274-281). Prospect Heights, IL: Waveland Press.

Goodlad, J. I. (1960). Classroom organization. In C. Harris (Ed.), *Encyclopedia of educational research* (3rd ed.) (221-226). New York: Macmillan.

Gordon, M. M. (1964). *Assimilation in American life.* New York: Oxford University Press.

Gould, S. J. (1981). *The mismeasure of man.* New York: W. W. Norton.

Heath, S. B. (1982). Questioning at school and at home: A comparative study. In G. D. Spindler (Ed.), *Doing the ethnography of schooling: Educational anthropology in action* (pp. 102-131). New York: Holt, Rinehart & Winston.

Herberg, W. (1955). *Protestant-Catholic-Jew.* New York: Doubleday.

Here they come, ready or not: An education week special report on the ways in which America's population in motion is changing the outlook for schools and society. (1986, May 14). *Education Week,* pp. 14-28.

Hess, R., & Shipman, V. (1965). Early experience and the socialization of cognitive modes in children. *Child Development, 34,* 869-886.

Jensen, A. (1969). How much can we boost IQ and school achievement? *Harvard Educational Review, 39*, 1-123.

John, V. P. (1972). Styles of learning—styles of teaching: Reflections on the education of Navajo children. In C. B. Cazden, V. P. John, & D. Hymes (Eds.), *Functions of language in the classroom* (pp. 331-343). New York: Teachers College Press.

Kaestle, C. E. (1983). *Pillars of the republic: Common schools and American society, 1780-1860.* New York: Hill & Wang.

Kallen, H. M. (1915). Democracy and the melting pot: Part I. *The Nation, 100*(2590), 190-194.

Kallen, H. M. (1915). Democracy and the melting pot: Part II. *The Nation, 100*(2591), 217-220.

Labov, W. (1969). The logic of non-standard English. *Georgetown Monographs on Language and Linguistics, 22*, 1-31.

McLaughlin, M. (1992). *Social constructions of students: Challenges to policy coherence, P92-147* (pp. 1-26). Stanford, CA: Center for Research on the Context of Secondary Teaching.

Montero-Sieburth, M., & LaCelle-Peterson, M. (1991). Immigration and schooling: An ethnohistorical account of policy and family perspectives in an urban community. *Anthropology and Education Quarterly, 22*(4), 300-325.

Oakes, J. (1985). *Keeping track: How schools structure inequality.* New Haven, CT: Yale University Press.

Ogbu, J. U. (1987). Variability in minority school performance: A problem in search of an explanation. *Anthropology and Education Quarterly, 18*(4), 313-334.

Persell, C. H. (1977). *Education and inequality: A theoretical and empirical synthesis.* New York: Free Press.

Phelan, P., Davidson, A. L., & Cao, H. T. (1992). Speaking up: students perspectives on school. *Phi Delta Kappan, 73*(9), 695-704.

Philips, S. (1972). Participant structures and communicative competence: Warm Springs children in community and classroom. In C. B. Cazden, V. P. John, & D. Hymes (Eds.), *Functions of Language in the Classroom* (pp. 370-394). New York: Teachers College Press.

Philips, S. (1982). *The invisible culture: Communication in classroom and community in the Warm Springs reservation.* New York: Longman Press.

Portes, A., & Rumbaut, R. G. (1990). *Immigrant America: A portrait.* Berkeley: University of California Press.

Powell, A. G., Farrar, E., & Cohen, D. K. (1985). *The shopping mall high school: Winners and losers in the educational marketplace.* Boston: Houghton Mifflin.

Ravitch, D. (1983). *The troubled crusade: American education 1945-1980.* New York: Basic Books.

Reibeiro, J. L. (1980). Testing Portuguese immigrant children: Cultural patterns and group differences in responses to the WISC-R. In D. P. Macedo (Ed.), *Issues in Portuguese bilingual education* (87-112). Cambridge, MA: National Assessment and Dissemination Center for Bilingual Education.

Shamai, S. (1987) Critical theory of education and ethnicity: The case study of the Toronto Jewish community. *Journal of Education, 169*(2), 89–114.

Silberman, C. E. (1985). *A certain people: American Jews and their lives today.* New York: Summit Books.

Suarez-Orozco, M. M. (1987). 'Becoming somebody': Central American immigrants in U.S. inner-city schools. *Anthropology and Education Quarterly, 18*(4), 287–299.

Suarez-Orozco, M. M. (1989). *Central American refugees and U.S. high schools: A psychosocial study of motivation and achievement.* Stanford, CA: Stanford University Press.

Superintendent's Monthly Enrollment Summary. (1915). *Proceedings of the Board of School Directors of Milwaukee* (p. 34).

Turner, F. J. (1920). *The frontier in American history.* New York: Henry Holt.

Tyack, D. (1974). *The one best system.* Cambridge, MA: Harvard University Press.

Zangwill, I. (1909). *The melting pot.* New York: Macmillan.

CHAPTER 1

THE PROCESSES OF CULTURE AND PERSON: CULTURAL THERAPY AND CULTURALLY DIVERSE SCHOOLS

George Spindler and Louise Spindler

Our basic premise is that culture is not simply a factor, or an influence, or a dimension, but that it is in process, in everything that we do, say, or think in or out of school. As a teacher, a student, a delinquent, a superlatively good student, or a miserably inept student, or an antagonistic, alienated, or resistive student, we are caught up in cultural processes. With this in mind we designate the school as a mandated cultural process and the teacher as a cultural agent. Of course the school is also a political and a social institution and a lot more.

We regard education as a calculated interference with learning. This applies to all education but particularly to that which is the most massive interference in learning in Western society, and except for total institutions in Goffman's (1961) sense, such as prisons and monasteries, the most massive interference cross-culturally—namely, the school. What we intend to convey is that schools teach selected materials, skills, and ideas. They also carefully exclude a great deal of cultural content that is being or could be learned by the students. Schools define what is not to be taught and what is not to be learned as well as taught and learned. A great deal goes on in schools other than calculated "intervention" (which we will now use rather than "interference") in learning. The calculated interventions themselves have unanticipated consequences. The students learn a great deal from each other that teachers don't control. Students also bring to school a lot of learning that teachers would rather they hadn't acquired. A combination of what children bring to school and what they learn from each other causes teachers trouble. It is this "trouble" with which we are concerned in this chapter.

27

INTRODUCTION

Our strategy here will be to describe and discuss certain models that we have generated in our research over the years in our attempts to understand how human beings adapt to changing circumstances in their lives. The chapter has a certain egocentric quality because we are not directly concerned with the models our colleagues have generated, although they have certainly been helpful.[1] We offer this chapter and the model of cultural therapy we promote as in process, exploratory, and in places, tentative. We intend it as a way of getting into a dynamic and significant area of relationships and communication that is present in various forms in all schools, in schooling, and in the act of teaching. We will doubtless modify our thinking as we receive feedback and as we and our colleagues attempt further applications of the model in school situations.

Much of what we have done as anthropologists of education, as teachers of anthropology, as consultants in schools, and as authors of books and papers is intended as cultural therapy. We have, for example, long taught the introductory course in cultural anthropology to Stanford students as a form of cultural therapy—to widen their cultural horizons and their appreciation of diverse lifeways. We teach education graduate students ethnographic methods and self-examination as approaches to understanding cultural diversity. We work as consultants with individual teachers or with faculty groups through simulations of cultural experience and interpretation designed to increase understanding of cultural diversity. We have rarely labeled what we do as such. When we do label anything we have done "cultural therapy" people get quite excited and want to know very specifically what we mean by it. The answer that we just gave, that cultural therapy is virtually everything that we do as professional anthropologists, is usually not very satisfying. One of our purposes in this chapter will be to clarify what we mean by this phrase.

As a preliminary orientation we can state that cultural therapy is a process of bringing one's own culture, in its manifold forms—assumptions, goals, values, beliefs, and communicative modes—to a level of awareness that permits one to perceive it as a potential bias in social interaction and in the acquisition or transmission of skills and knowledge—what we later refer to as "instrumental competencies." At the same time one's own culture, brought to this level of awareness, is perceived in relation to the other culture, so that potential conflicts, misunderstandings, and blind spots in the perception and interpretation of behavior may be anticipated. One's culture as well as the other's culture becomes a third presence, removed somewhat from the person, so that one's actions can be taken as caused by one's culture and not by one's personality. A certain comforting distance and objectification becomes possible, and relationships, such as those between teachers and students, can be explored without getting personal (or unduly upset) about it.

In our work with individual teachers we have found, excepting in cases where psychopathology is indicated, that the sociocultural position and experience of the individual is a better predictor of classroom behavior, particularly in respect to selective bias (on the part of the teacher) in perception of and interaction with students, than psychological factors as such, as indicated by psychological tests or interviews. In the case of our classic 5th-grade teacher, Roger Harker, for example, his troubled relationships and identity problems with his father, and his overidentification with his mother and sister did not have significant effects on his behavior as a teacher, but his narrow, upper-middle-class, white Protestant cultural background did (Spindler & Spindler, with Trueba & Williams, 1990).

Doing cultural therapy, as we do it, has psychological concomitants, but they are not the focus. The focus is the culture of the teacher and the way it biases relationships with children in classrooms. For teachers, cultural therapy can be used to increase awareness of the cultural assumptions they bring to the classroom that affect their behavior and their interactions with students—particularly students of color. For teachers, cultural therapy is an intervention that can be used as a first step to impact and change behaviors, attitudes, and assumptions that are biased (and often discriminatory) and thus detrimental to students whose cultural backgrounds are different from their own. Our use of cultural therapy has been directed at helping teachers and other adults to understand their own cultural positions and to reflect on and analyze the reasons why they might find the behavior of a culturally different person objectionable, shocking, or irritating.

For students, cultural therapy is essentially a means of consciousness raising—that is, to make explicit unequal power relationships in the classroom, the school, and the larger society. Further, cultural therapy can be used to help students clarify the steps necessary to obtain the instrumental competencies they need to gain access to opportunities within the school system (and hopefully the larger society). For example, many students of color do not have access to the "cultural capital" necessary to compete equally with the cultural majority for resources, knowledge, and experiences. The goal of cultural therapy for students (particularly minority students) is to empower rather than to blame them.

The experiences of our colleagues working with minority youth suggest that many students fault themselves for their inability to navigate the educational system. Almost none are aware of the implications of tracking; of the fact that they often receive inadequate help and assistance with respect to coursework, college application procedures, and so forth; or that attitudes, values, and beliefs, as well as pedagogical methods and school policies, frequently mitigate against their ability to succeed. Cultural therapy, as we conceptualize it, is intended as a method to increase students' understanding of the factors that work against them and to empower them to fight against the obstacles they encounter (rather than blaming themselves or engaging in behaviors that impede their access to skills and competencies necessary to ensure their access to power and opportunity).

With this preliminary understanding, we can turn to certain experiences and results from our field research as anthropologists in the manifold context of education.

REFLECTIVE INTERVIEWING IN SCHOENHAUSEN AND ROSEVILLE

For some years we have been researching in Schoenhausen, a village of about 2000 in a semirural but urbanizing area in *Land* Baden Württemburg, Southern Germany. Schoenhausen was known, and still is to a considerable degree, as an *ausgesprochner Weinort* (emphatically, a winemaking place). The native born are Swaebisch and Protestant. The Grundschule (elementary school) is charged with the responsibility of educating all of the children and preparing them for a changing Germany and world. Its 127 children are distributed in four grades staffed by 6 teachers, a Rektor (principal), and various other special services personnel.

The Roseville Elementary School, located in central Wisconsin, includes kindergarten through 8th grade and is somewhat larger than the Schoenhausen school, but is comparable in every other respect. The school district is rural but has many commuters who work in nearby towns, some of them as many as 40 or 50 miles distant. The majority of the children attending the school come from small dairy farms. The predominant ethnicity of the Roseville School District is German.

Over the years we have applied many different research techniques, some of which will appear in other parts of this chapter, but for our purpose at the moment we wish to emphasize some material that came out of an interview technique that we have most recently developed—the "cross-cultural comparative reflective interview" (CCCRI). It was applied in Schoenhausen for the first time in 1985 and had been applied in Roseville in 1983 and subsequently.[2] The CCCRI is designed to stimulate dialogue about the pivotal concerns of natives in comparable cultural systems. Some form of audiovisual material representing two or more cultures is used to bracket the interview. That is, the interview is conducted as an inquiry into the perceptions, by the native, of his or her own situation and that of the "other," and the assumptions are revealed in reflections about those perceptions. We regard both the perceptions and the assumptions as cultural phenomena.

We had taken films in both the Schoenhausen and Roseville classrooms and our basic procedure was to show these films to our interviewees and thus elicit reflective discussion of their own situation and that of the others. We did this with teachers, administrators, and children in both research sites. A very rich body of material was generated by these interviews, from which we selected only a few instances from the interviews with two teachers, "Mrs. Schiller" in the Roseville school and "Frau Wanzer" in Schoenhausen.

The Roseville School

> *GLS:* Now with respect to your underlying objectives as a teacher, that is Linda Schiller as a teacher, not necessarily what you get in the education courses, what would you say your basic purpose is?
>
> *Mrs. Schiller:* To teach them to be an individual, to be all they can, to the limits of their abilities and if I can get them to be a happy person as well as get them to do their best, then I think I've done my job. [Further discussion of the individual, of activity, and of disruption in class.]
>
> *GLS:* Here in Roseville wouldn't you be able to walk out of the classroom, go down to the office, leave your class for 5 minutes or more?
>
> *Mrs. Schiller:* Ah, yes. I left the 1st graders up in front without any assignment just the other day, and Jeremy grabbed the pointer and started "A, B, C, D", etc., and the whole class repeated and then went on through the alphabet several times. I said, "That was so nice. You didn't waste any time!"

Mrs. Schiller went on to discuss how the children knew where the materials were and could get them when they wanted them or had time for them after they had finished their assigned task. She expected them to work quietly and either individually or with others. The children used charts, tape recorders, flash cards, and so forth. She says, "They're all little teachers, it's just built in." She claims that she doesn't really arrange the materials beforehand; they know where everything is and just go and get what they need.

> *Mrs. Schiller:* I have a lot of faith in kids. I think kids are neat! If you have high expectations, 98% of the time they will fulfill your expectations.
>
> *GLS:* What would you feel like if you went out in the hall or someone called you to the phone and you came back after 5 minutes and found things in considerable disorder?
>
> *Mrs. Schiller:* Well, I would tell them right off, "I am *very* disappointed! I had this important phone call and you couldn't sit still for 5 minutes while I answered it." I would let them know it hurt me personally. It's kind of a personal thing. Oh yes! You start building that up the first day of school. Then they feel "we can't hurt our teacher."

She went on to describe an instance where a little girl had to go to the dentist and she had to take her out to the car where her mother was waiting. She came back and found such a nice class and praised them for being so nice and quiet. "They just love praise!"

There was a great deal more in this interview about how she depended upon the personal trust between the children and herself and how she cultivated the feeling that they couldn't "hurt their teacher." She also discussed curriculum. She pointed out that the teachers in the Roseville school had direct input into the curriculum, in contrast to the situation in Schoenhausen where the curriculum plan (*Lehrerplan*) comes down from the State Board of Education (its American equivalent).

Schoenhausen Grundschule

For the first few minutes we talked to Frau Wanzer about what we wanted to do in her classroom and explained that we wanted her procedures and goals to be clear to the Roseville teachers when we showed the films taken of her (Frau Wanzer's) classroom. She had seen the Roseville films already.

> *Frau Wanzer:* Ya, it was really difficult for me to see what was intended. Perhaps that was the ground for the feeling that many of us had, *Was lernen sie eigentlich?* [What are they learning really?].
>
> *GLS:* We explained that the films shown were typical for this class

and the *friewillig* [free will] character of the classroom activity
was indeed characteristic.

Frau Wanzer: I can scarcely understand how the teacher working
at the table with some of the children would work on without
looking to see what the other children were doing in the rest of
the room. How do the children working alone know what they
are supposed to do? With us there are difficulties and fighting.
This was apparently not the case with the Roseville school!

GLS: Naturally, the children have specific lessons, but then when
they are finished—they can do what they will.

Frau Wanzer: Sie können tuen wassie wollen! [They can do what they
want!]

GLS: Well, they have various opportunities—such as tapes, comput-
ers, the library, flash cards, charts, posters, and so forth.

Frau Wanzer: There is naturally a great difference as compared to
our school. In America they have so much more time and so
when they are finished with their lessons they can do what they
want, but with us there is no time.

GLS: To go back a little, so for every hour there is a specific goal
you must reach?

Frau Wanzer: I have in my curriculum plan the goal that I must
reach. Every hour has a part of goal. I must find out as the hour
progresses if I'm going to have enough time to reach that goal.
It depends on whether the hour goes well or badly, how much
time I will spend.

Here she is speaking of the *Lehrerplan* [curriculum plan] from the Baden
Württemburg [province] office of education.

GLS: Well, if you did have free time, how would you arrange it?

Frau Wanzer: I would arrange materials beforehand that belonged
to a specific theme. But in the framework of this theme, the
children could do what they wanted. But I wouldn't just leave it
up to them to choose from unorganized material. I would have
the fear that they [would] choose things that were just play.

She goes on at some length to describe just how she would work this
out and what kind of product she would expect, then ends with the comment: "This kind of procedure would work, but *volligfrei* [fully free]? *Dass
macht nichts* [that makes nothing—that's of no use]!"

We went on to discuss what would happen if she left the room and
came back and found chaos.

GLS: What would you do if you heard a disturbance in the room when you returned?

Frau Wanzer: I would talk to the class. I would attempt to reach an understanding. Scolding does no good. Sometimes I have said that I am *traurig* [sad].

GLS: Would you say that you are *beleidigt* [hurt]?

Frau Wanzer: No, never *beleidigt, nür traurig* (only sad).

GLS: Do you make the children feel guilty [*schuldig*]?

Frau Wanzer: I feel that guilt is not understandable for children of this age. How can they understand who is guilty—the one who started the trouble or the one who responded to the trouble and who carried it on further?

We carried on discussions of this kind with Frau Wanzer several times and her interpretation of her own behavior in the classroom and that of the Roseville teachers she had seen on film was consistent. She saw the Roseville classrooms, as did the other teachers, as tending toward being directionless, without specific goals, and not organized for the attainment of whatever goals existed. She did find the quiet orderliness of the Roseville school impressive and as exhibiting good "teamwork."

Interpretation

Frau Wanzer and Mrs. Schiller are two experienced teachers of about the same age who teach the same grade, about many of the same things, in quite similar schools in parallel communities in Germany and in the U.S. Yet their handling of their classrooms and the assumptions that guide their behavior are significantly different at some critical points. And their perceptions of each other's classroom reflect these differences. Mrs. Schiller's classroom is relaxed, quiet, low-keyed, and diverse. Children carry out various activities on their own, in addition to those carried out by the teacher and the small group she is leading through a specific learning task. There is little or no disruptive behavior. These qualities were confirmed in many sessions of observation by us, are apparent in the films we showed to the Schoenhausen teachers, the principal, and the Schulamtdirektor (superintendent of schools) and his assistants.

Frau Wanzer perceives Mrs. Schiller's classroom as undirected, as almost without goals. At the same time, she acknowledges that there appears to be "teamwork," but that this method would be unlikely to work well in the Schoenhausen Grundschule.

These perceptions are apparent in the interview. Frau Wanzer's assumptions are clear: if children are undirected they, or at least a significant proportion of them, will do nothing at all, become disruptive, or choose to play rather than work. She also reports that when children have clear directions on an interesting topic they can become very enthusiastic about learning and will work hard at it. Frau Wanzer explains the differences observed in terms of time, which is short in Schoenhausen, and the fact that the curriculum plan there defines the goals to be reached quite precisely. She does not see these as cultural attributes, but as given, as practical, and as preconditions to what she does, and what the children do, in her classroom.

The differences run deep. Mrs. Schiller assumes that her goal is to help each individual develop to his or her fullest degree—to the limit of their individual capacities. Frau Wanzer assumes, as does the Schulamt-direktor, that her purpose is to help each child attain the standards set forth in the *Lehrerplan*—that some will meet them fully and others only minimally. Frau Wanzer takes for granted the existence of a *Lehrerplan*, which is furnished to the school by the state education office, and will directly guide her management of her instruction. Mrs. Schiller takes for granted the fact that teachers in her school district develop their own curriculum and that it is only an approximate guide. Frau Wanzer assumes that the children eventually learn to continue working when she leaves the classroom, but that one can't expect too much of the younger 1st and 2nd graders. Mrs. Schiller expects her 1st and 2nd graders to be responsible for keeping a quiet, on-task classroom when she is gone for a few minutes. Frau Wanzer would talk to her class if there were a disruption, but she would not act "hurt," only "sad," and she would not try to make her children feel "guilty." Mrs. Schiller would develop personal liking and trust with her children, would be "hurt" if they misbehaved, and would leave them all feeling guilty if they did. These two teachers have quite different conceptions of guilt. For Frau Wanzer guilt has to be established—there is a perpetrator, a reinforcer, and perhaps a victim. For Mrs. Schiller there is a feeling state—guilt is internalized. The children feel guilty about their irresponsible behavior and about hurting their teacher.

These are the assumptions, as we see them, that lie behind both the behaviors of the two teachers in their classrooms and their perception of each other's behaviors *in situ*. These are cultural differences, we believe, that are expressed in and derived from the German and American historical experiences. In our own terminology, they reflect the German and the American heritage cultures.[3]

The claim we made in the preceding paragraph always arouses criticism and rebuttal. We are properly abashed by the rashness of our interpretation. However, we do feel that the elicited dialogue represents something that we can call "German" culture and "American" culture. We have recently represented the latter as a "cultural dialogue" (Spindler & Spindler, 1990), and we can understand certain of Mrs. Schiller's interpretations as expressions of (for instance) individualism, achievement, and internalization of authority and guilt, as a part of this dialogue. We can understand some of Frau Wanzer's discourse, and that of the Schulamtdirektor (district director of education), as expressing certain aspects of a long-term German dialogue about authority, efficiency, collective effort, and the attainment of standards. To claim that the little elementary schools in Roseville and Schoenhausen somehow express their respective national *Zeitgeisten* goes further than most of us want to go, and yet the implications are tantalizing and, we think, important. The action in these classrooms and the interpretations by the natives seem to be the tip of a cultural iceberg. The part of the iceberg that is under water is the enormous complexity of the national whole and its history. Just how to make the analytic connections remains obscure. Nevertheless, we feel that it is essential to take into consideration broad, pervasive aspects of cultural dialogue, such as those represented, when we talk about classrooms and confrontations in them. If the teacher goes into the classroom with undeclared, and possibly unverbalized (even to herself), culturally patterned assumptions of this kind and the students come with other kinds of assumptions, also undeclared, there will be serious difficulties in communication. "Cultural therapy" in this instance would be to make it possible for both the teacher and the students to verbalize these basic assumptions. This is often done in "rap sessions," but the purpose of such discussion is unclear and there is usually little reinforcement of what is expressed or pursuit of any misunderstandings that may have occurred.

THE ENDURING, SITUATED, AND ENDANGERED SELF

In 1987 we were invited to participate in a panel for the American Anthropological Association meeting on the fieldwork experience in anthropology. Rather than simply talk about our experiences in what is now some 28 field trips in five different cultures, we decided to talk about the "self" and we treated this ambiguous concept in three dimensions: the enduring, the situated, and the endangered self in fieldwork.

The *enduring self* is that sense of continuity one has with one's own past—a personal continuity of experience, meaning, and social identity (Hallowell, 1955). It provides the ego-syntonic functions of the self and functions as an integrating principle of the personality phenotype (Levine, 1984). It seems to have, at least in our own experience and that of some of our informants, a romantic-ideal quality that may be quite lacking in the more pragmatic situated self.[4]

The *situated self* may be thought of as encompassing those aspects of the person required to cope with the everyday exigencies of life. This self is situated and contextualized. It is instrumental in the sense that we use the concept (Spindler & Spindler, 1989a, 1989b). This self is linked to the attainment of ends defined within the framework of a lifeway or social context. One's sense of self-efficacy—a concept used by learning psychologists—is a product, as we see it, of instrumental success or failure. Whereas the situated self is oriented to the present and the contexts (situations) one finds oneself in, the enduring self provides a sense of personal continuity with the past. This may imply that the enduring self is entirely conscious, and indeed much of it is—particularly the idealized features of identity, obscured by time and selected out of memory. But there are events and situations that occurred in the past, which contribute to contemporary feelings and self-evaluation, that are not readily conscious. For our purposes this is not too important, but in individual cases it may be of great significance and would be brought out in extended counseling or therapy. For us, what is important is that any given student or teacher will have a sense of self that is relatively independent of the situation one finds oneself in. If this sense of self (the enduring self) is violated too often and too strongly by the requirements of the situated self that is constructed as an adaptive response to situational contexts, the enduring self will be damaged, or may even become the *endangered self*. This can occur in anthropological fieldwork and certainly occurs as children and youth of diverse cultural origins confront school cultures that are antagonistic to the premises and behavioral patterns of their own culture. This helps account, for instance, for the resistance of some minority youth to learning in school, where learning some aspects of what is being taught and accepting how it is taught may be regarded as a "sellout." We would regard this as evidence of a conflict between the enduring self and the situated self.

In 1970, in "Being an Anthropologist," we wrote that the ethnographer

> if successful, is in truth friendly, in truth concerned with the welfare of his or her respondents, but in truth an observer. The job is to find out what the people think and feel as well as what they do. One must penetrate beyond the facade of rationalizations and diversions that all humans throw up around their activities and sentiments. But the ethnographer must not become one of the people being observed, though from the outside he or she may seem to become one. The ethnographer must keep his or her identity while he studies theirs. One may well observe oneself—this self-knowledge is necessary. But when the distance between oneself and one's respondents is lost and between oneself in the sense of personal identity and in the sense of

the role as participant-observer, the ethnographer has lost his or her use-fulness as a field anthropologist. (p. 298)

Another point of view was expressed by Michel Leiris (1978) in "Das Augen des Ethnographen" in anticipation of an expedition to Africa:

> ... for me the trip has a prospect of fulfilling a certain childhood dream—the possibility of fighting against age and death—to go against the river of time—to lose my time-bound person in contact with humans very different than myself. I also wish that my artistic and literary friends could travel with me, not as tourists but as ethnographers, and therefore come into contact (with the "natives") in enough depth to forget their white, middle-class manners and to lose what they under their identity as intellectuals compre-hend. (p. 34)

There are dimensions of the self embedded in these statements, and we will comment on them shortly in terms of our personal experience, but for the moment it is clear that the ethnographers, both ourselves and Michel Leiris, were doing what persons coming into a new cultural situ-ation must do if they wish to get along and learn, and at the same time, to keep their identity. These are the problems, in our view, of the ethnic minority student or the lower class student in a middle-class school envi-ronment.

The problem, of course, is how to do this. The ethnographer has a role and in varying degrees is trained for it. The ethnographer is also highly motivated to perform adequately in an alien cultural setting. When we did our first in-depth field work with the Menominee Indians of Wis-consin, we risked our health and at times even our lives to get along and obtain our data.

We found the tradition-oriented group of Menominee most compat-ible. They were also culturally the most different (from us). They then (in the 1950s) lived in self-made shacks well back in the woods far away from the highway or amenities such as utilities, sewer systems, or electri-fication. These people carried on a way of life that was more than remi-niscent of an aboriginal central woodlands culture. The ceremonial round, subsistence activities, language usage, burial customs, sorcery, and reli-gious beliefs all exhibited specific traditional cultural features (Spindler & Spindler, 1984).

We were most interested in this group, spent the most time with them, wrote the most about them, and identified with them to a greater degree than with any of the four major groups of Menominee that we eventually described. We never thought we were Menominee Indians, but we felt that we were members of that group, and, indeed, were treated as such in many respects. None of this is too surprising. There was an obvious match between our romanticized, idealized, enduring selves and the place and people we found interesting.

What was not clear to us at the time and did not become so for some years was that the majority of the Menominee in that tradition-oriented group also bore enduring selves that were romanticized and idealized in the same direction.

All of the people in this group who were under 50 years old had extensive experience with the outside world—in schools and in the work force. Most had become disillusioned. They had come back to the "old people," as they put it, to learn and live their own lifeway again. All of them had traditional socialization experience, often with grandparents. All had experienced disruption and discontinuity. They came back, literally, to find themselves. The tradition-oriented group, we came to feel, was a kind of revitalization movement, guided by the surviving handful of knowledgeable elders. Of course, the individual life careers varied. We are speaking of over one-half of the total members of that group.

It is an oversimplification, but it is not wrong to say that both the tradition-oriented Menominee and we, the anthropologists, were engaged in the same quest—rediscovering and reasserting our enduring, romanticized selves. But they were more clear about that than we were.

We were less objective than we thought. We managed our situated selves effectively and maintained a working balance between objectivity and involvement. We would not do it differently if we had to do it over again but we understand better now our strong attraction toward this group. Other anthropologists who have worked with the Menominee were not similarly attracted. We think that such relationships are probably more common in fieldwork and are reflected more often in interpretation than is generally acknowledged.

We think that our experience, sketched above, suggests how complex self-other relationships may be. We were living and working in a social and cultural situation very different than the one to which we were accustomed. We were stimulated by this, as most anthropologists are in the field, and found it compelling in all sorts of ways. Our attraction was positive and we made a viable adjustment. But we did not fully understand what was happening—why we were so attracted to the traditional group of Menominee and also why we were not attracted by the acculturated portions of the Menominee population. To us, the latter seemed stuffy—too much like the people in small towns, or in big cities, for that matter, who we have tended to avoid in our personal lives. We might have seen the convergence in our romanticized-idealized-enduring selves if we had had those concepts worked out at the time, but we might not have seen the convergence between ourselves and those of the traditional Menominees.

A matching of selves, whether enduring or situated, is not simple. The fact that a kind of convergence could occur in our case may suggest that there are all sorts of ways in which convergences may occur between students and teachers and between students and school situations that are not apparent on the surface. There are, apparently, divergencies as well. These kinds of relationships require a deeper penetration than we can provide at this time, but they are suggested.

In this panel discussion at the AAA meeting we also dealt with dangers to the self, both enduring and situated, that might be inherent in the fieldwork process. We felt that there were some dangers. For example, we feel permanently marginalized in our society. Many of our colleagues must feel this too. Knowing our enduring self as we do and having found an alien identity with which to reinforce it, we feel we have left to us only our situated self to be played out in our own society. Our relationships to all of our everyday affairs and aspirations seem at times shallow. But we cannot go back. Our friends and informants in the tradition-oriented Menominee group are either dead or have themselves left behind much of their revitalized native identity. Even their rituals, some of which they still carry out, seem removed from the traditional context in which we first saw them. The echoes of the past are faint and only the sociopolitical realities of the day seem alive. But is this feeling anything more than simple nostalgia for our own youth and the reinforcement of the enduring self that we found there among the Menominee?

This is a situation peculiar to the field ethnographer, perhaps, and yet the feeling dogs us that the children from a minority group who attend a mainstream-dominated school must have many of the same kinds of feelings. They enter marginalized and their marginalization is reinforced. This is exactly parallel to what happened to us. We entered the field situation with the Menominee already somewhat alienated and disenchanted with much of mainstream society as we knew it. We found reinforcement for this marginalization and emerged from the 7 years of intermittent field experience permanently marginalized. We do not claim that our experience and marginalization are directly comparable to that of a minority child or youth. We are empowered by our position, our status, and our ethnicity. They may not be. Nevertheless, our experience in the field where we made our adjustment to other's realities is suggestive and gives us, at least, some basis for empathy.

What may be most important here is that we learned how to make situational adaptations without destroying our enduring selves. Perhaps this is what many minority students with strong ethnic identities must do. They must keep their identity since this identity, in the sense of the enduring self, is essential to the maintenance of life itself. And yet they must get along in the world as it is. It is a world where instrumental competencies have to be acquired that are not required by the enduring self or one's ethnic identity; a sense of pervasive self-efficacy must be developed in order to cope with the exigencies of life as they happen in a complex technological society. Somehow minority youth as well as mainstream youth must be enabled to make this kind of adaptation, and they will be helped in doing this if the necessary instrumental competencies can be de-emotionalized—removed from the value matrix of mainstream culture. Perhaps if we have clear concepts of enduring self and identities, and situational adaptations, and can verbalize them, make them explicit and applicable to everyday lives, we can help ourselves to make good working adjustments.

We end this section with another quote from our chapter from "Being an Anthropologist":

> We have never had a truly bad time in the field, though we have not, to be sure, endured some of the extreme exigencies that some of our colleagues have. But we have fallen ill, been cold, wet, and insect bitten, suffered from having to struggle along in someone else's language, been rejected by the very people we wanted to know, harassed by children when we wanted to work with their elders, repulsed by offensive sights and odors (given our culturally conditioned sensibilities). Our lives have been threatened by people and by impersonal forces. But it was all the very essence of living. (1970, p. 300)

If somehow the struggle of the minority student could be converted to a struggle with some glory in it—as there was and still is for us—getting along in school would be perceived differently and reacted to with energy and determination rather than alienation. This may seem to be another kind of "blame the victim" concept but it need not be if cultural therapy could somehow incorporate some elements from this kind of orientation, the orientation of the ethnographer. Perhaps both teachers and students have to become ethnographers, studying each other and themselves.

GETTING ALONG IN THE REMSTAL

One of our major research efforts in Germany has been to study the ways in which people perceive and make instrumental adaptations to the changing environment in which they live. The Remstal in Germany is an area of some 21 communities, ranging from very small villages to mid-size towns, but it is rapidly urbanizing and modernizing. One tool that we used, of our own invention and derived from field experience in

Germany (and in all of the other places we worked as well) consists of some 30 line drawings of significant activities in which a person may engage or conceive of engaging in. These drawings are of occupations, houses, social situations, clothes, recreation, and places. They are clustered around two poles—the traditional way of life and a modern, increasingly urbanized way of life. The activities, the line drawings, and the conception of what is traditional and modern must be refit, of course, to each research site. The technique is emic in its evocative stimuli, but the underlying model or theory of relations, which is etic, remains constant. Respondents are asked to choose activities they would like to engage in, which means choosing certain line drawings, and to explain why they chose them. The drawings may be selected by the individual from the whole pile of drawings, as the Blood Indians (Kanai) insisted on doing, or presented one by one in any predetermined order. Alternately, the pictures may be presented in preselected pairs to groups of some size with two slide projectors, as we did in the Remstal with school children, their parents, and their teachers. The respondent makes choices, then defends the choices, either in writing or orally under conditions of individual ministration.

Though not initially designed for that purpose, the Instrumental Activities Inventories (IAI) elicits data that seem relevant to concepts of self and personhood. We can say that we become what we choose as instrumentalities. The advertising profession recognized this long ago, and we are bombarded with invitations to identify with the sophisticated by drinking Perrier and to become members of the "now generation" by drinking Diet Pepsi.

We cannot engage in a detailing of the results, which we found to be complex and revealing, but what became abundantly clear was that there are indications of the enduring self and the situated self in the responses of the Remstäler. The enduring self is clearly ideal-romantic. It is represented in choices of *Weingärtner* (vintner) profession, *Selbständiger* (the independent small shop owner), the *Kleinbauer* (small farmer), the *Grossbauer* (big farmer), the quiet evening at home, the traditional *Fachwerk* (open-beam structure) house, and the *Weinlese* (grape harvest). Images and values constituting an idealized lifestyle, now disappearing rapidly, were woven together in the defenses of these choices, the friendly village, kin, family, land and nature, fresh air and sunshine, history, beauty, independence, fresh natural food, freedom, and health. This cluster was represented in every IAI protocol, even when instrumental choices of a more pragmatic orientation were expressed. This cluster we regard as an expression of the romantic-idealized enduring self (Spindler & Spindler, 1989b).

The pragmatic lifestyle, represented in the choices expressing the situated self, centered around choices of the modern rowhouse, white-collar work, factory jobs, the machinist and technical draftsman trades, the modern church, and the evening out in a festive pub. It is constructed of a cluster of quite different images and values: physical comfort, convenience, shopping, access to entertainment and medical care, regular income, paid vacations, less hardship, and clean work. This was the contemporary lifestyle actually available to most of the respondents. The ideal-romantic cluster represented in the enduring self was literally almost unavailable to the majority of the respondents.

We saw the cognitive management of these two opposing selves and supporting cultural clusters, the traditional vs. the urban-modern ways of life, as the primary task that the children learned in school and the teachers and parents taught. All teachers know that they themselves live, and that the children they are teaching will live, in the framework of the situated self (though they do not phrase it this way). And yet every teacher expressed the cluster of the ideal-romantic pole of the enduring self as desirable. Somehow the people of the Remstal seem to have been able to hold both the enduring-ideal-romanticized self, and the pragmatic-situated self, together without major breakdown. If they can do it, why do we have such difficulties with it in our schools?

We think that the answer is that the enduring self is related to the traditional Swaebish culture, which is of long standing in the Rems Valley. It is the traditional culture. There is a literature in Swaebish, the royal family of Baden Württemberg is Swaebish. The local Heimat-museums are about Swaebish home life, Swaebish artifacts, Swaebish quilts, and so forth. People speak Swaebish at home. The teachers, even though some of them are not from the Remstal area, speak Swaebish when they have to. The "newcomers," now third generation, from the outlying areas of Germany that had to be vacated after World War II, and from what was then the "East Zone," understand Swaebish. Although there are jokes about *die dumme Schwabe* (the dumb Swaebish) and their *unbeweglich* (unmoving) character, they are not really prejudiced against, nor regarded as lower-quality, low-status, or undesirable people. The fact that all children learn both Swaebish and *hoch Deutsch* is an indication of this. Speaking Swaebish is not discouraged in school, but the teachers teach in hoch Deutsch except when they have to explain something to a very young child whose primary language is still Swaebish. In short, children are raised and teachers work in an environment where cultural differences and distinctions are taken for granted and not considered invidiously. The problem in America and in American schools seems to be that in order to establish some kind of identity, mainstream American culture poses itself as dominant, supreme, moral, "right," to be observed, and to be taught at all costs to everyone. In the not-too-distant past this involved punishing children for speaking their native language, shaving their heads and "delousing" them (in residential Indian schools, for example), and in general letting them know that if they weren't pretty much Anglo-Saxon Protestant, or acting like they were, they were inferior, on the back burner, and to be shaped up or shucked off. We are reaping the harvest of our history, and although we are making efforts to change it, such efforts are not fast enough, thorough enough, or deep enough in our own psyches. There are very few consciously racist teachers but there are many teachers, perhaps even all teachers, who have very strong biases that are quite unmovable because they are integrated with their own sense of identity and self—in many cases the enduring self. If we could just adopt a Remstal attitude, it would help. Cultural therapy involves some self-examination along these lines on the part of both students and teachers. We do not mean by this that there should be a simple confession of sins by teachers, and in effect a kind of apology to children (though sometimes this seems in order), but rather that there be an analysis of the cultural persuasions involved on all sides. We are currently doing this in an experimental course for people with Bachelor of Arts degrees now returning to Sonoma State University to become teachers.

THE SELF AND INSTRUMENTAL COMPETENCE

It is not difficult to conceive of a global relationship of self, and particularly self-esteem, to instrumental performance, for which schooling, in modern complex societies, is a major arena. Children with various sociocultural backgrounds attend schools predicated on mainstream, largely middle-class, and largely white, Anglo-Saxon, Northern-European, Protestant cultural assumptions. Such children acquire deficits in self-esteem when they fail to master essential instrumentalities in this context. This self-esteem is damaged not only by actual failure but by negative perceptions and low expectations of these children by teachers and other students. The processes for failure begin when a child enters school.

The equation is direct. When instrumental competence is acquired and displayed in school settings, positive self-esteem and good self-concept is often the result. In turn, this can lead to competent school performance. In contrast, lack of instrumental competence in the school setting leads to negative self-esteem and poor self-concept and in turn to incompetent school performance, and possibly alienation and dropping out. One condition feeds another, which in turn continues to feed the first.

But the problem is more complex than that. The assumption that the whole self-concept is dependent upon school performance may be quite incorrect. The concept of self-efficacy, a subset of self-esteem, seems useful here. We define self-efficacy as a prediction that one will be able to meet the demands of the situation effectively. A student with feelings of self-efficacy thinks that he or she can answer questions, pass exams, read adequately—get the work done as well or better than most others.

Self-efficacy varies across different behaviors in different situations (Bandura, Adams, & Howells, 1980). This concept, like "instrumental competence," is not passive, as in Cooley's "looking glass self" (Gecas & Schwalbe, 1983). It is constructed of self-determined perceptions and predictions of behavior that interact with those of others in situations such as classrooms that are not simply a reflection of those others. Instrumental competence and self-efficacy seem quite similar, though stemming from unrelated research projects and quite different disciplines. Instrumental competence requires that one understands what activities are linked to what goals and how to perform the activities. Self-efficacy in our terms is an expectation that one can exhibit instrumental competence in the appropriate context.

For example, minority children often fail to acquire instrumental competence in test taking. The importance of tests in Anglo-oriented schools is not appreciated. The skills and motivations necessary for students' getting control of the content they are to be tested on (and then letting it drop), the significance of time in testing, and the need for hurry and tensed, focused excitement (even anxiety)—the whole pervasive complex of configurations of test taking in our schools—is not understood nor are the motivations for meritorious performance under the imposed and quite artificial conditions of test taking at present. The crucial linkage between goals, values, assignments, and priorities, and actual skills are not made. The child suffers failure, instrumental competence is not achieved, and self-efficacy is eroded.

Instrumental competence and self-efficacy are situational and may be considered to be expressions of the notion of situated self as employed in our interpretation of the Remstal case. We hypothesize that for minorities, as well as for Remstäler, there may be an enduring self that is sustained above and beyond the situated self or estimates of self-efficacy in school situations.

Children may fail in school because they do not perceive, understand, or master the instrumental relationships upon which schoolwork is predicated. They may develop low self-esteem and low estimates of self-efficacy in the school situation. But they may preserve an enduring self or identity that is comparatively intact and positive, formed and sustained in nonschool contexts.

Cultural therapy as relevant to these ideas would consist of trying to help children and teachers to acquire understanding of these instrumental competencies required in school. We are not thinking here of simply the competencies of test taking, or writing well, or doing math, but the broader context into which specific competencies are imbedded. The test-taking example is relevant here. There is not only the content of the test, the rightness or wrongness of answers, but also the test-taking cultural complex. We see this every day in our teaching at Stanford. Stanford students have been selected out for test-taking instrumental competence in its most complex and subtle sense. They are not always necessarily the best students. Much of school is ritualized, complicated, made difficult for those who are not raised in its shadow in ways that are irrelevant to ultimate instrumental competence. Part of our effort within the framework of cultural therapy would be to try to come to an understanding of what essential competence is as against ritualized, culturalized, competence—instrumental competence that has been imbedded within the framework of the majority culture but is not necessarily a part of minority cultures. Teachers need to understand this and children need to understand it, though we are not sure that teachers would find it entirely comfortable to have students understand too much.

ADAPTATIONS

There is a further complication—if we read the possibilities correctly. Our researches have convinced us that under conditions of personally experienced culture conflict, especially where the conflict creates conditions for instrumental failure, people respond in certain predictable ways. These modes of response we can sum up as follows: reaffirmation, withdrawal, constructive marginality, biculturalism, and assimilation (Spindler & Spindler, 1984, 1989a). There are various subsets to each of these modes, "withdrawal," for example, can be vegetative or self-destructive. "Assimilated" can be adjusted or compensatory.

Among the Menominee, where our ideas about these modes of adaptation first emerged, the reaffirmative adaption was represented by the native-oriented group. It was composed of a few older people who were essentially cultural survivors from the traditional past and a larger number of younger people who had met mainstream culture head on in schools and in the work world and who were trying to recreate and sustain a recognizable Menominee way of life—and escape from the mainstream. They sought participation in the Dream Dance, Medicine Lodge, Chief's Dance, Ghost Feast, and tried to live Indian style. They were fully aware of their choice. It could be called a strategy of adaptation (Spindler & Spindler, 1984).

Various forms of withdrawal were represented by others who were so torn by conflict that they could not identify with either the traditional or mainstream cultural symbols or groups. Many drank to oblivion and sometimes death. Others did nothing—they vegetated. "Constructive marginality" is represented by a number of Menominee who made a viable adaptation to culture conflict by avoiding strong identification with any group or any one set of symbols. They formed a personal culture that is instrumentally productive but is usually constituted of several different segments—some mainstream. They distanced themselves in greater and lesser degree from much of the conflict and maintained a wry view of it.

Among the assimilated Menominee there were some "150 percenters"—people who were more respectable than most respectable mainstream whites and who wondered how we could live and work with those "dirty Indians." They were compensators. There were others who were undifferentiated culturally from mainstream whites in the surrounding areas and who did not denigrate others who were more traditional. In fact they were interested in Menominee traditions, as described by Walter Hoffman, Alanson Buck Skinner, and Felix Keesing—anthropologists who had worked with the Menominee decades before we did, and who described the traditional culture in detail. There were also a few who appeared to be assimilated who had made a bicultural adaptation. They seemed equally at home in the traditional and mainstream context though the latter was socially dominant. This adaptation is extremely difficult to make because the distance between the two cultures is very great—we think greater than that for most minorities.

There's one other adaption represented by the Peyote Cult, or Native American Church. Menominee Peyotism synthesized Christian religious belief and traditional Menominee belief and symbolism. The Peyote tepee, for example, has 13 poles, one for Christ and 12 for the disciples. There does not seem to be anything exactly like Peyotism in the current adaption of minorities, though one could probably make a case for it.

The underlying principle is that conflict resolution is likely to take defensive forms, particularly when self-esteem is threatened. For example, the reaffirmative mode is characterized not merely by a return to a traditional or neotraditional pattern of behavior but also by the exclusion of perceived elements from the sociocultural context where one has suffered loss of self-esteem and has a low estimate of self-efficacy (contemporary resistance theory is an expression of this in a different theoretical framework). The assimilative mode may be characterized by a similar exclusion, but of perceived traditional cultural elements if these elements are perceived as a handicap or cause for instrumental failure. We hypothesize that something similar happens to many minority students. When instrumental competence is not attained in school and situational self-efficacy is damaged, the individual response may be to reaffirm, withdraw, or compensate. There can be an active rejection of the whole schooling context, and a reaffirmative celebration of street life, home life, or diffuse ethnic images and symbols, or a withdrawal characterized less by compensatory reaffirmation and exclusion of threatening elements than by self-destruction. There may be important differences in the adaptations between males and females that, to our knowledge, have not been explored in the existing literature (Spindler & Spindler, 1990; L. Spindler, 1989). We could go on exploring these possibilities, but we hope that our general intent is clear.

Cultural therapy with respect to this line of thought would consist of being able to bring out in free discussions the kinds of adaptations that students are making to the school, its culture, and its representatives. We are not inferring that the only adaptive strategies that are possible are included somewhere in the framework that we have delineated, but we do think that the framework orients us to some of the kinds of adaptation that are possible.

Knowing what one's adaptation is, one then can make a more cognitively based decision about whether or not this is the right strategy at the right time. It is very clear that some students are doing a kind of reaffirmative identification and in doing so withdraw from or become actively confrontive with school culture and purpose. Boundaries are created, and in fact boundaries are necessary for this kind of identity work. These boundaries may seem quite irrational and destructive to outside observers who are not "in the skin" of the adapter. The ultimate driving force is to maintain self-esteem, to at least not seriously damage the enduring self, and to make the situated self, in relation to the enduring self, tolerable.

CONCLUSION

Cultural therapy is an orientation for remedial efforts directed (by us) primarily at teachers or teacher trainers, and by others at students—both mainstream and minority. The essential features of cultural therapy are: making explicit the nature of conflict in cultural terms, the involvement of the enduring and situated self in this conflict, and the requirements for instrumental competence in the school situation. Cultural awareness, both of one's own culture (familial, ethnicity, class, gang, and so on) and of the other (usually mainstream or minority) culture is crucial for both students and teachers. When the nature of the problem is seen in this objectified manner, self-determined choices may be made on a realistic and less self-damaging basis.

ACKNOWLEDGMENTS

We wish to acknowledge the advice, reactions, and criticisms of colleagues and students at Stanford, The University of California at Davis, Sonoma State University, and the State University of California at Sacramento on the occasion of various presentations and colloquia on cultural therapy—and particularly to Patricia Phelan, Frank Logan, and Ann Locke Davidson at Stanford and Henry Trueba at the University of Wisconsin at Madison.

NOTES

1. We have drawn heavily in this chapter from our papers: "Instrumental Competence, Self-efficacy, Linguistic Minorities and Cultural Therapy" (1989a); "Crosscultural Comparative, Reflective Interviewing in Schoenhausen and Roseville" (1993); and "The Enduring, Situated and Endangered Self in Fieldwork: A Personal Account" (1992).

2. We presented the first paper on the CCCRI at the American Anthropological Association meetings in November, 1986. The first publication demonstrating it was not by us, but by Mariko Fugita and Toshyuki Sano (1988) who had been instructed in it by us. The reflective interview technique was not inspired by recent work on reflective teaching or inquiry into teaching processes, though this work is not irrelevant to our purposes. It stems from anthropological concerns emerging particularly in the writings of postmodernists on reflective and reflexive ethnography and interpretation, anticipated by work of people such as Mead and Collier. (The idea was inspired by Margaret Mead's chapter on evocative stimuli in fieldwork in *The Making of Psychological Anthropology* (1978); and by the work of John Collier Jr. and Malcolm Collier in *Visual Anthropology* (1986).) It has occurred to us that one way to encourage reflective, self-analytic, and self-aware teaching is to use culturally bracketed interview techniques such as the CCCRI. Our chapter in Schratz (in press), "Crosscultural Comparative, Reflective Interviewing in Schoenhausen and Roseville" describes the technique, locates its origins, and demonstrates the results.

3. Our emphasis is on culture as a dynamic process (rather than a static historical experience) where the values and experiences of diverse groups of people play a significant role in an ongoing American cultural dialogue that is constantly being renegotiated. (We write about this topic extensively in *The*

American Cultural Dialogue and Its Transmission [Spindler & Spindler with Trueba & Williams, 1990].)

4. Our interest in the "self" is of long standing, as evidenced by Louise Spindler's memoir on *Menomini Women and Culture Change*. G. Spindler used self-other concepts in his early research in California schools (see G. Spindler, 1959). The notion of a "situated" self was stimulated by a symposium paper presented at Stanford University by Dorinne Kondo (1987). There are other possibilities, such as the "constructed" self, made from the interaction of the enduring and situated selves, or the "saturated" self, which is overwhelmed by input from frenetic, divisive, fragmented social communication, or "multiple" selves, more diverse than the enduring self but more cohesive as reactive systems than situated selves. We find the "enduring" and "situated" selves as representing the poles of cohesion and diversification possible in the normal psychocultural constitution, and the "endangered" self as a consequence of severe conflict between the two.

REFERENCES

Bandura, A., Adams, N. E., & Howells, G. N. (1980). Tests of generality of self-efficacy theory. *Psychological Review, 84,* 191–215.

Collier, J., Jr., & Collier, M. (1986). *Visual anthropology.* Albuquerque: University of New Mexico Press.

Fugita, M., & Sano, T. S. (1988). Children in American and Japanese day-care centers: Ethnography and cross-cultural interviewing. In H. Trueba & C. Delgado-Gaitan (Eds.), *School and society: Learning content through culture* (pp. 125–163). New York: Praeger.

Gecas, V., & Schwalbe, M. (1983). Beyond the looking glass self: Social structure and efficacy-based self esteem. *Social Anthropology Quarterly, 46*(2), 77–88.

Goffman, I. (1961). *Asylums.* New York: Anchor.

Hallowell, A. I. (1955). *Culture and experience.* Philadelphia: University of Pennsylvania Press.

Kondo, D. (1987, February). *Company as family? Ideologies of selfhood in a Japanese family enterprise.* Paper presented at the Stanford University Colloquium, Stanford, CA.

Leiris, M. (1978). Das Augen des Ethnographen. *Ethnologische Schriften, 2,* 34–55. Frankfurt/M: Syndikat.

Levine, R. (1984). *Culture, behavior and personality.* New York: Aldine.

Mead, M. (1978). The evocation of psychologically relevant responses in ethnological field work. In G. Spindler (Ed.), *The making of psychological anthropology* (pp. 87–139). Berkeley: University of California Press.

Spindler, G. (1959). *The transmission of American culture.* The Third Burton Lecture. Cambridge, MA: Harvard University Press.

Spindler, L. (1962). *Menomini women and culture change* (Memoir No. 91). Menasha, WI: American Anthropological Association.

Spindler, L. (1989). A comment: Gender differences neglected. In H. Trueba, G. Spindler, & L. Spindler (Eds.), *What do anthropologists have to say about dropouts?* (pp. 135–136). London: Falmer Press.

Spindler, G., & Spindler, L. (1970). Fieldwork among the Menomini. In G. Spindler (Ed.), *Being an anthropologist: Fieldwork in eleven cultures* (pp. 267–301). New York: Holt, Rinehart and Winston. (Reprinted 1984, Waveland Press)

Spindler G., & Spindler, L. (1984). *Dreamers with power: The Menominee Indians.* Prospect Heights, IL: Waveland Press. (First published by Holt, Rinehart and Winston as *Dreamers without power: The Menomini Indians,* 1971)

Spindler, G., & Spindler, L. (1989a). Instrumental competence, self-efficacy, linguistic minorities, and cultural therapy: A preliminary attempt at integration. *Anthropology and Education Quarterly, 10*(1), 36–50.

Spindler, G., & Spindler, L. (1989b). The self and the instrumental model in the study of culture change. *Proceedings of the Kroeber Anthropological Society* (pp. 109–117). Berkeley: University of California Press.

Spindler, G., & Spindler, L. (1990). Male and female in four changing cultures. In D. Jordan & M. Swartz (Eds.), *Personality and the cultural construction of society* (pp. 182–200). Georgia: University of Alabama Press.

Spindler, G., & Spindler, L. (1992). The enduring, situated, and endangered self in fieldwork: A personal account. In B. Boyer (Ed.), *The psychoanalytic study of society* (pp. 23–28). Hillsdale, NJ: Analytic Press.

Spindler, G., & Spindler, L. (1993). Crosscultural, comparative, reflective interviewing in Schoenhausen and Roseville. In M. Schratz (Ed.), *Qualitative voices in education research* (pp. 53–93). London: Falmer Press.

Spindler, G., & Spindler, L., with Trueba, H., & Williams, M. (1990). *The American cultural dialogue and its transmission.* London: Falmer Press.

CHAPTER 2

STUDENTS' MULTIPLE WORLDS: NAVIGATING THE BORDERS OF FAMILY, PEER, AND SCHOOL CULTURES

Patricia Phelan, Ann Locke Davidson, and Hanh Cao Yu

First, you must understand and digest the fact that children, all children come to school motivated to enlarge their worlds. You start with *their* worlds. You do not look at them, certainly not initially, as organisms to be molded and regulated. You look at them to determine how what they are, seek to know, and have experienced can be used as the fuel to fire the process for enlargement of interest, knowledge, and skills. You do not look at them in terms of deficits: what they do not know but need to know. Far from having deficits, they are asset rich. You enter their world in order to aid them and you to build bridges between two worlds, not walls. (Sarason, 1990, p. 164)

This study[1] focuses on understanding students' multiple worlds and the transitions between them in an effort to provide information that will assist teachers, administrators, and others who work with students to build bridges between their worlds and the world of school. Our purpose is twofold: first, to describe family, school, and peer worlds, and the inter-relationships among them, and in particular how meanings and under-standings combine to affect students' engagement with learning; second, to understand students' perceptions of boundaries and borders between

This research was conducted under the auspices of the Center for Research on the Context of Secondary School Teaching with funding from the Office of Educational Research and Improvement, US Department of Education, Cooperative Agreement #OERI-G0087C235.

worlds and the adaptation strategies they employ as they move from one context to another. We are especially interested in features in school environments that aid or impede students in making the transition between their worlds and the world of school.

We use the term "world" to mean the cultural knowledge and behavior found within the boundaries of students' particular families, peer groups, and schools; we presume that each world contains values and beliefs, expectations, actions, and emotional responses familiar to insiders. We use the terms "social setting," "arena," and "context" to refer to the places and events within which individuals act and interact. Students employ cultural knowledge acquired from their family, peer, and school worlds in social settings and contexts. Social settings and contexts may be found within the bounds of any one world (e.g., a student having dinner with family members) or may include actors from various worlds (e.g., students interacting with friends in classrooms or friends in each others' homes). In the latter case, people in the same social setting may or may not share the same cultural knowledge acquired from the constellation of their individual worlds.[2]

Similar to Erickson (1987), we refer to boundaries as real or perceived lines between worlds, settings, or contexts that are neutral and where sociocultural components are perceived to be equal by the people in each setting. When boundaries exist, movement between worlds occurs with relative ease—social and psychological costs are minimal. Alternatively, borders are real or perceived lines that are not neutral and that separate worlds not perceived as equal. When borders are present, movement and adaptation are frequently difficult because the knowledge and skills in one world are more highly valued and esteemed than those in another. Although it is possible for students to navigate borders with apparent success, these transitions can incur personal and psychic costs invisible to teachers and others. Moreover, borders can become impenetrable barriers when the psychosocial consequences of adaptation become too great.[3]

Although the concepts we use are not new, prior research generally has focused on families, peers, and schools as distinct entities. We know that any one can affect powerfully the direction in which adolescents will be pulled. For example, dynamic teachers, vigorous schools, and programs targeted to override the negative effects associated with low socioeconomic status, limited motivation, and language and cultural barriers can produce committed, interested, and academically engaged individuals (Abi-Nader, 1990; Edmonds, 1979; Heath, 1982; Johnson & Johnson, 1981; Joyce, Murphy, Showers, & Murphy, 1989; Rutter, Maughan, Mortimore, & Ouston, 1979; Sharan, 1980; Slavin, 1988; Slavin & Madden, 1989; Vogt, Jordan, & Tharp, 1987; Walberg, 1986). Likewise, research on peer groups has described the potency and force with which members pull young people toward the norms of groups (Clasen & Brown, 1985; Clement & Harding, 1978; Coleman, 1963; Eckert, 1989; Larkin, 1979; Ueda, 1987; Varenne 1982). We know too that family indices, such as socioeconomic status and parents' educational levels, are important predictors of students' engagement with educational settings (Jencks et al., 1972), as are cultural expectations and beliefs (Clark, 1983; Erickson, 1987; Fordham, 1988; Gibson, 1987; Hoffman, 1988; McDermott, 1987; Ogbu, 1983, 1987; Spindler, 1987; Spindler & Spindler, 1982; Suarez-Orozco, 1985, 1987; Trueba, 1988; Trueba, Moll, Diaz, & Diaz, 1982).

In other words, we know a great deal about how aspects of families, schools and teachers, and peer groups independently affect educational outcomes. But we know little about how these worlds combine in the day-to-day lives of adolescents to affect their engagement with school and classroom contexts. Steinberg, Brown, Cider, Kaczmarek, and Lazzaro (1988) also note this neglect in educational research: "Virtually absent from the literature are studies that examine student and contextual influences in interaction with each other" (p. 43). Further, while it is in these different arenas that young people negotiate and construct their realities, for the most part, their movements and adaptations from one setting to another are taken for granted.[4] Although such transitions frequently require students' efforts and skills, especially when contexts are governed by different values and norms, there has been relatively little study of this process.

In this study our focus is on the individual as the mediator and integrator of meaning and experience, in contrast to single context approaches that compartmentalize aspects of students' lives (studies in which peer groups, family, and school variables are studied independently of one another). Although research in these areas has provided a great deal of important information, it is the researcher who determines the focus. Our emphasis is rather on the worlds of the individual child. Studies focusing on peer groups alone may miss the significance of school and classroom features that determine the choice or effects of a peer group. Likewise, studies of teachers and pedagogy can obscure features of adolescents' lives, such as peer group interactions or cultural background factors, which combine to impact students' engagement with learning.

Educators attempting to create optimal school environments for increasingly diverse populations need to know how students negotiate borders successfully, or alternatively, how they are impeded by barriers (and borders) that prevent their connection, not only with institutional contexts, but with peers who are different from themselves. We feel that it is particularly important to direct attention to school features that enable smooth transitions, and transform borders, real or perceived, into passable boundaries.

THE STUDENTS' MULTIPLE WORLDS STUDY

During this 2-year longitudinal study, the student study team has had an opportunity to know 54 students in 4 high schools increasingly well. The large, urban, desegregated schools in our sample are paired across districts: "Maple High School" ("Montevideo District") and "Explorer High School" ("Bolivar District") have experienced fairly dramatic changes in the demography of their student populations, whereas "Canyon High School" ("Montevideo District") and "Huntington High School" ("Bolivar District") have had more stable, middle-class student populations.[5] A majority of the students, selected to represent some of the diversity found in many of California's large urban high schools, were in their first year of high school when the study began in the fall of 1989. Students vary in a number of dimensions, including gender, ethnicity, achievement level, immigrant history, and transportation status. An equal number of academically high- and low-achieving students were selected from each school and both minority and majority students are included in the two achievement categories. Students were asked to participate by school personnel.

Four in-depth interviews with each of 54 students provide information on students' perceptions of classrooms and schools, the importance and influence of friends and peer groups, and the family conditions that are significant to their lives. In addition, informal conversations and interviews with 10 of the 54 students supplement more formal data collection methods. Observations in classrooms furnish documentation of interactions between adolescents and their teachers and peers in classroom contexts. Student record data (which include standardized test scores, grades, teacher comments, and attendance and referral records) contribute a picture of achievement patterns and teacher perceptions of individual students over time. Additionally, we obtained demographic and descriptive information about students and their families. Finally, we interviewed teachers about their perceptions of students' academic performance, classroom interactions, social and peer group behavior, and family background.

As the study began, our emphasis was on students' descriptions of school factors that affect their engagement with learning—for example, classroom organization, teacher attitudes and behaviors, pedagogy, and overall school climate. However, the use of open-ended interviews allowed students to talk about other features of their lives (i.e., peers and family) that are relevant to their feelings about school. "I wouldn't let them put me in a higher track because I wanted to be with my friends," reported one student. "At least in my family it's sort of expected that you're going to try to get A's or something close," said another. "Being Mexican means being popular, cutting classes, acting crazy," reported yet another student.

As a result, a model evolved to describe students' multiple worlds and the relationships among them. Particularly important is our focus on the nature of boundaries and borders between worlds, as well as strategies that students employ to move between and adapt to different contexts and settings. As depicted in Figure 2.1, the meanings drawn from each of these worlds combine to influence students' actions. For example, if parents emphasize school achievement but friends devalue good grades, young people must incorporate and manage these different perspectives while deciding on their own course of action. The emergence of the Multiple Worlds model is an important development of this investigation. Unlike most other approaches, which focus attention on stable characteristics of individuals (e.g., gender and ethnicity) or concentrate on language acquisition or achievement level alone, the Multiple Worlds model

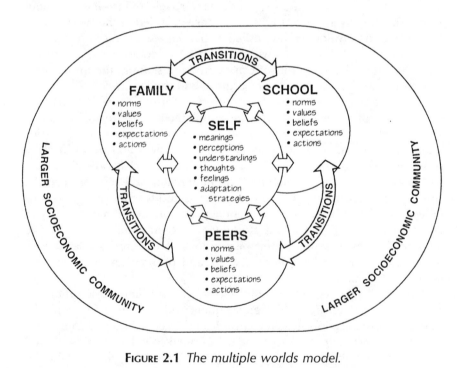

FIGURE 2.1 *The multiple worlds model.*

is generic. It is not ethnic, achievement, or gender specific, but transcends these categories to consider multiple worlds, boundary crossing, and adaptation for *all* students. The generic nature of the model is particularly useful for understanding diversity within ethnic groups. For example, we have seen that students—Latino, Asian American, African American, and European American—may perceive borders very differently and utilize various adaptation strategies as they move from one setting to another.

By focusing on transitions, we have been able to identify a number of different types of borders that students encounter. Psychosocial, sociocultural, socioeconomic, linguistic, gender, and structural borders all impede students' connection with classroom and school contexts. Borders are created in several ways and each type is characterized by distinctive properties that are important to understand as educators attempt to identify strategies that will enable students to make transitions successfully.

Borders

Psychosocial. Psychosocial borders are constructed when children experience anxiety, depression, apprehension, or fear at a level that disrupts or hinders their ability to focus on classroom tasks, or blocks their ability to establish relationships with teachers or peers in school environments. Psychosocial borders can also prevent students' connections with peers or family. It is certainly possible that psychosocial borders are secondary to or result from a child's response to sociocultural, socioeconomic, or linguistic borders. However, other events in children's lives can also create psychosocial borders, for example, stress and anxiety resulting from a physically or sexually abusive home situation; a parent's serious illness; the death of a pet; or other non–border-related events. In some cases, psychosocial borders are temporal in nature. In other words, anxiety and stress connected with a particular event can be reduced as circumstances change.

Sociocultural. When the cultural components in one world are viewed as less important than those in another, sociocultural borders are created. A number of authors have defined and directed attention to the significance of sociocultural boundaries and borders: Delgado-Gaitan and Trueba (1991); Erickson (1987); Barth (1969); McDermott and Gospodinoff (1979); Erickson and Bekker (1986). Like Erickson (1987) and Delgado-Gaitan and Trueba (1991), we believe that cultural differences per se do not necessarily create barriers to school participation and learning. In fact, it is certainly possible to view cultural differences as assets rather than as liabilities.

Socioeconomic. Socioeconomic borders are generated when economic circumstances create severe limitations. For example, the economic situation of a family may require a student to work outside the home thus making school participation (academic, social, and extracurricular) difficult or impossible. Or a student, economically constrained, may be precluded from involvement with peers whose economic circumstances are greater. And finally, socioeconomic borders can result from students' community and neighborhood conditions that contrast with their school environment—this is particularly true for students who are transported. Although sociocultural and socioeconomic borders combine frequently, this is not always the case. We feel the distinction is worthwhile when intervention strategies are considered.

Linguistic. Linguistic borders result when communication between students' worlds (home and school, peer and home, and so on) is obstructed, not because of different languages per se, but because one group regards another group's language as unacceptable or inferior. As Delgado-Gaitan and Trueba (1991) state:

> The very act of learning English as a second language is a cultural variation, but it does not necessarily create distress for children. A conflict ensues when children, limited in English proficiency, are taught all of their academic curriculum in English in such a way that their native language and culture are invalidated. (p. 28)

In our study, language differences became borders when teachers or students saw language as a problem.

Gender. When the school as an institution or the people in it promote roles, aspirations, or estimates of worth to women that differ from those it offers to men, gender borders exist. Gender borders can be found in both the substance and the process of the educational experience—in the content of the curriculum (i.e., when the history and accomplishments of one group are fully or partially excluded from the curriculum), in pedagogical styles and methods (i.e., when teacher attention and encouragement are more frequently directed towards one group), and in attitudes and expectations (i.e., when the sensibilities, problems and assets of one group are viewed differently than those of the other). Gender borders not only undermine self-confidence and block students' perceptions of what is possible for themselves and others, but also discourage or impede the acquisition of skills necessary to pursue specific careers.[6]

Structural. Structural borders occur between students' home or peer worlds and the world of school. We define structural borders as features in school environments that prevent, impede, or discourage students from engaging fully in learning—social or academic. Three types of conditions give rise to structural borders:

1. *Availability*—In this case, the school environment lacks adequate resources and supports to meet students' needs, for example, inadequate tutoring, no counselors, insufficiently equipped libraries, inadequate second language training, and so forth.
2. *Bridges*—Services and opportunities for students exist in the school setting but there are no bridges to connect students with available resources. In other words, students do not have information about the programs and opportunities that are available to them or, if they possess such knowledge, no one in the environment assists them in accessing resources that may be potentially beneficial.
3. *Match*—Structures and services are available and visible to students but either they do not match student needs or they actually impede students' connection with school and classroom settings, for example, an anti-abortion poster hung on a counselor's office door, tracking, severe and punitive discipline policies, and so on.

Although there is often overlap between these distinctions, we believe that the development and implementation of successful intervention strategies depends on the ability of teachers and others in school environments to recognize and identify not only where and when borders exist (e.g., between peers and schools, school and home, and so on), but also the nature of the borders that students encounter.

TYPOLOGY OF ADAPTATION

As our study has proceeded we have found a good deal of variety in students' descriptions of their worlds and in their perceptions of boundaries and borders. At the same time, we have also uncovered distinctive patterns among students as they cross settings. We use a typology to illustrate four patterns:[7]

Type I: Congruent Worlds/Smooth Transitions
Type II: Different Worlds/Border Crossings Managed
Type III: Different Worlds/Border Crossings Difficult
Type IV: Different Worlds/Borders Impenetrable

The patterns we describe are not necessarily stable for individual students over time, but rather can be affected by external conditions such as classroom or school climate conditions, family circumstances, or changes in peer group affiliations.[8]

Each of the four types includes the variety of combinations possible with respect to perceived boundaries and borders (e.g., between family and school, peers and family, peers/family and school, and so on) and each combination is characterized in different ways by different students. Our descriptions of students illustrate only some of the combinations possible. Both enabling and limiting patterns of behavior are contained in this typology. We will see that some of the superficially approved styles of adaptation can be as potentially restricting as those where discordant patterns seem to dominate.

Type I: Congruent Worlds/Smooth Transitions

For some students, values, beliefs, expectations, and normative ways of behaving are, for the most part, parallel across worlds. Although the circumstances of daily contexts change, such students perceive the boundaries between their family, peer, and schools worlds as easily manageable. Movement from one setting to another is harmonious and uncomplicated. This does not mean that students act exactly the same way or discuss the same things with teachers, friends, and family members, but rather that commonalities among worlds override differences. In these cases, students' worlds are merged by their common sociocultural components rather than bounded by conspicuous differences.

"Ryan Moore". Ryan Moore, a European-American middle-class student at Explorer High School in the Bolivar School District, typifies an adolescent whose worlds are congruent. According to Ryan, all of the people in his life essentially believe and value the same things. When Ryan leaves his family in the morning and joins his friends to walk to school he does not have to shift gears. His friends and their parents esteem the same things as Ryan and his parents—family cohesiveness and education are primary values.

> *Interviewer:* So it sounds like you sought out the kids who have the same values you do?
> *Ryan:* Yeah, it works better that way because all the people that don't really get good grades in our group, they want to get

good grades and they're always working. It's not like they're just here because the state says they have to be. (ES37STA:421–432)[9]

In fact, when Ryan's peers deviate from known and accepted ways of behaving, not only are eyebrows raised but friends reaffirm, with each other, what is acceptable.

> *Interviewer:* So you don't have to explain or become ridiculed for doing homework and that sort of thing?
>
> *Ryan:* No. No, like I remember one of our friends, he was trading baseball cards the day before finals, and it got around—'he's trading baseball cards!' And everybody else was going to people's houses to study and then here's this guy sitting out on his front lawn with a couple of other guys trading baseball cards and it was like 'You know what I saw him doing?' (*with shock*) No way! (ES37STA:434–448)

At school, teachers' language and communication styles, teachers' conceptions of the necessary strategies for success such as compliance, hard work, and academic achievement, and pervading upward mobility norms match the values, beliefs, and behaviors of Ryan's family, making transitions between home and school unproblematic. Further, Ryan learned quickly how to function successfully in the school setting—who has the power, where to go for help, what things can be changed, and what things can't. According to Ryan, "You just have to learn the rules of the game." Ryan not only has learned the rules, he has become an expert player. For example, unhappy with an experimental freshman history course, Ryan and a friend initiated a meeting with the school principal and history department faculty to suggest changes. Transferring elements from his home world, Ryan is able to affect his own school experience.

> *Ryan:* If it's really affecting me, I'll say, 'I've got to change this just because I figure, why sit around when you can change it?' . . . [that's how] it's always been . . . with me. It's also like my parents from the beginning, you know, [said] 'If you want something [to be different], go out and change it.' It's just been like, if I wanted to make something work, I just did it.
>
> *Interviewer:* In this situation you weren't intimidated by the people?
>
> *Ryan:* Basically, I go on and I'm nice and cordial and if you're nice to me then that's fine. And if you're not, if you're like closed to what I have to say then it just makes me want to win

more. I guess I'm highly competitive. I know that from my
sports and stuff. And so, it's kind of like a competition is how I
guess I view it. If I got a B in the class it's like I lost. And I want
to change that, or let it be known that it was unfair.
(ES37STAB:555–587)

Although Ryan likes some teachers better than others, his academic performance is unaffected by his preferences—he does well across subjects.
For the most part, his long-term goals and aspirations allow him to overlook, ignore, or rationalize classroom circumstances that are not optimal
in his view. Working toward future aspirations takes precedence over any
immediate discomfort he may feel because of a particular class or teacher.
However, when he perceives his future to be threatened (e.g., by an unfair
grade), he quickly takes steps to rectify the situation.

Across his worlds, people's perceptions of Ryan are remarkably similar. Parents, friends, and teachers all report that Ryan is an excellent student, a thoughtful learner, and a "really nice kid, well-liked by everybody."
Everyone expects that Ryan will get good grades, will behave in a thoughtful and mature manner, and will no doubt attend a prestigious college.
Ryan's expectations of himself are not dissimilar.

> *Ryan:* Everybody wants to get good grades because I mean now,
> everybody sees their future. And they realize that you can't mess
> around in school—you can mess around after school but you've
> got to be serious while you're here.
> *Interviewer:* What do you see yourself doing in four years?
> *Ryan:* Oh, I want to go to Polytechnic 'cause my dad went there. I
> like it there, it seems like the kind of school I'd like.
> (ES37STA:454–470)

An important feature binding Ryan's worlds together is that the actors
in his life move across boundaries as well. For example, Ryan's parents
have always been actively involved in school affairs, and currently both
of his parents participate in parent programs at Explorer High School.
Ryan's teachers either know his parents or are aware of their school
involvement. Ryan describes his parents as supportive of his school activities and he is proud that they take an active role. Likewise, Ryan's friends
live in his neighborhood, "hang out" at his house, and interact comfortably with his parents. There is nothing about Ryan's family (culturally or
socioeconomically) that sets him apart from his friends or their families.
Getting together with friends also reinforces these similarities.

> Well, we'll go to somebody's house and watch movies or they'll come to my house and we'll play ping pong. Just basically just get together. The big thing is being together. We get to talk everything out about the week and complain about what [we] want to complain about. Everybody has the same complaints. (ES37STB:535–543)

Ryan's friends also cross into his school world—he does not, for example, leave his friends in the neighborhood to go across town to a distant school. At school, Ryan and his friends are in an accelerated academic track and frequently have the same teachers. As a result, teachers not only know Ryan's friends but they also know or at least have some knowledge of his family.

Rarely, however, do Ryan and his friends intermingle with students in other peer groups. At Explorer High School, students describe borders between groups as rigid and impenetrable. Ryan's response when asked if ethnic groups intermingle illuminates his view of students' differences and illustrates border maintenance measures:

> If they speak Spanish and don't speak English, or they speak Vietnamese but hardly any English, they tend to hang together. But if they speak English well, they'll hang around with other people, except for the Hispanics—they tend to hang around in gangs.
>
> Not formal gangs, just—they're kind of like a group that goes around and you see and you realize, 'okay, they're here, I want to be there. When they're there, I want to be here.' It seems like they don't want to be bused here. So they're going to make our lives miserable here and bring with them the way they hang downtown . . . it's because they think, well we had to get bused down here because somebody spoke up, and now we don't want to be here, so let's let them know that we don't want to be here. (ES37STA:490–530)

Ryan and his friends have little contact with or knowledge about students different than themselves. Classroom and school climate features at Explorer exacerbate these circumstances. For example, tracking in some subjects serves to segregate Ryan and his friends from students in lower-level classes. In Ryan's untracked general science class (which he was required to take as a freshman) pedagogy is teacher dominated and there is little interaction or discussion among students. When answering end-of-chapter questions, Ryan works exclusively with his friends and views other students in the class, who are not as academically successful, as responsible for an unchallenging curriculum. None of Ryan's classes offer cooperative learning techniques and few provide opportunities for students to work together or to discuss ideas. Further, most of the curriculum includes limited information about people of color or wider socioeconomic issues dealing with reasons for stratification and unequal opportunities. In general, Explorer's school environment provides little opportunity for Ryan or his friends to move (intellectually or physically) outside of their bounded, congruent worlds. For the most part, school features mitigate against the development of intergroup understandings.

"Joseph Foster". Other students in our sample also describe congruent worlds where boundary crossing is not a problem. This type is not unfamiliar, and, not surprisingly, it frequently includes European-American, middle- to upper-middle-class, high-achieving adolescents. However, not all of these students are high achieving. For example, Joseph Foster, a middle-class European-American student at Canyon High School in the Montevideo School District, maintains passing grades (mostly D's and C's) and has no desire to achieve at a higher level. Nor do Joseph's teachers or parents expect him to do so. Joseph's teachers and counselor say that he is performing as well as he can and his parent's primary expectations are that he pass his classes and graduate from high school. Nobody, including Joseph, expects that he will go to college.

However, Joseph is clear about his future and everyone (parents, friends, and teachers) supports his goals. Like his father, Joseph plans to enter the construction business and aspires to own his own company.

> *Joseph:* I want to be a contractor. . . . well, that's what my dad is. Yeah, I want to have my own business. [My dad], well, he wants me to do that, and my mom, she sees that my dad does good, so she thinks it's a good idea.
> *Interviewer:* What about their expectations in terms of school?
> *Joseph:* Well, they just want me to get by [by] passing. I mean, they don't want me to be an A student, they just want me to pass. I'm not gonna go [to college]. My dad didn't go to college either. (OR11STB:200–256)

Family, peer, and teacher expectations of Joseph are similar, allowing him to move without dissonance between worlds. Joseph's actions in school are in accord with acceptable standards of behavior—teachers believe that his academic work is up to the limits of his capability, they perceive him as pleasant and agreeable, and they view his active participation in school sports as evidence of his involvement. Further, Joseph has specific plans for the future that include definite occupational goals, well in line with culturally acceptable work patterns. His counselor and some of his teachers know Joseph's older brother (who also attended Canyon) and his parents, who participate in school affairs by attending parent conferences and sporting events. They describe Joseph as "coming from a really nice, supportive family." Joseph is not a student teachers worry about.

Type II: Different Worlds/Border Crossings Managed

For some students, family, peer, or school worlds are different (with respect to culture, ethnicity, socioeconomic status, or religion), thereby requiring adjustment and reorientation as movement between contexts occurs. For example, a student's family world may be dominated by an all-encompassing religious doctrine in which values and beliefs are contrary to those found in school and peer worlds. For other students, home and neighborhood are viewed as starkly different than school—particularly for students of color who are transported. And for still other students, differences between peers and family are dominant themes.

Regardless of the differences, in Type II, students' perceptions of borders between worlds do not prevent them from managing crossings or adapting to different settings. However, this does not mean that crossings are always easy, that they are made in the same way, or that they always result in the same personal and psychic consequences. Indeed, we have uncovered three strategies students adopt to make these crossings, each associated with various emotional benefits and costs.

First, some students adapt completely, conforming to mainstream patterns of academic and social interaction while at school and hiding aspects of their home lives that might differentiate them from the majority of their peers. Frequently these students devalue or disparage aspects of their home worlds, their voices reflecting an internalization of roles and an acceptance of the status quo that some scholars refer to as "internalized oppression" (Delgado-Gaitan & Trueba, 1991; Gaventa, 1980). As Delgado-Gaitan and Trueba (1991) state, "Here is where the cultural and social conflicts between home and school can become a nightmare of contrasting demands that confuse or lead to rejection of the home culture or language, and even in some extreme cases to rejection of one's own self" (p. 31).

A second strategy occurs when students adapt situationally, conforming to mainstream patterns of interaction when they are in the minority, returning to home or community patterns of interaction when with their peers in social settings. These students do not devalue or seek to distance themselves from their different worlds, but rather, adapt as a practical matter. The students in our study who exhibit this pattern seem to suffer the least psychosocial stress. They fit in and operate successfully across a variety of social settings.

Finally, using a third strategy, some students develop a capacity to blend aspects of their different worlds, often maintaining high levels of academic achievement without hiding or devaluing the aspects of their home or community lives that differentiate them from their majority peers. These students both value and criticize aspects of their multiple worlds, drawing elements from each to create an identity that transcends conventional categories. Yet, the assertion of this transcultural identity (Rosaldo, 1989) can bring with it emotional costs as well as benefits. For in not succumbing to the normative press to fit in (in community, peer, and school worlds), these youth open themselves up for criticism from actors in their various worlds who expect adherence to social rules and expectations.

"Elvira Buenafe". Elvira Buenafe, a junior Filipina-American student at Canyon High School, illustrates the use of the first adaptation strategy vividly, as she describes her efforts to conform to mainstream patterns of academic and social interaction at school. Elvira entered Canyon High School in the spring of her 10th-grade year (the school includes grades 10 to 12) and has since maintained a 3.67 grade point average. She rises at 5:20 A.M. and, as a participant in the school district's desegregation program, catches a bus to Canyon High School, located in an affluent, upper middle-class neighborhood almost an hour from her home. Eighty percent of Canyon students go on to college. As Elvira describes her reasons for choosing to attend this school, she illustrates her perceptions of the sociocultural and socioeconomic borders between her home in a predominantly Filipino neighborhood and Canyon High School:

> Oh, they said the people were friendlier up here and the population—'cause some of my friends . . . they get tired of seeing so many Filipinos and they want a different atmosphere so they come up here . . . most of the Filipino guys down south are like hoods or involved in gangs and stuff, and [I] don't want that. They have long hair and when you come up here it's a little bit more different . . . also down south there's a lot of like girls that are involved in gangs too. I just get lazy cause I don't like to do my hair a lot and lots of the girls down south, they always fix their hair every

day and put on like black eyeliner. When they look at you, they just like think you're weird or something. (OR09STA:62–85)

It's like they live life more freely up here and that's what I like about it—they have cars, they can go out to lunch . . . I just like go home to do homework. (OR09STA:766–773)

. . . up here for some reason it looks so much cleaner and nicer and it makes you feel happy to be here, you know? Cause I just like stand on our upper floor [of the school]—if you play softball you just look at those condos or whatever those are, it's called New Age Living [pseudonym] and just look over there. (OR09STB:674–682)

Culture, ethnicity, and trying to work out her own place in divergent worlds are repetitive themes throughout Elvira's interviews.

Elvira views her family and neighborhood as a rigidly bounded Filipino enclave. "There used to be some real Americans, but then they moved," she said. As Elvira crosses the border between her home and school worlds, one of her primary objectives is not to stand out. She poignantly describes her horror of being the target of blatant discrimination because of her status as a transported student.

And well, most of the people here are friendly. There are a few that are like kind of not . . . I don't know, I guess they are not willing to integrate or they don't really want to. Sometimes I'm fine. But like, walking with a friend, there are these two guys and they're like saying, 'New York City, here comes de' program.' [referring to Elvira and her friend as transported students] I hate that, it's like 'Oh my God,' and I try to ignore them but. . . . (OR09STA:113–128)

As part of her effort to adapt, Elvira has completely disengaged herself from any involvement with her sister's friends. Maria, who is one year younger, has chosen to attend the family's neighborhood high school rather than participate in the district's transportation program. According to Elvira, her sister is "into her own race" and frequently mentions hating European Americans. Many of her sister's friends are in gangs, "two have been stabbed, another has stabbed someone." Though peripherally interested in these events, Elvira remains distant from any involvement. I think it's pretty interesting, but . . . it's their business. It's their business but it's not really my concern" (OR09STA2:56–59). In order to embrace the school world at Canyon, Elvira has had to consciously separate herself from her sister's peer group, whose values and beliefs would militate against her successful adaptation to the Canyon environment.

Although Elvira is clearly fascinated by her "clean, nice" Canyon environment, the social adjustment has been painful and difficult. Her daily transitions to and from school are characterized by dissonance, as she has few neighborhood friends who attend Canyon and has found it difficult to connect with the Canyon peer culture. When asked about friends, she replied:

> . . . two or three people . . . introduced me to some of their
> friends and other people in my class. But . . . still it's a problem
> because during lunch time I get lost and I don't know who to
> hang around with and there [are] so many cliques . . . they grow
> up together, especially like the natives up here at Canyon. They're
> just already there, cause you can sense it in most of your classes.
> They're just, you know, 'We went to so and so's house . . . to a
> party . . . did you go to that party the other day?' And 'Guess who
> I saw the other day?' (OR09STA:167–180)

Elvira feels she is an outsider to the social interactions of Canyon's neighborhood students. To cope with her isolation, Elvira has adopted strategies to overcome the barriers she perceives. For example, finding it difficult to "hang out" at lunchtime, Elvira has joined a dance group that practices at noon. In classes, she tentatively initiates talk with peers who sit nearby. Further, interviews suggest that Elvira is an astute observer of the actions and behaviors of others, thereby enabling her to adopt styles and practice interaction patterns similar to students with whom she is attempting to connect. Although transition to the peer world at Canyon has been difficult, Elvira is slowly making progress at acquiring new friends.

Another strategy Elvira has adopted to manage the difficult crossing to this school environment is to turn her complete attention to schoolwork.

> . . . when I do my homework or my other work, I usually put all
> my effort into it. So it's kind of hard when you get a bad grade,
> cause other people, you know, they don't do anything and . . .
> copy other people or whatever and they just pass with a C and
> they're happy but you know I want to do better or do more.
> (OR09STB:62–71)

Observing Elvira in classes confirms that her attention is on her lessons. Even in classes that seem dull or in which students harass the teacher, Elvira is attentive. Elvira, having internalized norms of upward mobility, equates academic achievement with achieving her goal of crossing the socioeconomic border between her home and school communities:

> [I want] a higher life, a higher status. It's like my standards of living are higher than what my parents have. It's like I don't know. I guess it's just a dream but . . . the ultimate would be living either in a nice little house in Hawaii, or a nice big house in Crespi [the Canyon neighborhood]. With some nice car. I don't know what kind of car. Right now I want a Cabriolet. A white one with a white top. But I don't really know. Crespi is the best, they're so nice. (OR09STB:1243–1259)

The actors in Elvira's life rarely cross the borders between her worlds. In fact, acutely uncomfortable with the differences between her worlds, Elvira expends energy to keep everyone apart. Since she has been at Canyon, her parents have visited the school twice: once to attend a dance performance, another time to attend a meeting for parents about college application procedures. On each occasion Elvira describes being nervous and uneasy. "I wondered if they would be the only Filipinos there." Nor do the few nontransported friends Elvira has made at Canyon visit her home—she worries what they would think if they came.

Despite Elvira's perception of the stark differences between her home and neighborhood and school, there are also similarities. For example, Elvira's parents, as well as her teachers, expect her to achieve academically. When asked about her parents' expectations, she replied:

> Oh I guess mostly it's like do your own things . . . well, not get F's and D's. . . . I think they mostly expect As and Bs, 'cause that's what I've been getting all along. They expect us to get grades higher, not lower, than a C . . . because my sister got a D in PE once and . . . he (my father) was so mad. (OR09STA:426–446)

> . . . well, I don't know, I guess they don't know what to expect, they just want us to live a successful life, kind of like theirs. . . . As long as we're getting good grades. (OR09STB:335–340)

Elvira's parents know the importance of good grades to her future education. Elvira says they ask her frequently, "Are you going to go to college?" Their hopes and expectations for her future are clear. Likewise,

Elvira's teachers and counselor also expect that she will attend college and assist her in moving towards that goal.

There are elements in Elvira's school and home worlds that help her to make these difficult transitions. The concern of her teachers and counselor, the positive response to her academic achievements, and an opportunity to develop an expanded vision of what is possible are helpful to Elvira. The general belief by others in the school environment, that she can and will do well, is reinforcing. Her parents' support and expectations for her future are congruent with those of her teachers and counselors at the school. However, although Elvira's quiet classroom manner, good grades, and nondisruptive behavior invoke positive descriptions from her teachers and counselor, no one at the school is aware of the psychic costs she experiences while crossing these borders. Indeed, some school features impede her progress. For example, Elvira's classes are rarely structured to allow students to interact with each other. Although this type of classroom organization has not affected her grades, it certainly has not facilitated her connection with other students. Moreover, peer interaction is something Elvira would like. She emphasizes, "I want to be someplace where I'm socially accepted."

"Carla Chávez". Whereas Elvira adapts to different worlds by hiding those aspects of her home world that differentiate her from her peers, Carla Chavez, a Latina sophomore at Huntington High School who also manages border crossings, adopts a different strategy. Carla, who maintained a 3.5 GPA in her advanced classes through her sophomore year, conforms to mainstream patterns of interaction in classrooms where she is in the minority, and returns to typical home and community behaviors with her Latina peers in social settings, both in and out of school.

For Carla, the borders between her home and school worlds are primarily sociocultural and structural, growing out of her majority peers' negative expectations of Latino youth and her need to rely on these same students for information about how to succeed in the school environment. Carla's classes are dominated by European-American and Asian-American students; she is the only transported Latina female from her sophomore class enrolled across Huntington's advanced classes. When asked about how she feels about being there she says:

> *Carla:* Well, I kind of feel uncomfortable. Not many Mexicans and Hispanics are in those classes. And so it kind of makes me feel uncomfortable.
> *Interviewer:* What about that makes you feel uncomfortable?
> *Carla:* . . . they probably think of me as weird . . . [they] probably

have this view that most Hispanics are dumb or something.
[They] have that opinion, you know, get bad grades. So, I don't
know why I feel uncomfortable . . . [it] means you're not really
with any other . . . many people. (RA28STD:540–562)

Because Huntington High School has no academic or personal counseling services, and because neither Carla's mother nor her father attended
college, Carla is forced to rely on her peers for academic information:
how to get on a teacher's good side, how to best complete a homework
assignment, what needs to be done to prepare for the SAT, how to obtain
information about college. Indeed, when Carla does receive information
from her teachers about college application, she lacks the cultural capital
to distinguish between good and bad advice:

Interviewer: What about in terms of getting information about
    college?
Carla: Mr. Cao [advanced English], I think, gives a lot of informa-
    tion about college, so does Mr. Quince [driver's education] . . .
    they really know about colleges. . . .
Interviewer: Can you tell me what kinds of things they've told you,
    that have been helpful?
Carla: . . . people ask questions, you know, what would be . . . like
    Trish . . . she wants to go to Stanford also [like me]. And she
    already has her tuition paid and everything, her parents already
    have the money . . . I'm all, 'Whoa!' And then Mr. Quince
    found this out, and [said] 'Of course she's going to get into
    Stanford if her parents pay, you know, up front.' If they paid
    like before time? Is that true?
Interviewer: No.
Carla: No?
Interviewer: No.
Carla: He was telling us that, I don't know if it's true or not. He
    was telling us other things about which schools would be good
    for certain things . . . he was telling about that it's better to go
    to a two-year junior college, and then switch to a regular college
    because they teach you the same things. He was telling us our
    parents probably think . . . they don't like this because they
    think the people up there don't know. 'Oh your child goes to a
    junior college?' They'll think like that's not as good as a regular
    college, and you know it's the same thing. They teach the same
    thing. And, he was just telling us that kind of stuff. (RA28STD:
    865–875, 894–959)

For Carla to cope with teacher and peer pressures to adapt and with her need to get information, she conforms to European-American, middle-class norms of interaction and behavior in her classes. She speaks white ("standard") English, works individually, and divorces her personal experience from her conversations with high-achieving peers:

> You don't really share your personal life with them, cause you really aren't, you know, the culture isn't quite [the same]. We don't talk about that. We just talk about school or school things. We just talk about school. (RA28STD:1248–1259)

The one behavior Carla does not adopt is the 'competition for the floor' that characterizes many high-achieving classrooms. Most of the time she is quiet, rarely expressing her opinions. One teacher describes her as a student who is easily overlooked; "she doesn't stand out—either as a nuisance or as a top student" (RA076ST1:38–41).

Despite the fact that she feels her heritage is devalued, Carla has maintained a positive orientation towards her Latino background. When asked how she feels about her heritage, she replies:

> Well, I'm proud of it. I feel that, you know, that Latins aren't stupid. I'd like to be one of them that could achieve something. Cause most people think that Latins aren't . . . you know, that they can't do nothing, that they're just going to become like in the lower class. And, I think that that's not true. I think that everybody's the same. You can do anything you want to. (RA28STEN:125–136)

Carla's positive orientation toward her home world manifests itself during the school day. During her free time at school and at home, Carla spends time with her family and Mexican peers, speaking Spanish and English. Carla's closest friend and her older brother have dropped out of school. Carla's conversations with her Mexican friends center around neighborhood rumors and boys, rather than school. Carla says that she feels most comfortable around these friends because their values are similar to her own.

There are aspects of her home and peer worlds that assist Carla in her efforts to make transitions. For example, Carla's friends are supportive of her academic achievement:

> *Carla:* Well, all of my friends expect me to get . . . good grades. And most of them are dropouts. They expect more from me than [from] other people.

Interviewer: Can you talk a little bit about how they would talk to you about that?

Carla: They're 'Yeah, Carla's going to become a doctor. We're going to get free [health care]' you know, like that. And then when I get bad grades they're all 'Uught-uh!' (RA28STEN:602–616)

Carla's parents also offer emotional support as she works to cross into her advanced classes:

Carla: . . . they're proud. You know, they show . . . like when my grades are good, they go telling people . . . 'You're doing really good,' and telling their friends, 'Yeah I think she's gonna become what she wants to, she's the only one in our family who can achieve what she wants.'

Interviewer: And how do you feel about that? When they say 'yeah, she's the only one in our family'?

Carla: It feels good . . . I like the thought 'cause it just gives me more hope that I could become what I want. So it's a little bit easier on me, instead of having parents who are always putting me down, all 'You're no good' and things like that. (RA28STB:558–565, 586–599)

At the same time, Carla describes her parents as having little understanding of the difficult sociocultural and structural borders she faces as she moves into her classes:

Carla: Well, yeah, well they don't really expect much from my brothers because they really don't get that great of grades. But ever since I've been getting [good] grades they expect me to keep up with them, to get good grades. Like they can't understand the classes are getting harder, and it's more responsibility . . . everything that I'm doing. They think that . . . they don't believe me that it does. That it gets harder, the classes, the grade as you go up.

Interviewer: Um-hmm.

Carla: Things get harder to do. You have more responsibilities. And they can't understand that's why my grades are dropping . . . they just look at my report card and 'Uh-huh, B's? What happened to your A's?' (RA28STD:75–97)

Carla's strategy of adapting situationally as she crosses sociocultural and structural borders between home and school aides her in achieving academically. But her chances are tenuous for using the school as a stepping-stone to further educational opportunities, for Carla is left to navigate borders without the assistance of the adults in her school environment. Teachers and others, unaware of the complex adaptations she makes, fail to provide resources that will assure her continued access to quality education.

Type III: Different Worlds/Border Crossings Difficult

In this category, like the former, students define their family, peer, and school worlds as distinct. They say they must adjust and reorient as they move across worlds and among contexts. However, unlike students who manage to make these adjustments successfully, these students find social transitions difficult. For example, a student may do poorly in a class where the teacher's interaction style, the students' role, or the learning activity are oppositional to what takes place within the students' peer or family worlds. Likewise, some students in this category describe their comfort and ease at school and with peers, but are essentially estranged from their parents. In these cases, parents' values and beliefs are frequently more traditional, more religious, or more constrained than those of their children, making adaptation to their home world difficult and conflictual. Still others cite the socioeconomic circumstances of their families as factors that work against their full engagement in school. A youth might have to work to help support his or her family, for example.

For youth in this type, border crossing involves friction and discomfort, and, in some cases, is possible only under particular conditions. For example, students who do well in one class may fail all others—and frequently they do not know why. Often, these students are less successful in classrooms in which norms and behaviors are not only different from, but oppositional to, those they encounter with their families and friends. This pattern often includes adolescents on the brink between success and failure, involvement and disengagement, commitment and apathy. These are some of the students for whom classroom and school climate conditions can mean the difference between staying in school or dropping out.

"Donna Carlota". Donna Carlota, a Mexican/European-American student at Huntington High School, is an example of a student who faces difficult socioeconomic and sociocultural borders in her transition to school. A fourth-generation American, and the oldest of four children in a single-parent family, Donna is working to be the first in her family to graduate from high school. Donna's mother dropped out of school in the 9th grade and has been on welfare since Donna was born; financial difficulties have

been a central feature of Donna's home world throughout her high school years. For example, Donna has moved three times in the two years since 9th grade began, first to her grandmother's so that her mother could save money for Donna's younger sister's 15th birthday party, and second, to a motel when a conflict between Donna's mother and grandmother left the family homeless for two months while her mother searched for a new place to live.

Even when her living situation is stable, Donna is an example of a youth who thrives academically when the values, beliefs, expectations, and normative ways of behaving are consistent across her family, peer, and school worlds, and who disengages from school when they are not.

At home, Donna maintains a position of authority and responsibility with respect to school, the household, and her younger siblings. For example, her mother leaves many decisions related to schooling entirely to Donna (e.g., whether or not to attend school on a given day and whether or not to do homework). Overseeing her brothers' and sisters' homework assignments is also left to Donna. According to Donna, these responsibilities are indicative of the trust her mother has in her judgements. Relationships and experiences in Donna's peer world are similar to her relationship with her mother. Popular with her friends, she holds a position of leadership and responsibility in her Mexican-American peer group, often organizing outings or acting as a mediator when arguments flare. Predominant peer-group norms include helping one another and putting others' interests first.

In both Donna's family and peer worlds, emotional openness is valued. For example, according to Donna, her true friends know all there is to know about her, and she knows all there is to know about them. Family problems are not hidden, but discussed openly. The most striking aspects of Donna's peer and family worlds is the lack of separation between them. Unlike many teens, Donna is proud to be seen with her mother and her family and she treats her mother as one of her girlfriends:

> Yeah, my mom knows most of my friends, my girlfriends that is. And she'll go out with us, shopping or whatever. Like last weekend, Anita and I were going shopping and we invited my mom to go, but she was too tired. And my friends will talk to her about all sorts of things. Like my mom, you can talk to her about guys, she likes to talk about guys. She's not like a lot of parents, really strict about that. (RA52STC:285–296)

For Donna's friends, school achievement is secondary to having fun, maintaining friendships, and developing relationships with the opposite

sex. Peer expectations, such as putting others' interests first, can negatively affect school performance. When, for example, Donna half com-
pletes a school assignment due in 20 minutes and a friend has not begun,
she will neglect her own work in order to help her friend. If Donna is
hurrying to class, and a friend calls out to her, she will stop to talk. Her
friend's needs outweigh the negative aspects of the tardy mark she will
receive. When she is given detention, she expects the same friend to stay
after school with her for several days to keep her company. When there
are troubles with family and friends, Donna's attention to her school work
declines.

Overall, Donna has maintained a C average at Huntington High
School, though her grades fluctuate across classes. In some of Donna's
classes, teachers encourage discussion and the sharing of ideas. In others,
cooperative learning techniques are used. Donna identifies these classrooms as easy, and does well, while her teachers describe Donna as a
mature and model student. In other classrooms instruction is primarily
teacher centered, interaction among students is discouraged, and students
are usually expected to be passive learners. Donna tends to daydream in
these classes, identifies them as difficult, and does poorly academically.
Further, these teachers barely recognize who she is.

> There's a lot of my teachers who tell me to keep up the good
> work, and they just compliment me, and tell me to keep getting
> good grades and stuff, which is fine. They always tell me, 'I want
> you to be a good student,' and they, a lot of them say 'I really
> appreciate having you in class' and stuff. And it's nice. The class
> I'm getting an F in, he to me seems like, he doesn't really pay
> attention to anybody in particular in class. It's just a whole class,
> and this is math but . . . there's really no one who could talk
> about him. So I don't know what he actually means. He doesn't
> look at me, and he knows when I do work, I do work, and I do
> listen to him. (RA52STB:1249–1268)

Donna does well in classrooms where she perceives the teacher as caring
and where the norms and behaviors that characterize her family and peer
worlds—group over self, listening and empathizing with others, and media-
tion skills—are required. In classroom contexts where these skills are not
utilized and the teacher is perceived as remote, Donna's attention shifts
to peer-group concerns. In these situations, Donna finds crossing the
border from peer to school worlds difficult.

There are significant features within Donna's home and peer worlds
that assist her in her efforts to cross school borders. Most important to

Donna, her mother demonstrates concern and interest in her children's schooling and takes an active role to insure their best interests are served. For example, although the family lives outside Huntington High School's attendance area, Donna's mother met with and persuaded school authorities to allow both of her daughters to attend this school. She perceives Huntington's resources and location in an upper-middle-class area as extra protection that will ensure that her children graduate from high school. Donna is well aware of her mother's concerns.

> She really wants us not to be like her. She wants us to learn from her mistakes. And they're not really mistakes . . . she says that she doesn't regret none of them, but she regrets not going to school . . . really, mainly, she wants us to graduate out of high school. To go out, graduate, since she didn't really do that. She wants us to be responsible. You know, for my brothers. If someday they become fathers, she wants them to understand . . . she doesn't want them to go and be making mistakes, making something and just walking away from it . . . most of the pressure is on me, 'cause I'm the oldest. (RA52STB:1079–1104)

Moreover, although Donna's peers' expectations of friendship may run counter to her teachers' expectations of students, Donna's friends are opposed to school failure, which is considered shameful, rather than something to be proud of.

> . . . if I get a bad grade, Anita will say 'What's this D, Donna? A D? Come on!' My friends might feel like they're low or something, but they're not proud of getting straight F's or nothing like that. And not all of my friends get bad grades. Some of them get good grades. . . . You usually don't find out that they got a bad grade unless one of them gets grounded. Then you know that report cards just came out. And also, if one of them does badly they'll just change the subject real quick. That's how you know they don't want to talk about it. (RA52STC:346–375)

In short, although Donna's peers do not rank school first in their concerns, they do support Donna in her efforts to graduate from high school. *"Manuella Rios"*. Other students in our study are not dissimilar to Donna, though many are in more danger academically. For example, Manuella Rios, a second-generation Mexican/Filipina-American student at Maple High School in the Montevideo School District, faces psychosocial and sociocultural borders daily. Manuella has received A's and B's in two academic classes but is failing all the rest. Her school records through the 7th grade reveal high grades and test scores; in fact, in junior high school, Manuella was an identified gifted student. In the 8th grade Manuella's grades began to drop. In high school, they have plummeted. Involvement with peers who devalue school success and attend instead to family expectations (e.g., extended trips to Mexico to visit relatives; helping with a family business) divert her attention from school. The two classes in which Manuella has done well have been organized to promote student-student interaction. For example, in history Manuella and four other students work regularly as a group on class assignments. In this situation Manuella serves frequently as a resource to the others, and the classroom arrangement makes it unnecessary for her to make the transition from peers to a more traditional teacher-dominated environment. Further, Manuella perceives her teacher, "Mr. Castaneda," as particularly caring, concerned, interested in her personally, and capable of understanding her family pressures. "I can really talk to Mr. Castaneda," she says.

In contrast, classes that Manuella is failing are characterized by teachers who lecture, work that is often limited to reading textbook chapters and answering end-of-chapter questions, and interaction that is confined to students' responding to teacher-initiated questions. In these classes Manuella withdraws, shuts down, and tunes out. None of these teachers know that she has been successful in other classroom contexts, and they believe her failure stems from a lack of motivation and self-discipline.

Type IV: Different Worlds/Borders Impenetrable

For some students, the values, beliefs, and expectations are so discordant across worlds that border crossing is resisted or impossible. When border crossing is attempted, it is frequently so painful that, over time, these students develop reasons and rationales to protect themselves against further distress. In such cases, borders are viewed as insurmountable and students actively or passively resist attempts to embrace other worlds. For example, some students say that school is irrelevant to their lives. Other students immerse themselves fully in the world of their peers. Rather than moving from one setting to another, blending elements of all, these students remain constrained by borders they perceive as rigid and impenetrable.

"Sonia Gonzales". Sonia Gonzales, who attends Explorer High School in the Bolivar School District, typifies a student who does not cross sociocultural borders. Sonia perceives the border between her home and peer worlds and that of school as insurmountable. A second-generation American, Sonia entered school speaking Spanish. By the 5th grade she was

classified as English proficient. Growing up in a Mexican barrio, Sonia has maintained her orientation toward her Mexican heritage. At home and with her friends—the majority of whom are bilingual—Spanish is the language of choice. Mexican traditions and practices are emphasized in her family and among her friends. However, there is no question that Sonia is bilingual and possesses bicultural skills. For example, her academic history through the 8th grade is relatively optimistic. During this time she earned mostly B's and C's. In high school her grades have declined—as a freshman she failed 4 out of 5 academic classes and the first semester of her sophomore year, she did not pass any.

According to Sonia, the border between her school and peer worlds became impassible when she moved into a socially prominent, female "Mexicano" peer group. Sonia's peer world consists of sociocultural components fundamentally different from and opposed to those that are required both for success in school and in the wider society.

> I don't know, but Mexicans are more crazier than white people. It's like we have like different kinds of thinking I guess, I don't know. Like we want to do everything, it's like they [white people] take everything slowly you know . . . and I don't know, it's just that they think about the future more and stuff. And us, you know what happens, happens. And it's just meant to happen. And it's like, we do crazy things, and we never think about the consequences that might happen.
>
> And like white people over here in this area right here, like everything's more quiet, more serious, you know. You don't see like, it's really rare to see a teenager pregnant, it's like more Mexican and black people are the ones that come out pregnant. And you don't see like white people screwing around. And when you go to Juvenile, you never see like a white person in there, cause they have their act together and Mexicans, they just tend to screw around all the time. . . . (ES56STB:965–1032)

Expectations in Sonia's peer group include being available to give advice, listening in good times and in bad, and doing "crazy" things such as taking risks and having fun. There is an explicit recognition among group members that proschool behavior is not congruent with group norms and expected behaviors.

> *Interviewer:* Do you have any of the same classes together?
> *Sonia:* No, unfortunately. Well in a way it's better because if we were together we would have really screwed up. 'Cause like

> when me and her get together, we just screw around all the
> time. And so it's better to stay away from each other. . . . 'Cause
> otherwise we don't care about school or anything when we're
> together. 'Cause we have a lot of fun together. (ES56STB:234–
> 250)

With these friends, Sonia skips classes, ignores homework, gets into trouble with school authorities, and gets involved—both as a sympathetic onlooker and as an accomplice—in the gang activity carried out by male friends.

According to Sonia, her family has little influence on her school behavior. Her relationship with her father, a production worker, is distant and antagonistic, and he has little involvement in her life. In contrast, she has a close, sisterly relationship with her mother, who was raised in an upper middle–class family in Mexico where she graduated from high school. Sonia talks to and seeks advice from her mother about her friends, boys, and school. In turn, her mother shares her concerns about her marriage with Sonia. According to Sonia, her mother constantly urges her to raise her grades and to consider going to college. However, she is unable to assist Sonia with homework and is uncertain as to what role she should play with respect to school involvement. Sonia believes that her mother is uncomfortable crossing into the world of school because she has no knowledge of or experience with the American educational system. Because of this, most of the responsibility for seeking and getting educational assistance is Sonia's.

Sonia sees her situation as starkly different from that of many of the students at Explorer High School who do well academically. She vividly describes the difficulty she experiences in crossing borders between her home and school worlds.

> It's really confusing. And some people that understand me, they
> say, 'It's really easy, what's wrong with you? It's easy.' But it's hard,
> it's hard. Probably it depends on what kind of background you
> have, too, 'cause if you have parents that been to college, they've
> been prepared, and they're pretty much prepared, you pretty
> much have a better idea what's going on, you like understand
> things better, 'cause you grew up in the kind of environment that,
> you know, they understand more. But if you have parents that
> dropped out and stuff like that, you know, it's different, it's harder.
> 'Cause you try to get help from them, you know, when you're doing
> your homework. They don't understand what you're doing, they
> don't know. And it's hard, it's harder. (ES56STB:793–814)

Sonia's difficulties in crossing the sociocultural border between family and peer and school worlds are exacerbated by the fact that she has few connections to school. Her comments and our observations reveal that she has little meaningful contact with her high school teachers. According to Sonia, she has never had a teacher who spoke adamantly about the successes and strengths of Mexican culture, or who spoke to her personally about her future. Further, she believes that her teachers communicate negative images about her ethnic identity:

> White teachers, some of them are kind of prejudiced. It's probably the way they look at you, the way they talk, you know, when they're talking about something, like when they talk about the people who are going to drop out. And Mr. Kula, when he's talking about teenage pregnancy or something like that, he turns around and looks at us [Sonia and her Mexican female friends]. It's like, he tries to look around the whole room, so we won't notice, but like he mostly like tries to tell us, tries to get it through our heads, you know. (ES56STB:1884–1911)

Sonia also perceives little support and even direct hostility from her non-Mexican peers. Her statements reflect the intense discomfort she feels in classes without her friends.

> 'Cause you feel uncomfortable in a class that, you know, where there [are] practically no Mexicans in there. So nobody you can talk to. And then the people in there, they're like really stuck up, you know. It makes me uncomfortable to be in that class 'cause they're like, you feel like they're talking about you or something. It's uncomfortable 'cause they're like stuck up, they don't like talking to you. You might say hi or hello and sometimes they don't answer back. And that's why I don't like them, you know. (ES56STB:855–874)

Sonia's description illuminates her feelings of being an outsider. There appear to be few features in her classes that operate to pull her in and ensure her inclusion as a respected and valuable member of the group. Further, none of her teachers are aware of the intense discomfort she feels. Security, acceptance, and a strong sense of belonging characterize Sonia's involvement in her peer world. These qualities are not replicated in the world of school. And why would Sonia risk jeopardizing her close friendships to embrace a school world that she perceives as hostile and cold? The combination of peer-group norms that devalue behaviors associated with academic success and school features that fail to address her individual needs create insurmountable borders.

"Jeffrey Hoffman". Students who describe borders as impenetrable also include those unable to cross into the worlds of peers or family. For example, Jeffrey Hoffman, a European-American student at Huntington High School, describes his experience of the psychosocial border between school and peers. "At school I really don't have any friends," says Jeffrey. Alienated from peers in his school environment, Jeffrey describes how difficult it is to concentrate on academics when all he can think about is how isolated he feels. Jeffrey's low grades (and high test scores) are indicative of his inability to focus on school. However, during his first semester at Huntington, Jeffrey went to a peer counselor who encouraged him to participate in Huntington's drama program. Jeffrey has subsequently become actively involved, not only in drama but also in peer counseling. These programs have helped Jeffrey make some friends but his standing with peers remains tenuous. Most of Jeffrey's teachers are unaware of the difficulties he faces—others do not consider the educational implications of his inability to transition to a peer world. For example, Jeffrey's science teacher directed students to work together in groups but did not notice that Jeffrey sat quietly alone.

Other students in this type perceive demarcated borders between peer and family worlds. In these situations, conflicts are frequently acute and students' energies and attention are diverted from engagement in learning. Locked in conflict with their families, these students see school involvement as extraneous to the other pressures in their lives.

REFLECTIONS: BORDER CROSSING AND ITS IMPLICATIONS

This chapter presents a model for thinking about the interrelationship of students' family, peer, and school worlds and in particular, how they combine to affect students' engagement with schools and learning. We have generated a typology to illustrate patterns of movement and adaptation strategies students use as they move between worlds and interact in different contexts and social settings. Although each of the four types contain variety with respect to students' perceptions, there are nevertheless some common themes.

In our sample, most of the students who describe congruent worlds and smooth transitions (Type I) are members of two-parent families that place a high value on family cohesiveness. Family values include an orientation towards the future, academic achievement or doing the "best one can," and conformity to acceptable standards of behavior. These students' friends reinforce the value of effort with respect to school, sports, and work. Further, the actors in their lives move across the boundaries of their worlds—friends go to each other's homes and are in the same classes at school. Parents attend school events (e.g., sports, drama) and participate in teacher conferences and parent organizations. It is well known by teachers, either personally or through word of mouth, that parents support teachers' efforts and are available if problems should arise.

Teachers frequently feel comfortable with these students, for they do not cause problems and rarely exhibit behaviors that are worrisome. Further, teachers perceive these students as being on the right track. For example, one of Ryan's teachers described him as "programmed for success." Other teachers, however, express concern that these "well-adjusted and successful" students are the ones who are forgotten. And in fact, we have found that these students frequently express tremendous pressures—anxiety about the future, living up to the expectations of those around them, maintaining high grades.

Further, students who are secure and comfortable within the bounds of their congruent worlds may have an especially difficult time connecting with peers unlike themselves. Many have little opportunity or reason to practice or acquire border crossing strategies. Distanced from students in other groups, it is these students who are particularly at risk for developing spurious ideas and stereotypes about others. Some of these students are not interested in getting to know or working or interacting with students who achieve at different levels or who have different backgrounds. Constantly reinforced for their "on-track" behaviors, they can be quick to denigrate divergent actions by others. In a sense, their view is limited and bounded by the congruency of their worlds.

Students whose worlds are different but manage to successfully traverse borders (Type II) are, like the previous students, are often overlooked by their teachers. They too present few problems—they appear to fit in, and their behavior is in accord with acceptable classroom and school norms. Nevertheless, these students are frequently an enigma to their teachers, who have no knowledge of their families or the reasons for their success. Their invisibility as individuals is illuminated by teacher descriptions that expose the lack of even the most fundamental knowledge about students' backgrounds.

Even though many students are able to cross perceived borders successfully, they are frequently forced to deny aspects of who they are. This is illuminated by these youths' efforts to keep the actors in their worlds separate, and the tremendous discomfort they feel when unable to do so. Because teachers view these students as "well-adjusted," the conflicts and difficulties they feel can be overlooked or discounted as unimportant. Teachers' relief that students "fit in," do well academically, and present few problems precludes their attention to important aspects of individuals' lives, for example, the energy and effort required to navigate different worlds successfully.

Students whose worlds are different, and who cross borders only under certain conditions (Type III), often teeter between engagement and withdrawal (whether with family, school, or friends). For youth whose family and peer worlds stand in contrast to that of the school, academic success occurs sporadically. In classrooms where students flourish, teachers know the students well, are attuned to their needs, and show personal concern for their lives. These teachers are aware of their students' precarious academic status and incorporate various pedagogical methods to ensure student involvement. In classrooms where students do poorly, teachers often classify them as overall low achievers and are unaware of their successes. For example, Manuella's math teacher, in whose class she had spent five hours a week for almost a full academic year, did not know who she was. Low expectations and pessimism about students' abilities characterize these teachers' views. Blame for students' failures is placed on students' personal characteristics or forces outside the school, for example, the students' family or peers. These teachers rarely suspect that classroom features, pedagogical style, or their own attitudes may powerfully influence students' ability to succeed and connect with the school environment.

Finally, students who describe borders as impenetrable (Type IV) say that attempts to embrace other worlds create stress and anxiety. As a result, these students gravitate toward situations where support is found and away from circumstances that exacerbate their discomfort. For example, students alienated from school may turn their attention to peers. Or students like Jeffrey, who are alienated from peers, spend time with extended family members. However, the inability of these students to cross borders does not necessarily imply that they are completely opposed to school. Students who view the differences between family or peers and school as unbridgeable say that classroom and school climate features do not support their needs. In fact, they frequently describe instances of insensitivity or hostility from teachers and other students that threaten their personal integrity or devalue their background circumstances (e.g., religious or cultural). Many voice a desire to obtain the skills necessary to cross successfully into the school environment.

The multiple worlds model has important implications for schools and learning. Perhaps most significant, it provides teachers and others a way of thinking about students in a more holistic way. Further, the model suggests a focus for educators as they think about school features that impact students' lives. From data gathered during the Students' Multiple Worlds Study, it appears that in our culture many adolescents are left to navigate transitions without direct assistance from persons in any of their contexts, most notably the school. Further, young people's success in managing these transitions varies widely. Yet students' competence in moving between settings has tremendous implications for the quality of their lives and their chances of using the educational system as a stepping-stone to further education, productive work experiences, and a meaningful adult life. In order to create environments where students are able to work together in classrooms, to solve problems jointly, and to have an equal investment in schools and learning, we need to identify institutional structures that eliminate borders without requiring young people to give up or hide important features of their lives. This requires more than understanding other cultures. It means that students must acquire skills and strategies to work comfortably and successfully in divergent social settings and with people different than themselves.

NOTES

1. This is a revised edition of an article originally published in *Anthropology and Education Quarterly*, 22(3), September 1991.

2. Our use of the term *world* corresponds closely to Spradley and McCurdy's (1972) definition of *cultural scene*. Likewise, the terms *social settings, arenas,* and *contexts* in this study parallel their definition of *social situations* (pp. 25–30).

3. As Erickson (1987) notes, the distinction between cultural borders and boundaries was made initially by Barth (1969) and has also been discussed in terms of schooling by McDermott and Gospodinoff (1979) and Erickson and Bekker (1986).

4. Ruth Benedict's (1938) observation over 50 years ago—that American institutions provide inadequate support in helping young people progress from one role to another—continues to have relevance today. She states, ". . . adult activity demands traits that are interdicted in children, and that far from redoubling efforts to help children bridge this gap, adults in our culture put all the blame on the child when he fails to manifest spontaneously the new behavior or, overstepping the mark, manifests it with untoward belligerence" (p. 432).

5. Although Huntington High School was selected originally because of its relatively stable student population, during the course of this study the minority student population has increased to approximately 50%. Nineteen percent of these students are eligible to participate in the district's transportation program.

6. Although gender borders are certainly present in the schools in which

we worked, the focus of our study has been on students' perceptions of the borders that impede their engagement with school. For the most part, they have emphasized psychosocial, sociocultural, and structural borders.

7. The types we identify are not inclusive of all students, but represent the majority of students in our sample. We are in the process of expanding our typology.

8. For example, 17 of the 54 students in our study have exhibited different patterns with respect to perceived borders and border-crossing strategies during the first year and a-half of this study.

9. Here and elsewhere, quotations are identified by interview file code (e.g., ES37STA) and line numbers. The interviews are part of a public-use file that will eventually be made available to interested researchers through the Center for Research on the Context of Secondary School Teaching at Stanford University.

REFERENCES

Abi-Nader, J. (1990). A house for my mother: Motivating Hispanic high school students. *Anthropology & Education Quarterly, 21*(1), 41–58.

Barth, F. (1969). *Ethnic groups and boundaries: The social organization of culture difference.* Boston: Little, Brown.

Benedict, R. (1938). Continuities and discontinuities in cultural conditioning. *Psychiatry, 1,* 161–167.

Clark, R. M. (1983). *Family life and school achievement: Why poor black children succeed or fail.* Chicago: University of Chicago Press.

Clasen, D. R., & Brown, B. B. (1985). The multidimensionality of peer pressure in adolescence. *Journal of Youth and Adolescence, 14*(6), 451–468.

Clement, D., & Harding, J. (1978). Social distinctions and emergent student groups in a desegregated school. *Anthropology and Education Quarterly, 9*(4), 272–283.

Coleman, J. S. (1963). *The adolescent society: The social life of the teenager and its impact on education.* New York: Free Press.

Delgado-Gaitan, C., & Trueba, H. (1991). *Crossing cultural borders: Education for immigrant families in America.* New York: Falmer Press.

Eckert, P. (1989). *Jocks and burnouts: Social categories and identity in the high school.* New York: Teachers College Press.

Edmonds, R. (1979). Some schools work and more can. *Social Policy, 9*(5), 28–32.

Erickson, F. (1987). Transformation and school success: The politics and culture of educational achievement. *Anthropology and Education Quarterly, 18*(4), 335–355.

Erickson, F. D., & Bekker, G. J. (1986). On anthropology. In J. Hannaway & M. E. Lockheed (Eds.), *The contributions of the social sciences to educational policy and practice: 1965–1985* (pp. 163–182). Berkeley, CA: McCutchan.

Fordham, S. (1988). Racelessness as a factor in black students' school success: Pragmatic strategy or pyrrhic victory? *Harvard Educational Review, 58*(1), 54–83.

Gaventa, J. (1980). *Power and powerlessness: Quiescence and rebellion in an Appalachian valley.* Urbana: University of Illinois Press.

Gibson, M. A. (1987). The school performance of immigrant minorities: A comparative view. *Anthropology and Education Quarterly, 18*(4), 262–275.

Heath, S. B. (1982). Questioning at school and at home: A comparative study. In G. D. Spindler (Ed.), *Doing the ethnography of schooling: Educational anthropology in action* (pp. 102–131). New York: Holt, Rinehart & Winston.

Hoffman, D. M. (1988). Cross-cultural adaptation and learning: Iranians and Americans at school. In H. Trueba & C. Delgado-Gaitan (Eds.), *School and society: Learning content through culture* (pp. 163–180). New York: Praeger.

Jencks, C., Smith, M., Acland, H., Bane, M., Cohen, D., Gintis, H., Heyns, B., & Micelson, S. (1972). *Inequality: A reassessment of the effects of family and schooling in America.* New York: Basic Books.

Johnson, D., & Johnson, R. (1981). Effects of cooperative and individualistic learning experiences on interethnic interaction. *Journal of Educational Psychology, 73*(3), 444–449.

Joyce, B., Murphy, C., Showers, B., & Murphy, J. (1989). School renewal as cultural change. *Educational Leadership, 47*(3), 70–77.

Larkin, R. W. (1979). *Suburban youth in cultural crisis.* New York: Oxford University Press.

McDermott, R. P. (1987). The exploration of minority school failure, again. *Anthropology and Education Quarterly, 18*(4), 361–364.

McDermott, R. P., & Gospodinoff, K. (1979). Social contexts for ethnic borders and school failure. In A. Wolfgang (Ed.), *Nonverbal behavior* (pp. 175–195). New York: Academic Press.

Ogbu, J. (1983). Minority status and schooling in plural societies. *Comparative Education Review, 27*(22), 168–190.

Ogbu, J. (1987). Variability in minority school performance: A problem in search of an explanation. *Anthropology and Education Quarterly, 18*(4), 300–335.

Rosaldo, R. (1989). *Culture and truth: The remaking of social analysis.* Boston: Beacon Press.

Rutter, M., Maughan, B., Mortimore, P., & Ouston, J. (1979). *Fifteen thousand hours: Secondary schools and their effects on children.* Cambridge, MA: Harvard University Press.

Sarason, S. B. (1990). *The predictable failure of educational reform: Can we change course before it's too late?* San Francisco: Jossey-Bass.

Sharan, S. (1980). Cooperative learning in small groups: Recent methods and effects on achievement, attitudes, and ethnic relations. *Review of Educational Research, 50*(2), 241–271.

Slavin, R. E. (1988). Cooperative learning and student achievement. In R. E. Slavin (Ed.), *School and classroom organization* (pp. 129–158). Hillsdale, NJ: Erlbaum.

Slavin, R. E., & Madden, N. A. (1989). What works for students at risk: A research synthesis. *Educational Leadership,* February, 12–14.

Spindler, G. D. (1987). *Education and cultural process: Anthropological approaches.* Prospect Heights, IL: Waveland Press.

Spindler, G. D., & Spindler, L. (1982). Roger Harker and Schonhausen: From familiar to strange and back again. In G. D. Spindler (Ed.), *Doing the ethnography of schooling: Educational anthropology in action* (pp. 20–46). New York: Holt, Rinehart & Winston.

Spradley, J. P., & McCurdy, D. W. (1972). *The cultural experience: Ethnography in complex society.* Chicago: Science Research Association.

Steinberg, L., Brown, B. B., Cider, M., Kaczmarek, N., & Lazzaro, C. (1988). *Noninstructional influence on high school student achievement: The contributions of parents, peers, extracurricular activities and part-time work.* Madison: National Center on Effective Secondary Schools.

Suarez-Orozco, M. M. (1985, May). *Opportunity, family dynamics and school achievement: The sociocultural context of motivation among recent immigrants from Central America.* Paper presented at the University of California Symposium on Linguistics, Minorities and Education, Tahoe City, CA.

Suarez-Orozco, M. M. (1987). Becoming somebody: Central American immigrants in U.S. inner-city schools. *Anthropology and Education Quarterly, 18*(4), 287–299.

Trueba, H. T. (1988). Peer socialization among minority students: A high school dropout prevention program. In H. Trueba & C. Delgado-Gaitan (Ed.), *Schools and society: Learning content through culture.* New York: Praeger.

Trueba, H. T., Moll, L., Diaz, S., & Diaz, R. (1982). *Improving the functional writing of bilingual secondary students* (Contract No. 400-81-0023). Washington, DC: National Institute of Education.

Ueda, R. (1987). *Avenues to adulthood: The origins of the high school and social mobility in an American suburb.* New York: Cambridge University Press.

Varenne, H. S. (1982). Jocks and freaks: The symbolic structure of the expression of social interaction among American senior high school students. In G. D. Spindler (Ed.), *Doing the ethnography of schooling: Educational anthropology in action* (pp. 211–239). New York: Holt, Rinehart & Winston.

Vogt, L. A., Jordan, C., & Tharp, R. G. (1987). Explaining school failure, producing school success: Two cases. *Anthropology and Education Quarterly, 18*(4), 276–286.

Walberg, H. (1986). What works in a nation still at risk. *Educational Leadership, 44*(1), 7–11.

CHAPTER 3

PERSPECTIVES ON LANGUAGE MAINTENANCE AND SHIFT IN MEXICAN-ORIGIN STUDENTS

Lucinda Pease-Alvarez and Kenji Hakuta

Recent perspectives on bilingualism across the disciplines of linguistics, anthropology, and psychology emphasize the positive side of being bilingual and living in an ethnic minority community. For example, a sizable literature on the cognitive functioning of language-minority children who are balanced bilinguals (i.e., with equal or nearly equal levels of proficiency in both of their languages) suggests that bilingualism may promote cognitive growth (Diaz, 1985; Duncan & DeAvila, 1979; Hakuta & Diaz, 1985; Kessler & Quinn, 1980). A growing body of ethnographic research focusing on the everyday lives of bilingual children, their families, and communities emphasizes the range and depth of the social contexts that surround and involve them as well as the skills acquired through operating across cultures (e.g., Moll & Greenberg, 1990; Vasquez, 1992). For example, translation, a common activity for many bilingual children from immigrant backgrounds, represents an occasion when children take on positions of responsibility in their homes and communities. Moreover, recent research suggests that children's involvement in this activity may enhance their metalinguistic awareness and language proficiency (Malakoff & Hakuta, 1991).

Despite these advantages, bilingualism is generally a transitional phase or way station on the road to Americanization for most immigrants (Fishman, 1966; Grosjean, 1982). Historically, children from immigrant families who become bilingual in English and their native language become the parents of English monolinguals (Lopez, 1978; Veltman, 1988).

The research reported in this chapter is supported by grants from the Spencer Foundation and the University of California Linguistic Minority Project.

According to survey data on the language choices of Latino groups, even Spanish—a language thought to be fairly enduring in the U.S. context and frequently discussed as an important marker of Latino identity—seldom lasts beyond the second or third generation. Despite this evidence of intergenerational shift toward English for most Latino immigrant groups, relatively little is known about the nature of language shift in the children and their families. That is, to what degree and at what level does shift characterize the experience of Latinos in the U.S.?

In this chapter we describe our experiences with two research activities that address this gap in our understanding about bilingualism in the U.S. Both of the studies investigate native language shift and maintenance in children of Mexican descent living in California. Thus far our findings seem to concur with that of other researchers: there is a rapid attrition of Spanish. However, upon closer inspection there are some interesting points to be made about our findings that may be of special significance to educators, especially from the perspective of those who value the maintenance of linguistic diversity in our student population.

Before proceeding with any description of research on language attrition, it is necessary to lay the groundwork by describing what is meant by language shift. Language shift is most often thought of in terms of three components: (1) an individual's actual proficiency in two languages, (2) an individual's language choice, and (3) an individual's attitudes toward the cultures associated with each language. Although these components are clearly related (for example, language choice by necessity entails sufficient proficiency in the two languages to make choice possible), they are related to distinct disciplinary perspectives—proficiency being the principal domain of psycholinguists, choice the principal domain of sociolinguists, and language attitudes of social psychologists.

THE WATSONVILLE STUDY

In the first study to be described here, Hakuta and D'Andrea (1992) looked at the patterns of language choice, attitudes, and proficiency in high school–aged students of Mexican descent and from different immigration backgrounds. These students were all residents of Watsonville, a community with a large Latino population. Direct assessments of students' language proficiency in Spanish and English and self-reported information on their backgrounds, language proficiency, language choice, and language attitudes were collected for these students. In order to capture the roles of generation and length of residence across the different components of shift, students were divided into six groups:

Group 1: Born in Mexico, arrived in the U.S. > 10 years old.

Group 2: Born in Mexico, arrived in the U.S. between the ages of 6 and 10 years old.

Group 3: Born in Mexico, arrived in the U.S. at age 5 or younger.

Group 4: Born in the U.S., both parents Mexican born.

Group 5: Born in the U.S., at least one parent born in the U.S.

Group 6: Born in the U.S., at least one parent and associated grandparents born in the U.S.

As shown in Figure 3.1, tests of language proficiency revealed the largest difference in English proficiency to exist between Groups 1 and 2. Also, we see that youngsters in Groups 2 through 4 are only slightly different from each other and have acquired English with very little loss of Spanish proficiency. Another way of saying this is that immigrant students who arrived between the ages of 5 and 10 are more similar to students whose parents were born in the U.S. (Groups 3–6) than they are to recently arrived students (Group 1) with respect to English proficiency.

However, in terms of Spanish proficiency, for youngsters born in the U.S. with at least one parent born in the U.S. (Group 5) there is a significant drop in their Spanish language proficiency. In a very real sense, then, Groups 2–4 represent a tremendous window of opportunity for full development of bilingual abilities.

Socially, however, a very different picture emerges from the data, as seen in these students' language choices. As evident in Figure 3.2, there is a trend toward the use of English across all of the groups, even within the groups that evidence strong bilingual proficiency (Groups 2–4). It is clearly this social aspect of language use rather than language proficiency that triggers the loss of bilingualism. In short, native language proficiency appears to be relatively resistant to attrition within generations even though there is a steady increase in the use of English.

Additional data were collected in this study on the attitudes of the students towards bilingualism and their own ethnicity. The results show that attitudinal factors are related to language choice for these students, but not to their language proficiency. Those with a maintenance orientation toward Spanish report that they used it more than students with a more assimilationist view. However, these same Spanish maintenance-oriented students do not necessarily score well on tests of language proficiency. It appears that the complexity of language loss and native language maintenance among bilingual students is considerably underestimated when one looks only at the cognitive and academic aspects of language proficiency. That is, favorable orientations toward the maintenance of

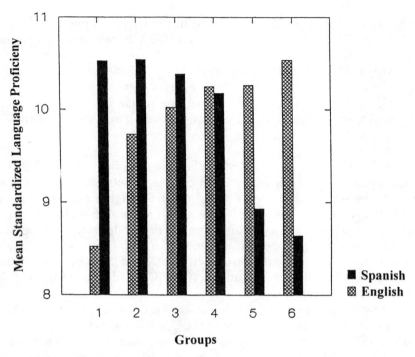

Figure 3.1 *Mean Standardized Spanish and English language proficiency measures for six groups (Group 1: Born in Mexico, arrived in the USA > 10 years old; Group 2: Born in Mexico, arrived in the USA between the ages of 6 and 10 years old; Group 3: Born in Mexico, arrived in the USA when 5 years old or younger; Group 4: Born in the USA, both parents Mexican born; Group 5: Born in the USA, at least one parent born in the USA; Group 6: Born in the USA, at least one parent and associated grandparents born in the USA). Source: Hakuta & D'Andrea (1992).*

Spanish may still hold true and influence children's decisions to use Spanish even though they do not predict their proficiency in that language.

THE "EASTSIDE" STUDY

Building on this work, we have undertaken a three-year study of variations in language proficiency, choice, and attitude in a suburban Bay Area community that we have called Eastside. Like many communities in Northern California, Eastside has become increasingly more diverse with regard to income and ethnicity. In the mid-1960s, the community was populated mostly by working-class Anglos; now it is home to immigrants from Southern Europe, the Pacific Islands, and Latin America. Among these groups, working-class immigrants from Mexico are the most numerous, and along with other Latinos, represent more than 50% of the school-age population. To illustrate the trend over time, Figure 3.3 shows the numbers of Hispanic and non-Hispanic students in the elementary school district since the beginning of this immigration trend in about 1964.

The "Eastside" Community

Before describing this study and our findings thus far, we feel that a few words about Eastside are in order. The presence of the Mexicano community is obvious in Eastside. The streets are alive with commercial and social activity reminiscent of Mexican towns, Spanish is commonly used throughout the commercial as well as the residential sectors of the

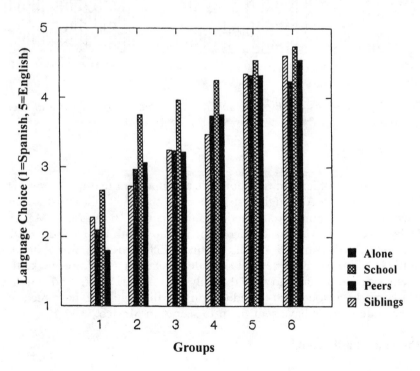

Figure 3.2 *Language choice with siblings, with peers, for academic purposes at school, and when alone, by group. Source: Hakuta & D'Andrea (1992).*

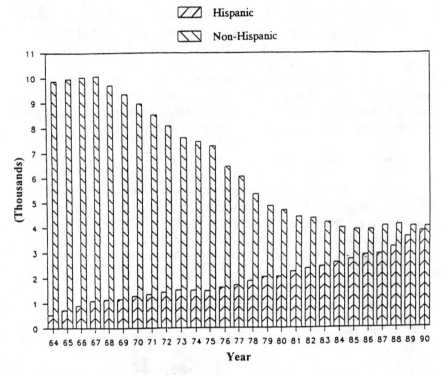

Figure 3.3 *Numbers of Hispanic and non-Hispanic students in the elementary school district that serves Eastside during 1964–1990.*

community, and Mexican traditions are an important feature of everyday life for Eastsiders. Although Eastside is more than 500 miles north of the Mexican border, community members maintain strong ties with Mexico. Many make yearly visits to Mexico to be reunited with family and friends. For others, their connections with Mexico fulfill needs that cannot be met in the U.S. For example, several Eastside families that we know make frequent visits to Tijuana to visit the only doctor they trust. And families who were dissatisfied with the education that their children have received in Eastside schools have sent them to school in Mexico.

The Study Participants

Participants in this study include 70 children of Mexican descent and their families. Thus far 38 3rd graders, their parents, and in some cases, their siblings have participated in interviews and activities investigating their language proficiency, attitudes, and choices. Unlike the work done in Watsonville, this study combines qualitative and quantitative techniques and relies on observational as well as self-report data. Again the focus is on children from a variety of immigration backgrounds, with somewhat refined distinctions from those used in the Watsonville study:[1]

MM: Both mother and child born in Mexico.
MU/A: Mother born in Mexico, child born in U.S.
        Mother moved to U.S. at age 15 or older.
MU/C: Mother born in Mexico, child born in U.S.
        Mother moved to U.S. at age 10 or younger.
UU: Both mother and child born in U.S.

Preliminary Findings

Although we are at the beginning stages of our research, we have found evidence that concurs with the findings from our previous study. In the case of a preliminary survey used to help identify our sample, we found evidence that participants in this study are also making a rapid shift towards the use of English. Within each of the groups mentioned above, the children use somewhat more English than the adults. The UU group (roughly, second-generation Mexican Americans) has shifted almost completely to English while the children of Mexican-born immigrants (MM, MU/A, and MU/C groups) rely predominantly on Spanish. Interestingly, children of mothers who came from Mexico as children (MU/C) rely on Spanish more than those from the other two immigrant groups. Also, the later-born children of the group whose mothers came as adults (MU/A) tend to use more English than their older siblings.

Though far from complete, our interviews with children and their parents about their language choices and attitudes toward bilingualism are an important source of information about the way they view their social worlds and the role that languages play in these worlds. For example, when we ask children to describe their reasons for using a specific language with a specific interlocutor, they usually tell us that the interlocutor's proficiency or choice of language influenced their language choices. However, some children also refer to ethnicity and culture as factors that influence their language choices (e.g., "Hablo español con él porqué es Mexicano/I speak Spanish with him because he is Mexican," "Hablamos ingles porqué ella es Americana/We speak English because she is American"), thus giving the impression that languages are to a certain extent delineated by people's cultural affiliations. Sometimes, though very rarely, this kind of talk leads to more intriguing discussions about the scope of these cultural affiliations. For example, one child felt that the negative attitudes that some Anglo children have towards Mexicanos would be diminished if Anglo children learned Spanish:

> Como dijo la niña, como aquella niña güera, a ella no le importaba los mexicanos, no le importaba ninguno. . . . Pero si ella supiera en español y sabía como muchas cosas bonitas que puede aprender uno en el mundo, entonces ella no diciera eso de los Mexicanos.
> [Like what that girl said, that Anglo girl. She doesn't care about Mexicans. But if she knew Spanish and knew about the many nice things that one can learn about the world, then she wouldn't say that about Mexicans.]

Parents have also talked about the degree to which languages are permeable across social contexts. This is most notable when we ask about the role Spanish plays and should play in their homes. All are committed to the maintenance of Spanish and advocate its use to varying degrees in their homes. Most are confident that their children will not lose Spanish, even though they can provide examples of other children who are no longer proficient in Spanish or who no longer want to use Spanish. Interestingly enough, the one parent who feels that her child is losing her ability to speak Spanish also talks about how the school has influenced language-choice patterns in her home.

> Mi esposo habla inglés con los niños ahora porque las maestras le han dicho a él que tiene que ayudarlos para que no atrasen en su ciclo escolar. Cuando los niños no entienden bien no pueden aprender. Entonces le decía la maestra que le hablara más a él en inglés y para las tareas.
> [My husband speaks English with the children now because the teachers told him that he has to help them so that they don't fall behind in school. When children don't understand well, they can't learn. So the teacher told him to speak with him (their son) in English (and when helping him with) homework.]

Despite their commitment to Spanish at home, parents do not agree about the role of Spanish in the school. Most are grateful to have their children enrolled in bilingual classes where teachers use Spanish when giving directions and explanations. One parent expressed the less common opinion that Latino children should have access to Spanish instruction throughout their elementary school careers to combat the loss of that language. As she reasoned:

> El inglés aquí lo van a ir aprendiendo. Me preocupa más el español–que no se les olvide. O sea que lo practican bien en escritura, en dictado, y en lectura porque cuando pasan a quinto, sexto grado casi no le van a dejar en español. Entonces yo quiero que adquieran muy buenas bases en español como están haciendo allí (at school).
>
> [Here they'll learn English. I'm more worried about Spanish– that they don't forget it. That is, that they practice writing, dictation, and reading because when they go on to 5th, 6th grade there won't be much Spanish (in school). So I want them to acquire a strong foundation in Spanish like they're doing there (at school).]

As the following comments indicate, some parents worry that the use of Spanish in the classroom will jeopardize their children's acquisition of English.

> Teachers should focus on the English just because I think they tend to speak too much Spanish to the Spanish speaking and they get lazy and they want to go the easy way which is the one they understand which is Spanish. I think that loses (confuses) them too sometimes in their English and their academics.
>
> Deberían de practicar mas inglés en la escuela porque casi saben todo el español. Entonces lo que necesitan es el inglés. Tengo mucho interés en que lo aprendan. Me gustaría que aprendan pronto. Mis hermanos tienen muchos años aprendiendo (inglés) y lo han aprendido escuchando puro inglés.
>
> [They should practice more English at school because they know Spanish. So they need English. I'm very interested in having them learn it. I would like them to learn soon. My brothers have spent many years learning (English) and they have learned by listening to only English.]

Overall, these findings are consistent with the attitudinal data toward language and schooling obtained from Mexican-American (and other ethnic minority) adults in the Detroit area (Lambert & Taylor, 1990), who find strong support for the maintenance of home language and culture, but some hesitation when it comes to the role to be played by the schools.

The data we have collected so far only begin to probe the complexities of language shift in this community. The data, for example, are based on interviews and thus allow inferences and explanations only about self-reported language practice (generally touching on the technical fields of social cognition and metalinguistic awareness). As we proceed, an important component of our studies will be observations of children's language-use practices, across a variety of settings, using case study methodology. For example, we will identify and describe key events when Spanish prevails in the lives of children and their families. We will also investigate the degree to which language issues—particularly those having to do with native language maintenance and loss—occupy the attention of parents and other community members. Finally, we will continue to work toward gaining a better understanding of the role of the two languages in the community. For example, it will be useful to know about the views and language-use practices of established and influential community members. We are interested in finding out the degree to which bilingualism really places people at an economic advantage and which bilinguals seem to reap the economic benefits of being bilingual. Thus, a series of questions will be used to explore the validity of the commonly held belief that bilingualism will lead to economic advantages and enhance one's standing in the job market.

Thus far, our research moves us towards a more explicit definition of shift for Mexicanos living in the U.S. Although by no means complete, our findings indicate the need to consider shift at two different levels: use and proficiency. From the standpoint of use, shift appears to be occurring both across and within generations, whereas shift in language proficiency appears to be an intergenerational phenomenon. Thus, children whose use of Spanish decreases with time may not lose their proficiency. However, as adults they may not be inclined to establish a Spanish-speaking home environment that will lead to Spanish-language development in their children.

COMBATING SHIFT/PROMOTING NATIVE LANGUAGE MAINTENANCE: IS IT POSSIBLE?

As both advocates of bilingualism and language educators, we are somewhat disheartened by the view of shift we have presented. We are constantly struggling with the sense that the phenomenon we are describing is inevitable and that much about the children's contexts and experiences contributes to shift. Certainly, the visibility of the English-only movement attests to the pervasiveness of antibilingual views in the larger society (Crawford, 1989). Schools, even bilingual education programs, have done little to counteract this trend. In fact, most bilingual education programs in this country have contributed to a deficit view of bilingualism. In general, the acquisition of English and eventual transitioning of language-minority students into an English-only curriculum is the primary goal of bilingual programs.[2]

A possible interpretation of our findings would be to recast shift as a problem of making sure children retain the kinds of attitudes that lead to their continued use of Spanish across settings. It is worth underscoring the fact that standard arguments for transitional bilingual education programs in this country have framed the issue around the importance of establishing cognitive and academic language proficiency in the native language as a basis for the development of those abilities in English (Cummins, 1981). Although a cognitive and academic base in the two languages is clearly important for school success, social and attitudinal aspects of language may perhaps be even more critical in the case of native language maintenance.

Thus, from our perspective of native-language maintenance, a worthwhile goal would be to influence the attitudes of those who are part of the social milieu available to children outside of their homes. Schools that foster positive attitudes about Spanish, as well as make bilingualism a goal for children from a variety of backgrounds, may represent a move towards this kind of social milieu. Another means of encouraging native-language maintenance would be for teachers to capitalize on the community- and home-based language-use practices involving Spanish that are available to bilingual children. By incorporating and building upon these language-use practices in the classroom, teachers would be providing students with familiar and authentic contexts for native-language development.

Drawing on our combined experiences, we have firsthand knowledge of two occasions when schooling has taken on one of these approaches. The first example is the instance of a school district taking an active role in advancing bilingualism as a goal for all students. What is particularly interesting is the evolution of this commitment in the context of a community not known for liberal attitudes toward bilingualism. In the case of the second example, a teacher organized her high school Spanish curriculum around translation, an activity that was part of the everyday experiences of her Latino students.

Two-Way Bilingual Education in a Northern California Community

Bilingual education has been part of the educational scene in a town we call "Lawson"—a community of 8500 people located in the Northern California wine country—since 1979. The goal of the original program was to move limited English proficient (LEP) students into the regular curriculum. According to former program participants, teachers barely proficient in Spanish themselves seldom used it in their classrooms.

In the early 1980s, "Antonio Vargas," a migrant-education teacher new to the district, began laying the groundwork for a bilingual program that would provide Anglo and Latino children with opportunities to develop oral fluency and literacy in Spanish and English. Vargas, who was well aware of the need for district, parental, and community backing for the program to work, embarked on a campaign to educate teachers, district administrators, community members, and parents about the benefits of bilingualism. His approach included informing board members of other maintenance-oriented bilingual education programs, involving them in a variety of relevant staff development opportunities (e.g., Spanish-language courses, methods of organizing instruction in two languages), and becoming a key figure in community activities (e.g., joining Rotary, organizing a sister-cities program with a Mexican community). In addition, he developed a good relationship with the staff of the local newspaper, which has continued to spotlight the accomplishments of the bilingual program to this day.

Vargas also enlisted the support of the district superintendent, who gave him and two of the district's elementary school principals the go ahead to write the Title VII grant that funded the bilingual education program from 1983–1988. In this new program, unlike many bilingual programs, student enrollment was fairly evenly distributed between Latino and Anglo students and the development and maintenance of Spanish as well as English was a central goal. According to Vargas, the superintendent supported his efforts and continued to give him free rein to seek ways to improve and build on the program once it was funded. One of the improvements he envisioned and worked toward was to set the stage for a Spanish-immersion strand so that Anglo and Latino children would receive almost all of their instruction in Spanish.

Once again, Vargas embarked upon a campaign of informing the community, the school board, and school administration about Spanish-immersion programs. Initially, he and the bilingual teachers in Lawson discussed articles describing immersion programs in Canada and the U.S. Later these articles were circulated among district administrators, school board members, and parents. With the administrators' support, Vargas invited an expert on Spanish-immersion education to make a series of presentations for parents in the spring of 1986. Afterward, Vargas took a group of ten Anglo parents to a nearby community to visit their two-way Spanish-immersion program. As one parent put it, "We were excited about immersion education before our visit. But we were convinced afterward."

In May of 1986, Vargas and a group of interested parents, most of them Anglo, obtained permission from the school board for a Spanish-immersion classroom at the kindergarten level. Because the district did not approve additional financial support for this pilot project, parents raised funds to buy Spanish-language materials and books and to send the immersion teacher to conferences on immersion education. They also recruited new parents into the program and worked with district administrators to determine criteria for admittance into the Spanish Immersion Program. By this time the parents interested in immersion education had joined together to form a Lawson chapter of Advocates for Language Learning (L.A.L.L.), which included, for the most part, Anglo parents interested in promoting the spread of second-language immersion education throughout the country. "John Dolan," the president of this group, says that his vision "is to have immersion education in 50% of the schools in this country because kids in immersion programs achieve academically as well as or better than if they were educated in English, plus they learn Spanish. They get everything and then some."

Since the program began, a grade level has been added each year so that at the time of this writing, the program has grown to include Spanish-immersion classes in kindergarten through 4th grade. Thus far, teachers use only Spanish with their students, both in and out of the classroom. Another teacher, aide, or parent offers 20 to 40 minutes of English language development, which usually consists of reading to children in English or participating in a hands-on activity. Students also participate in the range of special activities that are available to the entire school in English (e.g., music classes, art classes, assemblies). Initial literacy is introduced in Spanish and thus far teachers have decided to wait until the second half of 3rd grade before providing literacy instruction in English.

A number of factors contributed to the establishment of this two-way program for bilingual education. First and perhaps foremost, Vargas' visions and efforts have had an incredible impact on the development of bilingual education in the community. Administrators, teachers, and parents agree that he was responsible not only for getting the bilingual program off the ground but also for the dual-language development goal of the program. Vargas also made sure that other key figures shared his vision. He communicated his plan to teachers, administrators, parents, and community members and convinced them of its merit.

Although his success must be attributed, in part, to characteristics that are unique to him, he employed strategies that could be adopted by others. To convince those in power of the efficacy of a bilingual approach that capitalizes on students' linguistic resources, he backed up his ideas with articles and information about current programs. He also brought in experts to work with administrators and teachers. As he stated, "I did nothing that was a surprise," meaning he carefully laid the groundwork for each innovation he planned. Working gradually, he first presented the idea to key figures (e.g., the superintendent and school board members), he then showed them effective programs, and finally, he encouraged them to talk to experts in the field.

Vargas fostered an environment where teachers and parents, as well as administrators interested in bilingual education, felt that they had a voice in the decision-making process. Although in many ways Vargas brought bilingual education to the community, he was supported in his efforts by a superintendent who believed in giving his staff free rein. Moreover, once convinced of the efficacy of the approach, the superintendent actively supported Vargas and the teachers he hired in their efforts to implement and improve the bilingual program. Fortunately, the district's new superintendent also supports the program and continues to back the efforts of those involved in extending its scope to English-only classrooms.

The fact that Vargas and a core group of teachers shared a similar vision of bilingual education cannot be overlooked. Obviously, Vargas played an important role in laying the groundwork for this vision. However, many key players did not need Vargas to convince them of the benefits to be derived from a bilingual approach. As one teacher put it, "Many of us have been committed to bilingual education and dual language maintenance for years." Interviews reveal that many people in the community have had experiences that have led to or enhanced their appreciation of culture and linguistic diversity. For example, many program participants include former Peace Corps volunteers, the sons and daughters of farm workers living in California and the Southwest, immigrants from countries where bilingualism is respected, and people who have lived abroad for extended periods of time, most notably in Latin American countries.

The community context also played an important role in the establishment of this unique program. Our knowledge of the community suggests that school-related issues have not led to divisiveness across ethnic boundaries, a main feature surrounding the history of bilingual education and desegregation in other communities. This may, in part, be attributed to the more liberal (and possibly benevolent) attitudes of the Anglo residents of Lawson toward Latino immigrants. Anglo school administrators repeatedly reported that citizens of the majority community had a tradition of responding to the needs of Latino families. The churches were frequently cited as institutions that provide for needy Latinos. Latino as well as white residents of the community also reported that the conservative white growers and business people had more respect for Latinos, especially Mexicano immigrants, than their counterparts in other parts of the Southwest. As one Chicano teacher who has lived in many different regions of the Southwest put it, "Even the most rednecked ones are not as bad as they are in other places."

Finally, the size of the school district may have had a significant influence on the development of bilingual education in Lawson. Obviously, a small program, operating in a small district of only two elementary schools, can make certain changes more easily than a very large district. It is likely that communication between administrators and teachers follows a much more direct line than in larger districts, thereby contributing to an articulation of shared goals and inclusionary strategies for involving teachers in decision making. Also, because the Latino population has not yet reached the proportions of larger school districts, administrators have not had to deal with the complexities of a large immigrant population.

In many respects, the establishment of this program stands out as a laudable accomplishment. It is a rare example of an occasion when the linguistic resources of a minority community have been considered valuable and made available to the majority community. At the same time, we find certain features that led to the institutionalization of this program worrisome. The most notable has been the unequal involvement and access to the schooling process on the part of Anglo and Latino parents. Anglo parents, not Latino parents, played a critical role in generating the needed support and resources that led to the establishment of the Spanish-immersion program. They continue to wield more influence over the decision-making process. For example, a group of Anglo parents have demanded that they play a role in the hiring and firing of Spanish-immersion teachers. According to teachers, they are also much more inclined to question or complain about what goes on in their children's classrooms than Latino parents. In our opinion, there is something undeniably ironic about an instructional program that has done so much to recognize and incorporate an important resource of its minority students, in this case the Spanish language, in a school context where Anglo parents' voices and concerns predominate.

A Translation Approach to Teaching Spanish for Spanish Speakers

Our second example, one teacher's approach to teaching Spanish to Spanish speakers, has particular relevance to those interested in facilitating the development and maintenance of native languages in language-minority students. Providing native Spanish speakers with instruction in Spanish at the high school level is not new. However, these classes often resemble Spanish as Foreign Language classes that are available to nonnative Spanish-speaking high school students (i.e., the curriculum focuses on grammatical features of Spanish and communicative skills more appropriate for tourists than native Spanish speakers). From our vantage point, this approach to language learning does little to foster the kinds of language abilities and attitudes that contribute to native-language maintenance. These attitudes and abilities include student awareness about the psycholinguistic and sociolinguistic aspects of their bilingualism. By psycholinguistic awareness we mean the knowledge and appreciation of the formal aspects of language, such as phonology (e.g., the /p/ and /b/ sounds are distinguished differently in English than in Spanish) and grammar (e.g., Spanish systematically marks the distinction between imperfect and preterit past tense on verbs, whereas English does not). Sociolinguistic awareness refers to knowledge and appreciation of language use and variation, such as the fact that people from different regions of the country speak differently.

Aída Walqui, a high school teacher in Salinas, relies on translation as a means of enhancing language awareness in her Spanish-speaking students of Mexicano/Latino origin. As is the case for many language-minority students, translation is an everyday activity in their homes and communities. By involving students in translation and interpretation activities, Walqui's goals for them are to develop native-language and second-language proficiency, awareness of community language use and needs, and the ability to explore further education and job opportunities in the field of translation and interpretation. To achieve these goals, Walqui's students take part in translation and interpretation tasks, study sociolinguistic issues relating to both languages and multilingual situations (e.g., the English-only movement, dialect variation), and engage in community studies of bilingualism.

Interpretation tasks focus on a range of genres and contexts. For example, at the request of social studies teachers who teach in Spanish, Walqui's students translated texts about specific historical periods (e.g., materials on Nazi Germany) that were available only in English. In this activity, the students realized that they needed additional background information to translate the materials and conducted the necessary library research. In another project, students dubbed an English-only, Smithsonian-produced, video documentary on artist Diego Rivera. This project not only provided students with the opportunity to hone their research skills, it also fostered their appreciation for the painter's blending of painting and politics.

Walqui has also organized the classroom as a resource for the community. For example, one year the students advertised their services as translators over the radio and television and thus generated numerous requests for them to translate letters, official documents, and brochures for community organizations. By having students reflect on and critique translations, Walqui has also encouraged them to develop an appreciation for literary translations. Comparisons of translations to originals provides adolescents with a sense of the strategies that translators employ as well as the nuances in the kinds of meanings that different translations of the same text evoke.

A formal evaluation of Walqui's program was conducted in which students wrote essays that compared alternative translations of poetry (one which provided a more or less verbatim translation, and another that took greater liberties in interpretation). A content analysis of the essays revealed that students in the program gave more relevant and reasoned arguments for choosing the better translation, as compared to a group of high-achieving students in a Spanish-for-Spanish speaking class (Villarreal, 1990).

CONCLUSION

From our perspective, we are enjoying a period of increasing linguistic and cultural diversity in this country. In many schools, students who speak languages other than English are now in the majority. These bilingual individuals represent the best hope this nation has of developing competency in languages other than English. However, if history repeats itself— and if our own observations and the data of sociologists are correct—the native language of many of these students will not be passed on to their children. Our inquiry into the process of language shift suggests that shift is not a cognitive necessity, but one that is powerfully conditioned by social attitudes and beliefs. Further, we have pointed to some convincing demonstrations of school-based efforts to combat shift. Interestingly, these programs are not founded on cognitive principles, but rather, build on the social and community base of the language. We believe that in the absence of such social engagement, language proficiency, no matter how aggressively and elaborately developed, will not translate into sustained maintenance.

NOTES

1. The decision to make the mother the target parent was influenced by two factors: (1) a desire to adhere to a consistent criteria when selecting children in groups MU/A, MU/C, and UU, and (2) demographic information, con-

sistent with our impressions, that mothers play a more important role in language transmission to their children than do fathers. (Veltman, 1983)

2. In a nationally representative survey of programs for limited English proficient students conducted in the early 1980s, only 15% of the programs reported a maintenance philosophy (Development Associates, 1984).

REFERENCES

Crawford, J. (1989). *Bilingual education: History, politics, theory and practice.* Trenton, NJ: Crane.

Cummins, J. (1981). The role of primary language development in promoting educational success for language minority students. In California State Dept. of Education (Ed.), *Schooling and language minority students: A theoretical framework* (pp. 3–50). Los Angeles: Evaluation, Dissemination, and Assessment Center, California State University, Los Angeles.

Development Associates. (1984). *The descriptive phase report of the national longitudinal study of the effectiveness of services for LM/LEP students.* Arlington, VA: Development Associates.

Diaz, R. M. (1985). Bilingual cognitive development: Addressing three gaps in current research. *Child Development, 56,* 1376–1388.

Duncan, S. E., & DeAvila, E. A. (1979). Bilingualism and cognition: Some recent findings. *NABE Journal, 4,* 15–50.

Fishman, J. (1966). *Language loyalty in the United States.* The Hague: Mouton.

Grosjean, F. (1982). *Life with two languages.* Cambridge, MA: Harvard University Press.

Hakuta, K., &. D'Andrea, D. (1992). Some properties of bilingual maintenance and loss in Mexican background high school students. *Applied Linguistics, 13,* 72–99.

Hakuta, K., & Diaz, R. (1985). The relationship between degree of bilingualism and cognitive ability: A critical discussion and some new longitudinal data. In K. E. Nelson (Ed.), *Children's Language, 5* (pp. 319–344). Hillsdale, NJ: Erlbaum.

Kessler, C., & Quinn, M. E. (1980). Positive effects of bilingualism on science problem-solving abilities. In J. E. Alatis (Ed.), *Current issues in bilingual education* (pp. 295–308). Washington, DC: Georgetown University Press.

Lambert, W. E., & Taylor, D. M. (1990). *Coping with cultural and racial diversity in urban America.* New York: Praeger.

Lopez, D. (1978). Chicano language loyalty in an urban setting. *Sociology and Social Research, 62,* 267–278.

Malakoff, M., & Hakuta, K. (1991). Translation skill and metalinguistic awareness in bilingual children. In E. Bialystok (Ed.), *Language processing and language awareness by bilingual children* (pp. 141–166). Oxford: Oxford University Press.

Moll, L., & Greenberg, J. (1990). Creating zones of possibilities: Combining social context for instruction. In L. Moll (Ed.), *Vygotsky and education: Instructional implications and applications of sociohistorical psychology* (pp. 319–348). New York: Cambridge University Press.

Vasquez, O. A. (1992). A Mexicano perspective: Reading the world in a multicultural setting. In D. Murray (Ed.), *Diversity as a resource: A redefinition of cultural literacy* (pp. 113–134). Washington, DC: TESOL Press.

Veltman, C. (1983). *Language shift in the United States*. Berlin: Mouton.

Veltman, C. (1988). The future of the Spanish language in the United States. New York and Washington, DC: Hispanic Policy Development Project.

Villarreal, R. (1990). *Bilingualism as an educational building block for high school students*. Unpublished paper, School of Education, Stanford University, Stanford, CA.

CHAPTER 4

HISPANIC CULTURAL PSYCHOLOGY: IMPLICATIONS FOR EDUCATION THEORY AND RESEARCH

Marcelo M. Suarez-Orozco and Carola E. Suarez-Orozco

This chapter discusses some key themes in the cultural psychology of Hispanic immigrants and their children. We explore some important aspects of the Hispanic-American immigrant experience considering first- and second-generation individual, family, and group dynamics. We refer to some of the most interesting findings by our colleagues working with Mexican immigrants and Mexican Americans (the largest Hispanic group in the U.S.), as well as to our research findings among immigrants and refugees recently arriving from Central America (the newest Hispanic Americans). We also point out some notable findings of researchers working with Cuban Americans and mainland Puerto Ricans. We consider how certain enduring psychocultural features in the Hispanic experience may be of importance to understanding—and ameliorating—the educational condition of the various Hispanic subgroups.

It is impossible to discuss the Hispanic condition as if it were a monolithic phenomenon. Mexican Americans, Cuban Americans, mainland Puerto Ricans, and immigrants from Central and South America are distinct populations that share a number of unifying characteristics. These groups share various degrees of familiarity with the Spanish language and such cultural traits as the importance of the extended family (familism), an emphasis on spiritual and interpersonal relationships, respect for authority, and an emphasis on the "here and now" rather than the future time orientation valued by the dominant American culture.

Yet it is important to emphasize that Hispanics in the U.S. are a diverse demographic and sociocultural population. Hispanics come from many different countries and socioeconomic, educational, and professional backgrounds. Cuban Americans, for example, tend to have attained higher educational levels than all other Hispanic groups and they tend to have higher incomes as well. But more recent Cuban immigrants have included persons of lower socioeconomic status and poorer education. For example, over a few weeks in 1980 some 129,000 lower-status Cuban immigrants, the so-called Marielitos, came to the U.S. en masse. On the other hand, many of the original immigrants from Cuba were of upper-status professional background motivated to leave Cuba for political reasons following Fidel Castro's ascent to power in 1959. Some have argued that their professional and refugee background has given the upper-status Cubans in the U.S. "a sense of specialness which may have facilitated their adaptation to new environments and may be connected to their relative success [in the U.S.]" (Bernal, 1982, p. 197).

Conversely, mainland Puerto Ricans tend to have lower levels of education and the poorest economic condition of all Hispanic groups. A special issue facing mainland Puerto Ricans is the relationship between the U.S. and the island of Puerto Rico, a condition that provides American citizenship to them. Furthermore, the quasi-colonial nature of the relationship between the U.S. and Puerto Rico, in addition to the stresses of migration and minority status, has created some special problems in the mainland Puerto Rican community.

Mexican Americans and the immigrants from Central and South America tend to fall somewhere in between the Cuban and mainland Puerto Rican cases in terms of educational achievements and income levels. Mexican Americans are themselves a heterogeneous population including new arrivals from various regions of Mexico, as well as the descendants of those who were in the Southwest prior to the U.S. takeover of these formerly Mexican territories.

In the case of immigrants from Mexico, Central and South America, we find special problems relating to whether they entered the U.S. as documented or undocumented migrants; whether they came voluntarily or due to political persecution (many recent arrivals from Central America came in search of political refuge); whether they are seasonal migrants planning to return home, or plan to stay in the U.S. more or less permanently; and whether they came to the U.S. as a family unit or as individuals.

In the Mexican-American case, there is the important factor already noted that the Southwest of the U.S., where they are now the largest minority group, was once part of the United States of Mexico. Therefore, the Mexican Americans who were in the Southwest territories prior to their U.S. takeover from Mexico cannot be considered immigrants in the traditional sense of the term. Rather than their coming to the U.S., the U.S., so to speak, came to *them*.

All of these factors greatly impact opportunities and the migration experience. If we were to search for a common denominator of experience that holds true for most Hispanic immigrants it is that they are coming (or came) from relatively impoverished "developing" countries, and typically from the lower socioeconomic strata, into a more affluent, industrialized society. We must again point out that the upper-status early Cuban migrants and recent South-American professionals are exceptions to the rule.

OPPORTUNITY VS. DEPRIVATION

It is well recognized that immigrants often come as pioneers with a dream of making a better life for themselves as well as for their children. Their objectives are relatively clear: get a job, earn money, learn a new language, offer an education to the children, and improve their lot in life. The obvious difficulties that most immigrants face include language inadequacies, a general unfamiliarity with the customs and expectations of the new country (what anthropologists refer to as "cultural discontinuities"), limited economic opportunities, poor housing conditions, discrimination, and what psychologists term the "stresses of acculturation" (Rogler, Cortes, & Malgady, 1991, pp. 585–597).

Despite these obstacles, in many cases (although from the point of view of the host country their living circumstances may seem poor and disadvantaged) immigrants typically see their lot as having improved from what it was in their country of origin. As a result, immigrants may fail to internalize the negative attitudes of the host country towards them, maintaining their country of origin as a point of reference. Hence, immigrants commonly view and experience their current lot not in terms of the ideals and expectations of the majority society but rather in terms of the ideals of the "old culture."

This is the part of an immigrant's orientation that we have termed "the immigrant's dual frame of reference." That is, immigrants are constantly comparing and contrasting their current lot in the host society with their previous experiences and expectations in their country of origin. During the earliest phases of immigration, the new arrivals may come to idealize the new country as a land of unlimited opportunities. A new arrival noted,

Here [the U.S.] there are more opportunities to find a good job. There [Guatemala] we have no national funds, the national bank of Guatemala is empty. It is a big robbery. The different presidents come in saying that they want to help the country, and all they really do is take care of themselves. The people stay poor without anything. Now here you can study, you can better yourself. There are many opportunities here. I learned English here. Few people in Guatemala can learn another language. Here you can express yourself, you can complain out loud. There is no persecution like in Guatemala. There everything depends on who you know.

Note that as they idealize the new land, many new arrivals may at the same time concentrate on the negative aspects of life in the land left behind. Another new arrival from Latin America illustrated this principle when he said,

Life in my country is very backward. There we live in a humble way. You are remote from everything. The people are ignorant. You can't do anything there, you can't travel, you can't learn another language. Here people are open and there is freedom, here there are people from all over the world. This is a liberal country. This is the most modern country in the world. There kids grow up in the shadows of their mother's skirts. They train you to be obedient. Here I don't see that. . . . Here you have the freedom to do whatever pleases you. Here there are opportunities we do not have [in Latin America].

This pattern is also found among other Hispanic immigrants, including many coming from Mexico. Rogler, Cortes, and Malgady (1991) explore the psychosocial consequences of an important generational discontinuity between Mexican-born parents and their California-born children that relates to the immigrant's dual frame of reference. They write,

The selectivity of the migration stream from Mexico to California tends to create a psychologically robust first-generation immigrant population [that] feels less deprived because migration has increased their standard of living; in contrast, the Mexican Americans born in the United States feel more deprivation because of their much higher but unrealized aspirations. (p. 589)

We concur with this observation. The children of immigrants evaluate their experiences in the new country differently than did the immigrant generation. This is based, in part, on the fact that the children of immigrants (the second-generation) did not experience the limitations and economic hardships of life in the "old country." In fact, among the children of immigrants, the "old country" may be romanticized as a somewhat Edenic place (hence the desire of searching for one's "roots" in the old country among the children of immigrants) and not for what it was actually like in the land their parents left.

It is important to note that first-generation immigrants may not only increase their own standard of living but also the standard of living of the family members left behind. Hispanic immigrants almost universally help out their relatives left behind with regular and substantial remittances from the U.S. Hispanic immigrants send millions of dollars every year to Mexico and Central and South America.

"Maria," a new arrival from Mexico, illustrates how for many Hispanic immigrants the point of migrating is improving the lives of those left behind. Maria came to the U.S. in the early 1990s from the State of Mexico when she was 29 years old. Her husband's sudden death from cancer made their already precarious economic situation extremely problematic. In order to feed her four children, she said, the family decided Maria should come to the U.S. in search of work.

Two of her sisters, as well as many other friends from her *rancho* (village) in Mexico, had already come to the U.S. to escape the Mexican economic crisis of the 1980s. Word was sent back that in the U.S. Maria could find employment in the service sector and earn between 100 and 125 dollars a week. As a live-in maid in a middle-class suburb in Southern California, Maria now earns enough to send home between 200 and 300 dollars every month. This sum, Maria said, was more than double the minimum wage she was earning in Mexico before she left.

Maria says that the money she sends back goes to feed and dress her children, whom she left in the care of her parents. Now, Maria said with some nostalgia in her voice, they can even purchase for her kids an occasional toy, even a bicycle. Maria's remittances are also critical for purchasing fertilizer, animal feed, and the agricultural equipment used by her father and brothers in their small *rancho*. Maria's immediate dream is to obtain "her papers" (immigrant documents) so that she may bring her children to the U.S. to be with her.

In this case we see how a single person is responsible for ameliorating the standard of living of many left behind. The pain Maria suffered by leaving her family behind is lessened by her realization that it is by being away that she can best serve those she loves most. And this is the sad experience of many immigrants—enduring losses to be able to best help those left behind. Hence many immigrants in a new land experience losses, some marginality, and deprivation, but they know that they are making a tremendous difference to the lives of those left behind.

THE SECOND GENERATION: FROM IMMIGRANT MARGINALITY TO ETHNIC CONSCIOUSNESS

The children of immigrants (second-generation Mexican Americans) born in the new land, however, do not share their parents' dual frame of reference. Not being immigrants themselves, they can not frame their current experiences in terms of the old-country ideals, standards, and expectations. They are less likely to continue to send remittances back to the relatives in the old country. Rather than seeing themselves as better off vis-à-vis the old country (as their parents did), second-generation Mexican Americans may perceive their situation as one of deprivation and marginality vis-à-vis the majority-culture (American) dream (Horowitz, 1983). Thus, the second generation often faces the same discriminations and economic difficulties as their parents *without* the perceived benefits.

Ongoing discrimination and ethnic tension have an erosive effect, particularly on the very vulnerable children of immigrants. Villareal (1959) insightfully describes the phenomenon of ethnic prejudice in his classic novel, *Pocho*, in which the protagonist learns about the predicament of *pachucos* (second-generation Mexican Americans):

> Their bitterness and hostile attitude towards 'whites' was not merely a lark. They had learned hate through actual experience with everything the word implied. They had not been as lucky as he and had the scars to prove it. . . . [Their experiences, however,] were due more to the character of a handful of men than to the wide, almost organized attitude of a society, for just as zootsuiters were blamed en masse for the actions of a few, they in turn, blamed the other side for the very same reason. (pp. 150–151)

Anthropologists George A. De Vos (1980) and John U. Ogbu (1978) have argued that the specific problems facing immigrants and minority groups in general must be seen in the context of the distinct psychosocial experiences of each group as they enter a majority-dominant society. Ogbu (1978) describes what he terms "involuntary minorities." These are minorities that initially have been incorporated into a dominant society against their will (such as African Americans through slavery or Native Americans and the early Mexican Americans through conquest). In addition to their original subordination, these groups have been subjected to what Ogbu calls a "job-ceiling." Ogbu maintains that many of the involuntary minorities were traditionally given the most undesirable menial jobs in the opportunity structure and could not raise above these positions regardless of talent, motivation, or effort.

De Vos and M. Suarez-Orozco (1990) have noted that in addition to "instrumental exploitation" for economic purposes (for example, to maintain a pool of low-skilled, low-paid workers to labor the most undesirable but needed jobs), these minorities are also used for "psychological exploitation." That is, they may also be the target of psychological abuse such as stereotyping as "innately inferior," "lazier," and therefore less deserving of sharing in the dominant society's "dream." Economic exploitation and psychological exploitation are, in a sense, two sides of the same coin: psychological exploitation and disparagement rationalizes the dominant society's economic treatment of these groups.

The children of immigrants raised in a context of ethnic disparagement can either identify with the oppressing dominant group, and attempt to join them by leaving their own ethnic group behind ("passing"), or they may resolutely reject the society that rejects them and turn to others who share their predicament—their peers. From this second situation typically emerge countercultural groups or gangs that reject the dominant society and affirm their own ethnic identity.

Among Hispanics, poor achievement in school tends to be a serious problem (Suarez-Orozco, 1989). The reasons for this are complex. Vigil (1988) attributes this to the fact that many Hispanic immigrant parents have not had much education themselves and yet have attained a modest (relative from whence they came) degree of prosperity. Some parents may therefore be sending the message to their children, "We made it without a formal education, so can you."

A problem with this line of argument is that Hispanic parents generally say they want their children to have the formal education they themselves could not have. Scholars have noted that Hispanic families encourage youths to early employment, marriage, and childbearing, which may divert some youths from investing in formal education. Ogbu (1978) has approached the problem of poor Hispanic performance in school from a different but related perspective. According to Ogbu, there is a perception (often based in reality) among some Hispanics, particularly Mexican Americans and mainland Puerto Ricans, that high school graduates are not much more financially successful than those who dropped out and pursued jobs. Hence these Hispanic youths may not invest in school because they do not see that they will get any additional rewards in the posteducational job market.

School personnel are often indifferent (or even hostile) to the linguistic and other cultural needs, as well as the special circumstances of Hispanic immigrant families (Suarez-Orozco, 1989). This, coupled with the economic pressures of providing for a large family, may lead to negative attitudes toward school and the route of education. Consequently, a high dropout rate from school continues to be a severe problem in the Hispanic community (Horowitz, 1983; Suarez-Orozco, 1989; Vigil, 1988).

BETWEEN WORLDS

Stonequist (1937) described the experiences of social dislocation of "the individual who through migration, education, marriage or some other influence leaves one social group or culture without making a satisfactory adjustment to another find[ing] himself on the margin of each but a member of neither" (p. 4). Stonequist maintained that "wherever there are cultural transitions and cultural conflicts there are marginal personalities" (p. 4). These cultural differences create more difficulty in circumstances where there are sharp ethnic contrasts and hostile social attitudes. This may result in "acute personal difficulties and mental tension" for those individuals identified with aspects of both groups. Stonequist ascertained that the common traits of what he termed the "marginal man" evolved from the conflict of two cultures rather than "from the specific content of any culture" (p. 9).

In the best case scenario, Stonequist (1937) argues, certain individuals with the right potential can overcome these adverse circumstances and "return as creative agents" who "would be able to contribute to the solution of the conflict of races and cultures" (p. 15). Although this is undoubtedly true, such marginal status comes at considerable psychological cost.

The Immigrant Paradox: Instrumental Gains, Affective Losses

This brings us to the psychological toll to be paid for migrating to another country. Although immigration may bring about an improvement in economic conditions, migration also ruptures the "immigrant's supportive interpersonal bonds" (Rogler, Malgady, & Rodriguez, 1989, p. 25) well recognized to be crucial for psychological well-being. In addition, migration may psychologically represent a cumulative trauma. Migration often results in multiple losses, the effects of which are not always immediately apparent (Grinberg & Grinberg, 1989).

Rogler, Cortes, and Malgady (1991) summarize their recent overview of the literature on acculturation and mental health status among Cuban Americans, mainland Puerto Ricans, and Mexican Americans,

> Migration is likely to disrupt attachments to supportive networks in the society of origin and to impose on the migrant the difficult task of incorporation into the primary groups of the host society. The migrant is also faced with problems of economic survival and social mobility in an unfamiliar socioeconomic system. These uprooting experiences are accompanied by problems of acculturation into a new cultural system, of acquiring the language, the behavioral norms and values characteristic of the host society. (p. 585)

In those individuals who possess sufficient psychological resources to withstand the trauma and who have adequate available social support, the migration experience can result in personal enrichment and psychological growth. For many, however, the losses result in an exacerbation of psychological traits and problems. A study of mainland Puerto Ricans reports that those "with fewest psychological resources for coping with the new environment reported the worst stress outcomes" (Rogler, Cortes, & Malgady, 1991, p. 593).

Grinberg and Grinberg (1989) outline three typical patterns of psychological problems that may occur after migration. These include problems with "persecutory anxiety" (whereby the host environment is experienced as hostile and persecutory in nature), "depressive anxiety" (when the individual is preoccupied with his or her losses due to the migration), and "disorienting anxiety" (which results from disorientation about the "old" and the "new" ways of being, time, and space).

Persecutory anxieties may be manifested in the form of irrational fears of aspects of life in the host society. During the first days of the recent war in the Persian Gulf, a rumor rapidly spread among Mexican migrants in Southern California that all "undocumented" persons captured by the Border Patrol would be sent to fight in the front lines of the Gulf War! The (undocumented) immigrant's well-grounded fear of persecution by the Border Patrol metamorphosed into an irrational fear of being sent to war. Immigrants may also feel disappointment following a realization that their initial idealization of life in the new land was erroneous. This may occur with an insight that life will indeed be difficult in the new country. A recently arrived Hispanic immigrant said,

> [Now] I am so disappointed. I had so many ideas [about life in the U.S.]. When I was young, I remember the way people that went back [home] from the United States would bring so much money

with them! And they would tell us that life here was so different, [that it was] so easy to make money in the United States. Really, it is a big lie. These are the kind of people that work like slaves here, work, work, work, all day, and save all their money to use . . . when they go back . . . to show it off back there. They don't use any of their money here. So when I come in, I encountered all these problems here too.

As Grinberg and Grinberg (1989) describe it, an immigrant's sense of "depressive anxiety" is characterized by an excessive preoccupation with psychological losses. A young Hispanic immigrant speaks of the tremendous sense of loss he feels in the new land,

Here I have no family, I have no home. If I had my family and a home here I would be more optimistic. Now I feel tired. I am sure that if I had a home here, my mother would be waiting for me with my food ready. Now I come back home, and I have to make my own food. I get up in the morning to go to school, and I am all by myself. I make my own coffee, iron my clothes, do everything alone. I come back from work at night and I am all alone. I feel very low. I sit in bed all alone, and I lose morale. I think about my future and about being all alone. This depresses me a lot; I feel desperate.

Note the poignant longing for maternal nurturing suggested in the wish that his mother would be there waiting for him with his food ready. Mother's food, that is the food of the motherland, we must note, is typically laden with symbolic and expressive significance in the lives of immigrants. It is as if by eating their own ethnic foods, immigrants symbolically attempt to re-establish a link with the lost motherland.

The sense of anxious "disorientation" among new immigrants that is described by Grinberg and Grinberg (1989) is related to what anthropologists have termed the sense of "culture shock" one typically experiences when entering a radically different way of life. A Latin American immigrant articulated this point:

When we come here [from Latin America], we are afraid. We are even afraid of talking to people with the little English we speak. . . . At first I was so timid. I could not even engage in a conversation. I was afraid people would laugh at my English. We are afraid of this so we shut ourselves in our little universe.

When I came here, I noticed how different people are [from Latin Americans]. Here they dress differently, they talk differently,

they act differently. I did not know how to act here, I did not
know how to speak English, I did not know what to do or what to
say. So the first thing I did was try to dress like everybody else. I
did not want to stand out. Because people here notice if you are
dressed very differently. They may not say anything directly to
you, but they do notice. I did not want to look like a stranger, I
did not want to stand out. The next thing I did was to pay attention to what people here did, how they spoke and how they acted.
I tried to learn how and why they acted in a certain way because I
didn't know.

The children of Hispanic immigrants may become the repositories
of their parents' anxieties, ambitions, dreams, and conflicts. They are frequently vested with responsibilities (such as translating and sibling care)
beyond what is normal for their stage of psychological development. Due
to a lack of linguistic skills, Hispanic immigrant parents are often unable
to help their children in school-related tasks. This may bring about further anxieties and a sense of inadequacy in the parents. Perhaps because
of these feelings, Hispanic immigrant parents typically overrestrict the
activities of their children and attempt to minimize the host country's
influence.

Immigrant children may suffer shame and doubt, which compromise
and undermine their self-confidence and development. Feelings of inadequacy and inferiority commonly lead to a loss in faith in the child's abilities to "make it" in the new setting (Grinberg & Grinberg, 1989). A psychological choice for young adults seems to emerge: either dropping-out
of school or overcompensating in the form of overachieving (see the case
study of Richard Rodriguez and the high-achieving Central American
children described below).

ETHNIC IDENTITY, "MULTIPLE MARGINALITIES," AND GANG FORMATION

Grinberg and Grinberg (1989) and Vigil (1988) maintain that a critical issue facing the children of immigrants is that of developing a sense
of "identity." According to Erickson (1963), a sense of identity is the critical task in development during adolescence. In order to develop "ego-
identity" (a healthy sense of who one is), there must occur a certain
amount of complementarity between the individual's sense of self and the
social milieu. If too much cultural dissonance and role confusion exist,

there may be difficulties in an individual's developing a strong sense of identity.

Children of Hispanic immigrants may suffer from what Vigil (1988) terms "multiple marginalities," which in some cases compromise the development of a sense of identity. Vigil and others have noted that such children are likely to experience intense culture conflict on both individual and group levels. For many second-generation Hispanic American youths,

> Language inconsistency at home and school, a perceived gap in the status of their parents and the quality of their environment and those of the larger society, and the dangers and attractions of barrio streets create an ambiguity in their ethnic identity. Parents and older siblings are often unable to effectively guide youngsters in ways to reconcile the contrasting cultural worlds, and this results in an uneven adoption of acculturative strategies. (Vigil, 1988, p. 41)

In some cases, youths attempt to resolve identity issues by embracing total assimilation and a wholesale identification with mainstream American values. In other cases, a new ethnic identity, incorporating both Hispanic and dominant American culture is forged (in which cases bilingual fluency is often achieved). Yet in other cases the adaptation is not as smooth and a "subculture of cultural transitionals" (Vigil, 1988, p. 39) develops. These "transitional" youths are sometimes called *cholos*. Within the same family each child may adopt his or her own way individually, resulting in various siblings occupying very different sectors of the spectrum (from *cholo* to "anglicized," and from bilingual to "Spanglish" to English-only speaking) (Vigil, 1988).

Villareal (1959) poignantly articulates the effects of cultural marginality on the children of Mexican migrant workers. In this passage, Villareal's protagonist eloquently describes second-generation cultural identity issues:

> They had a burning contempt for people of different ancestry, whom they called Americans and a marked hauteur towards Mexico and toward their parents for their old-country ways. The former feeling came from a sense of inferiority that is a prominent characteristic in any Mexican reared in southern California; and the latter was an inexplicable compensation for that feeling. They needed to feel superior to something, which is a natural thing. The result was that they attempted to segregate themselves from both their cultures, and became truly a lost race. . . . That in spite of their behavior, which was sensational at times and violent at others, they were simply a portion of confused humanity, employing their self-segregation as a means of expression. (pp. 149–150)

It is precisely such identity issues that propel many second-generation Hispanic American youths to join gangs. In fact, Vigil (1988) con-
tends that gangs are largely a second-generation immigrant phenomena.
In his perceptive studies, Vigil traces the historical pattern of gang formation in urban areas since the beginning of large-scale Mexican immigration to the U.S. before the turn of this century.

Vigil (1988) accounts for several key factors in the development of
Hispanic gangs. These include: low socioeconomic status, urban poverty,
and limited economic mobility; ethnic minority status and discrimination;
lack of training, education, and constructive opportunities; and a breakdown in the social institutions of school and family. Vigil also points out
major causal factors in "a first- and second- generation conflict within each
ethnic group, which creates loyalty discord and identity confusions; and
a noted predisposition among youths to gravitate toward street peers for
sources of social associations and personal fulfillment" (p. 4). All of these
factors hold particularly true for many second-generation Hispanic American youths. In addition, we must note that "*cholo* gangs" have been a long-
lasting, rather than transitory phenomena, due to a unique situation of
continuous migration from Mexico, which brings in reinforcements of
the traditional culture, and new cycles of "marginality," on an ongoing
basis (Vigil, 1988).

Gangs provide a "mechanism of adaptation for many youths who need
a source of identification and human support" (Vigil, 1988, p. 6). The gang
provides a "reforging of Mexican and American patterns . . . creating a
culture [and language] of mixed and blended elements" (p. 7). Vigil maintains that "although *cholos* are Americanized, either by accident or design,
they refuse or are unable to be totally assimilated" (p. 7). They retain
certain Mexican customs, sometimes in caricature form, and a strong sense
of peer group (gang) as family, male patterns of machismo, and an ambivalent attitude toward authority (Horowitz, 1983; Vigil, 1988).

At the same time, youths in gangs may not feel "Mexican" and in
some cases may actually experience considerable antipathy towards Mexican visitors (Dayley, 1991) and disparage "wet-backs" [first-generation
undocumented immigrants] (Vigil, 1988). Often there is a perception of
"limited good" and competition over scarce resources (such as jobs, education, housing, and so forth) with the newer arrivals. Psychologically, the
second-generation may view the new arrivals as embodying aspects of
themselves that the second-generation may wish to disclaim.

Both Vigil (1988) and Horowitz (1983) have found that the individuals who are most heavily involved in gangs come from the most troubled
families: with absent parents, a history of alcohol or drug addiction, child
neglect or abuse. Vigil (1988) estimates that 70% to 80% of the heavily

involved gang members come from such family situations. For such individuals, in the absence of more appropriate role models, gang membership becomes incorporated into their sense of identity. Gangs offer their members a sense of belonging, solidarity, support, and warmth. Although many second-generation youths may look toward gangs for cues about dress, language, and attitude, most remain on the periphery and eventually outgrow the gang mystique after passing through adolescence. Nevertheless, the gang ethos provides a sense of identity and cohesion for marginal youths during a turbulent stage of development.

LABYRINTHS OF SOLITUDE: INSTRUMENTAL MOBILITY VERSUS EXPRESSIVE AFFILIATION

Second-generation Hispanic Americans who have the opportunity and choose to join mainstream American culture face very different day-to-day experiences but may continue to suffer from a marginal status:

> Individuals who choose to measure their competency in terms of the wider society rather than in terms of local identity risk a loss of emotional support from peers and kin. Trusting and close relationships must be developed with new people and on different terms. The movement away from the traditional sources of support and the traditional basis of social relationships can create feelings of acute loneliness. Little within the Chicano community prepares them for the competitive, individualistic Anglo world of social relationships in which they must face lack of acceptance and some degree of discrimination. They become caught between two worlds. (Horowitz, 1983, pp. 200–201)

Richard Rodriguez's (1982) autobiographical account of his experiences growing up in Sacramento, California, provides a rich illustration of an individual who attempts to integrate himself into the dominant society, actively rejecting his native tongue, social networks, and culture. Rodriguez is certainly very successful viewed from the standards of the dominant society. As a Stanford, Columbia, and Berkeley graduate and fellow of the prestigious Warbug Institute in London he came a long way from the Sacramento of his youth. However, a close reading of his controversial autobiography shows that Rodriguez suffers from a sense of marginality and alienation that is truly poignant.

Stymied in her own attempts to get ahead, Rodriguez's mother "willed her ambition to her children. 'Get all the education you can. With an education you can do anything'" (Rodriguez, 1982, pp. 54–55). His mother is told by the local nuns to stop using the "private" language (the language of intimacy—Spanish) and to start using the more instrumental "public" language (English) at home. Rodriguez admits to being "angry at them [his parents] for having encouraged me towards classroom English" (p. 52). He found himself retaliating by intentionally hurting his parents, by correcting them when they made mistakes in English. "But gradually this anger was exhausted, replaced by guilt as school grew more and more attractive to me" (p. 50).

The more Rodriguez (1982) was propelled into the public world of school and the dominant culture, the more alienated he became from his private world of family, ethnicity, and culture. This was fueled, in part, by his sense of shame over his parents' accents and their inability to help him even with his 2nd-grade homework. "Your parents must be proud of you. . . . Shyly I would smile, never betraying my sense of irony: I was not proud of my mother and father" (p. 52).

Unable to identify with his humble, silent Mexican father, Rodriguez (1982) turns to his powerful teachers. "I wanted to be like my teachers, to possess their knowledge, to assume their authority, their confidence, even to assume a teacher's persona" (p. 55). In carefully reading Rodriguez's account of his life, one senses that the only identification he is able to make with his father is with his silence.

With the acquisition of English and an education, Rodriguez (1982) faced both huge gains and huge losses. He gained the capacity to enter the public arena he so valued as well as the ability to understand and communicate within the dominant culture. However, he clearly loses emotionally on several levels. He loses his feeling of belonging to his family. With his transition to English, his family was "no longer so close; no longer bound tight by the pleasing and troubling knowledge of our public separateness" (p. 23). He loses the easy intimacy and open communication between family members. "The family's quiet was partly due to the fact that, as we children learned more and more English, we shared fewer and fewer words" (p. 23). He also loses interest in the affective nuances of language and becomes more concerned with content, "Conversation became content-full. Transparent. Hearing someone's tone of voice—angry or questioning or sarcastic or happy—I didn't distinguish it from the words it expressed" (p. 22). Rodriguez develops a sense of anomic withdrawal from his family. A numbness engulfs Rodriguez, separating him from his now-distant parents.

He makes a choice then, between instrumental mobility ("making it" in the world of the dominant society) and expressive affiliation. Rodriguez is profoundly alone—alienated from his family and alienated from his peers, finding few who are able or willing to take his path. He must then rationalize his choice with its consequent gains as well as losses. In doing

so, he becomes a vocal opponent of both bilingual education and affir-
mative action.

In reading Rodriguez (1982), one feels pity both for him and for his
parents. He is so alone that the only sense of intimacy he has is with his
readers: "encouraged by physical isolation to reveal what is most personal;
determined at the same time to have my words seen by strangers" (p. 187).
His parents lose what is clearly a favorite son. His mother's attempts at
intimacy and involvement are consistently rebuffed. The gulf between
them seems interminable and irreparable.

Rodriguez's controversial condemnation of bilingual education deserve further comment. Certainly it is true that by using "nonmainstream"
English (such as Spanglish, Black English, lower-class English) one is at a
disadvantage, as evaluations are constantly being made about oneself based
on language usage. However, we would question whether it is indeed
necessary to give up one's native language, one's affective language (along
with all the resulting accompanying losses) in order to "make it." In ideal
circumstances, it should not be an either-or situation.

Rodriguez's devastating account goes directly to the symbolic and
affective aspects of language. To see language as a mere instrumental tool
for communication is to miss its deep affective roots. To give up Spanish
to acquire English represents a symbolic act of ethnic renunciation: it is
giving up the mother tongue for the instrumental tongue of the dominant group.

It is in such contexts, when learning the language of a dominant group
is symbolically equated with giving up one's own ethnic identity, that language acquisition becomes a problem. The Dutch can speak English very
effectively at no emotional cost. In contrast, the Flemish-speaking people
in Belgium have faced historical difficulties in learning French—the language of the once dominant and oppressive Walloons. An understanding of the affective aspects of language also helps to explain why minority ethnic rights movements often pick up language as a symbolic banner
of belonging vis-à-vis dominant groups (e.g., the Basques in Spain, the
push for bilingual education in the U.S., the insistence that Black English
be given equal value to standard English, and so forth.)

IMMIGRANT GUILT AND COMPENSATORY ACHIEVEMENT

We turn now from the vicissitudes facing the second-generation children of immigrants (Richard Rodriguez and the *barrio* gang members) to
consider in more detail a psychocultural case study among first-generation Hispanic immigrants. In many ways, the first-generation immigrant

pattern presents a picture opposite to the Rodriguez and gang cases. In the example described next, we see a concern with achievement motivation, "trying to become a somebody," coupled with a wish to turn toward family and loved ones, to help them and to alleviate ongoing parental hardships.

This next section reports some findings of a psychocultural study of the experience of a group of Central American youths recently arrived in the U.S. Escaping the Central American wars and scarcity, such youths have been entering the U.S. by the tens of thousands within the last decade (Suarez-Orozco, 1989). In the process of resettling they came to share a dream with the earlier generation of Hispanic immigrants and refugees to the U.S.: to establish themselves in a way that would enable them to help loved ones still living and struggling in the old country. In pursuing their dream, these youngsters came to endure great sacrifices against an almost unshakable belief that their present hardships would in the future bring them and their loved ones the benefits of a more decent life (for a similar conclusion based on an ethnographic study among recent arrivals from Central America in Washington D.C., see Ready, 1991).

Our research was conducted in an inner city in the Southwest U.S., which has a large population of new arrivals from Central America. The study consisted of year-long participant observation (participating in and observing the daily lives of the immigrants) in the barrios, as well as systematic ethnographic interviews and psychological testing with some 50 youths (ages 14 to 19) from El Salvador, Guatemala, and Nicaragua. All had entered the U.S. in the early 1980s and had enrolled in inner-city schools trying to gain mastery of the English language.

Interviews with teachers in these conflict-ridden, inner-city schools revealed their general preference for new arrivals over the native-born ethnic populations found in the schools. Teachers noted that the new arrivals were generally better disciplined, more grateful, and, above all, very serious about learning the language (Ready, 1991; Suarez-Orozco, 1989; Vlach, 1984). A large percentage of the immigrants in this sample worked while attending school full time. The new arrivals worked mostly in the service sector of the U.S. economy. Most of them sent home remittances regularly.

Escape to Freedom

Universally, informants reported leaving Central America *por la situación* (because of the situation back home). These words came to be used by the youngsters as referents to a nightmarish world of "disappearances," systematic torture, random killings, bodies appearing in the streets with political messages carved in the flesh, kidnappings, and forced recruitments into conflicts foreign to their hearts.

In El Salvador over the last decade more than 70,000 civilian noncombatants were killed by government forces and "death squads" allied to them, and 750,000 or so (15% of the population) became refugees beyond its borders; 500,000 or so (another 10% of the population) became homeless or displaced within its borders. In Guatemala, it has been estimated that "as many as one million Guatemalans may be refugees" as a consequence of the genocidal campaign to crush the peasant revolt (Brown, 1985). During the bloody war to overthrow Somoza, an estimated 40,000 Nicaraguans were killed (see Buckley, 1984, p. 332; LaFeber, 1984, pp. 226–242), and some 200,000 Nicaraguans left their country in search of refuge in Mexico, other Central American nations, and the U.S. (For an overview of the psychosocial consequences of political terror see Suarez-Orozco, 1990).

There is ample evidence to document the political terror and severe economic scarcity currently prevailing in Central America. The personal experiences of *all* of the new immigrants had been in some measure directly affected by these conditions. The youths most often cited *la situación* as their reason for leaving, they had an increasing sense that the random political violence would sooner or later affect them directly. Some informants had fled following the actual assassination or disappearance of a relative, friend, or acquaintance. One youngster reported escaping El Salvador after his father, a factory guard, was assassinated. Another left Guatemala after the killing of a cousin. Still others left after their friends or acquaintances began to disappear only to reappear as mutilated corpses. Yet others were directly escaping a random military draft that would force them to participate in what they deemed senseless slaughter.

"Ernesto" escaped rural El Salvador during the crescendo of the killings in 1979. He was in his early teens when alone he embarked on the long, uncertain, and dangerous journey North. His story gives a human voice to the cold statistics of pain:

> The *situación* in my country is the reason I left. My mother was very worried about my future, she was afraid about my safety. I came here all by myself, because as you know the situation in my country was bad. I did not like politics—any politics. There were many murdered without any reasons . . . I was really afraid. Two of my cousins and two of my friends were killed, murdered in 1979 . . . we couldn't believe it! And many acquaintances . . . just

disappeared. People were killed by both sides, the death squads and the guerrillas. So one cannot be with one group or with the other; the best thing is to be quiet and not be involved in anything.

But then what happened to my friends made me afraid. I said, "Any time, something will happen to me. El Salvador is a place where it is a sin to be young." Life became impossible; I could no longer live like that . . . I would go to school, and the students would be protesting about something, and the next day a few would be dead. . . . I was afraid I was going to be recruited into the army. There they teach you to be a criminal; they teach you to kill, kill, kill. They make you crazy. The death squads are sadists. They kill anyone.

Most of the immigrants had one or more members of their nuclear family still residing in a Central-American nation. In all of these cases, sending a youth out to freedom was done in the context of other siblings and relatives having had to remain behind: for them, as members of the more modest classes in Central America, there simply were not enough resources to enable the entire family to pick up and leave. Young men were seen as being particularly vulnerable to the aggressive "recruiting campaigns" by the local military and guerrilla organizations. Hence, they were often given priority, over younger siblings and girls, for help in escaping.

Among these youngsters, a severe sense of responsibility about the fate of those who had so sacrificed to send them out to safety was evident. A key interpersonal concern among these immigrant youths was that many of their loved ones remained in an eerie scenario of collective terror and scarcity. This fact has created unique interpersonal and intrapsychic concerns in this cohort of immigrant youths. They all continued to be affected one way or another by the uncertain fate of the less fortunate folk at home. Indeed, an intense sense of duty to less fortunate relatives gains center stage in the psychosocial profile of many new arrivals. Guilt about one's survival coupled with emerging perceptions of opportunities in the new land not shared by those left behind, fueled the immigrant's ambition for a better tomorrow for themselves, and, most importantly, for their families.

Among many immigrants, particularly those with close relatives remaining behind in the war-torn region, something akin to "survivor guilt" has appeared (Bettelheim, 1980, pp. 274–314). The syndrome experienced by many of the recent arrivals from war-torn Central America is similar in some aspects to the guilt described by Bettelheim that occurred among survivors of the Nazi death machine. Bettelheim described how many survivors in the death camps shared a feeling that their lives were spared because others had died or suffered. To some degree, the Central-American informants manifested such a condition in thinking about their survival and that of their families in relation to the often inexplicable death and suffering of others.

We argue that the guilt found among the new immigrants arises in the context of a specific interpersonal morality. Any system of morality is rooted in a human awareness that action and thought may have positive or negative consequences for others. Developmentally, human beings become increasingly aware of their own capacity to "hurt" or "help" others by doing or failing to do something (Piaget, 1930).

In a normally adjusted person, an awareness that one's condition may create pain in others makes one prone to feelings of guilt. A proneness to guilt among these new Hispanic immigrants derives from (1) an insight that loved one's sacrificed much for them in securing their well-being, (2) their selection over others, often siblings, to escape to the U.S., and (3) the fact that they now enjoy the relative security and opportunities of the new environment when loved ones continue to face terror and scarcity.

Such awareness creates a ready propensity to intense guilt should they fail or become derelict in their social duties. Should these feelings occur, they can only be assuaged by expiatory reapplication to the task at hand. Feelings of desperation give way to a harsh sense of responsibility that they must now seize upon any opportunity in the affluent society. Working to ease familial hardships is intimately related to this psychosocial syndrome of proneness to guilt over one's selective survival.

"Becoming Somebody"

It is very difficult for anyone, even the most insightful individual, to articulate with ease the feelings and thoughts related to this emotionally laden syndrome. Most youths would only say "I feel bad my brother is still in El Salvador, he may be drafted any day, I am trying to help him get out." Or, "It bothers me that my mother *se mata* [kills herself] cleaning house so I can study," and so forth. As we became more intimate with the new immigrants, we began to sense the recurring nature of this basic concern.

It was their "projective" materials, particularly the immigrants' dreams and responses to the Thematic Apperception Test (TAT)—a "projective" test used by many anthropologists and psychologists—that more fully sensitized us to the psychosocial dynamics of these immigrant youths. The TAT consists of a series of pictures that are presented sequentially to the informants. A number of researchers have used the TAT in the course of their psychological and anthropological work (De Vos, 1983; McClelland, 1984; McClelland, Atkinson, Clark, & Lowell, 1953; Suarez-Orozco, 1989, 1990). Our interest in the TAT is not in its clinical, psychodiagnostic use. For the purposes of this work, we are not concerned with individual idiosyncrasies and psychopathology. Rather, we are concerned with how the TAT reflects shared, patterned thematic clusters when given to a specific population.

The informant is shown the card and is told to make up a story, out of imagination, giving a narrative with a past, a present, and a future based on what he or she sees in the pictures. The informant is simply asked: What are the characters in the pictures doing? Why? How do they feel? What happened before and how does the story end? The TAT rests on the logic that informants, when presented with vague stimuli such as these pictures, will reveal their interpersonal attitudes and ongoing concerns. The narratives they create will to a certain extent reflect their own wishes, fears, dreams, and worries. The test, when given to specific populations, can be used to postulate normative patterns of preoccupation for the group as a whole. Some scholars in psychological anthropology have argued that the TAT may serve as a powerful tool complementing participant observation and ethnographic interviewing to systematically elicit certain key, normative concerns, or the interpersonal "atmospheric condition" of a group (De Vos, 1973). We will add that, when properly used, after our achieving trust and rapport, and having gained some ethnographic depth in which to embed the TAT results, the test may facilitate investigation of shared, affect-laden preoccupations that may not be immediately visible or easily approached through other means of research. The TAT, then, serves as a medium to allow informants to explore certain emotional issues in a manner that is less threatening than, for example, direct questioning.

A variety of emotionally important concerns such as attitudes toward family obligations and suicide in Japan; changing Korean attitudes toward the discharge of traditional family roles, changing attitudes among kibbutzniks on the nature of their venture, macho attitudes among Mexican-American youths, the fatalism of Southern Italians, and rural Irish attitudes toward sexuality, have been elegantly documented with the TAT (for a review of these and other studies using the TAT see Suarez-Orozco, 1989).

In terms of standardizing data analysis with the TAT, De Vos (1973, 1983) and his colleagues (De Vos & Suarez-Orozco, 1990) have advocated setting explicit criteria for coding and analyzing narrative materials within a culturally specific framework that can be checked by others. This system of codification is concerned with establishing reliability of scoring on the basis of the manifest content of a story. Latent psychodynamic processes are not a major concern. Rather than searching in the narratives for hidden "deep structures" or for the "basic or modal personality structure" in a group, the system serves to identify main thematic clusters as they unfold in the sequential order given by the informants. In the broadest terms, this system heuristically divides human behavior into "instrumentally" oriented behavior (means to an end), and "expressive" behavior (an end in and of itself). Within the system there are several categories of concern that order data around universal themes in interpersonal behavior that are found in every culture. Examples of instrumental concerns are achievement-alienation, competence-incompetence, responsibility-irresponsibility, control-subordination, and cooperation-competition. Expressive concerns relate to nurturance-deprivation, harmony-discord, affiliation-isolation, pleasure-suffering, and appreciation-degradation (De Vos & Suarez-Orozco, 1990). Clusters of such thematic concerns are treated numerically, and their occurrence can be compared to that in other groups.

It is essential that any projective data be used only in the context of other data, careful interviewing, and ethnographic observation. The researcher must be intimate enough with the culture and language to embed the projective materials in the context of a larger data framework (for pro and con discussions of the TAT, see Suarez-Orozco, 1990).

The following are examples of the typical narratives told by the new Hispanic immigrants when they were shown card two of the TAT. This card depicts a country scene with a woman with books in her arms in the foreground. A man is working in the fields and an older woman is looking on in the background (Murray, 1943). Here are a few of the stories:

Narrative 1: She is looking at her poor parents working hard in the land so she can study, so she can become somebody. She wants to achieve something so that her parents do not continue to live in poverty, always working so hard. The mother is thinking that one day her daughter will do something for them. And that is why they give her the possibility to study. They work hard so that in the future their daughter may become someone, so she won't have to live through what they had to live. The daughter will get them out of poverty. She will get them out of their misery. She will study hard, she will become a good, educated person. She goes to school to become somebody.

Narrative 2: A father, daughter, and the mother. The mother is pregnant. The man is struggling so that his daughter can get ahead studying. This gives her a desire to continue studying. She dedicates herself to studying. She will win, she will get ahead. That way she shall pay back her parents for their sacrifice. She continues studying hard and is able to get her parents out of poverty.

Narrative 3: She has books. Her parents work the land. She wants to study to become somebody. She wants a career. Her parents are very poor. She wants a career to help her poor parents, so they do not have to suffer so much. She studies hard and becomes somebody. Her parents are so proud of her. With their help she is able to become a professional. Whenever they need help, she is there for them.

Narrative 4: She is the daughter of hard-working peasants. They sent her to school. She worked very hard in school to be able to get her family out of poverty. She became an important, educated, and outstanding person. She helped her family. She placed her family in a better environment.

Narrative 5: Her parents were poor. Peasants have few opportunities to study. But her parents did all they could to send her to study. They bought her books and paid for her schooling. At the end she was well prepared and worked hard to help her parents get out of the hard work they endured all their lives. She betters their way of life.

Typically, the new arrivals from Central America interpreted this card as depicting a family group enduring hardships and economic deprivation. The parental figures were most commonly seen as sacrificing, often to send the young woman to study. The young woman is seen as studying hard to avoid repeating her parents' cycle of hard work and deprivation (compensatory achievement). Through her studies, she eventually achieves high status, she "becomes somebody." Finally, and of importance to understanding the psychosocial profile of the new arrivals, rather than leaving her parents behind, as in the stories commonly told by more independent and individualistic North Americans (De Vos, 1983), the protagonist of our Hispanic immigrant stories commonly returns home to take care of her poor parents and to end their hardship with the fruit of her studies.

Indeed, in a sample of 50 recent arrivals from Central America (20 females and 30 males, ages 14 to 19), 56% of the narratives told to card two of the TAT were about achievement motivation (working hard to "become a somebody") coupled with nurturing concerns (such as returning home to help out the sacrificing parents). The pattern of compensatory achievement is in this case related to ongoing feelings of responsibility based on guilt over parental sacrifice. "Becoming a somebody" is thus a reparative act to end parental hardships.

In their narratives, these Hispanic immigrants demonstrate much greater preoccupations regarding nurturance and achievement motivation than do majority Americans. Indeed, such concern with familial interdependence, affiliation, and nurturance is a shared psychocultural feature characteristic of Hispanics be they of Puerto Rican, Cuban, Central and South American, or Mexican origin.

MOTIVATIONAL DYNAMICS OF HISPANIC IMMIGRANTS

The Hispanic motivational complex stands in sharp contrast to the work of David C. McClelland and his associates, who pioneered the systematic study of motivation with majority (non-Hispanic) Americans (McClelland, 1984). McClelland and his group concentrated their efforts on capturing achievement motivation, defined by them as the need for "competition with a standard of excellence" (McClelland, Atkinson, Clark, & Lowell, 1953, p. 161) as shown in the products of human fantasy. Concretely, they attempted to document achievement themes under various experimental conditions through the use of projective tests, including the Thematic Apperception Test. To summarize their model, achievement motivation, they argue, flourishes within a rather specific interpersonal climate that trains youngsters to become independent from others, family included. Indeed, the narratives told about card two of the TAT by high-achieving, majority (non-Hispanic) Americans included achievement themes in the context of gaining independence from the family. In these stories, the heroine of card two typically goes off to the city to become a somebody, but does not return home to nurture her relatives. In fact, the non-Hispanic American narratives capture an ethos in which achievement themes emerge in the context of attempting to gain independence from the family. This is in sharp contrast to the stories elicited from the new Hispanic immigrants.

McClelland's analysis of achievement motivation would suggest that the most highly motivated of the new Hispanic immigrants should be self-reliant individualists, traveling with "light affective baggage," wishing to leave their parents and other folk behind in their journey through the affluent society. Accordingly, these youngsters should be struggling for independence from their parents, perhaps to gain materialist self-advancement to make up for coming from economically "unsuccessful" families.

McClelland's model may correctly address achievement motivation themes among Americans of the middle-class dominant culture yet the achievement-individualism cluster does not fit well the subtle motivational dynamics encountered among Hispanic immigrants. Indeed, the interpersonal concerns running through the lives of most of these immigrants include a strong wish to achieve *to be able to nurture one's parents, and other unfortunate relatives.*

In fact, the interpersonal dynamics that fostered achievement motivation among the new Hispanic immigrants was almost the binary opposite of McClelland's model of familial dynamics. Among the new arrivals, perceptions of parental sacrifice are a subtle concern to be factored into the motivational patterns of the youngsters. Most immigrant youngsters are keenly aware of the continuities in a cultural chain of mutual nurturance and affiliation; many youngsters reported how their parents had to face hard work at a premature age in Latin America to help their own parents and siblings to make ends meet. Rather than viewing their parents as aloof and distant, the new arrivals portrayed them as warm and caring; after all, they said, their parents sacrificed tremendously to settle them in the safety of the U.S.

The Hispanic case does not fit the majority (non-Hispanic) American paradigm for achievement motivation. The most motivated of these Hispanic immigrants are not individualists searching for self-advancement and independence. As one informant put it, "now it is my turn to get them out of Central America," referring to his parents and younger siblings still in the crossfire. Our research captured other facets of this achievement-nurturance cluster: as we discuss elsewhere—the older, more experienced youth systematically helped the younger or more recent arrivals to find work, tutored them, and otherwise aided them in their first steps in the new land. And the immigrant youths who worked while attending school full time (about 68% in a sample of 50 informants) reported sending remittances back home regularly (Suarez-Orozco, 1989).

We hope that this research with new Hispanic immigrants has pointed to some of the basic cross-cultural limitations of a theoretical model derived from an Anglo-American research bias. Misapplying such models to explain the issues facing "other peoples in other places" has had certain subtle implications. For example, in the case of Hispanic Americans, it has been argued, in a simplistic fashion, that a somehow asphyxiating cultural matrix orienting individuals heavily to the family is responsible for crippling achievement motivation. Heller (1966) has argued that Hispanic families hinder mobility "by stressing . . . [such values as] family ties, honor, masculinity . . . and by neglecting values that are conductive to it, achievement, *independence* and deferred gratification" (p. 35). Such thinking is based on an erroneous juxtaposition of independence training as a sine qua non (requirement) for achievement motivation.

The inescapable image is that Hispanic family traditions of interdependence, cooperation, and mutual nurturance are somehow impeding the growth of achievement motivation. Some have argued that Hispanic children, not sufficiently trained in "independence" patterns, remain somehow caught in a family web of counterproductive values that hinder achievement motivation (Carter & Segura, 1979). Such reasoning typically leads to different variants of an assimilative genre, where cultural diversities are eventually truncated. Richard Rodriguez's (1982) tale as reflected in his autobiography, *Hunger of Memory*, is one such version. Again, achievement in his case was only possible at the expense of turning away from his family and his community. Yet, as we noted, the price of his achievement was a severe sense of loneliness and alienation from his ethnic group.

However, this need not be the only route; the permutations of the human spirit are too varied and complex to be reduced to single encompassing formulae. In the Central-American case, rather than encountering a pattern of rugged individualism and independence, we identified the emergence of a worldview that orients the self to others in the context of resettling in the new land.

But the achievement concerns in these new Hispanic immigrants were not similar to those reported for the majority Americans. Having witnessed a life-long pattern of parental deprivation and sacrifice, many Hispanic immigrant youths wish to maximize their new opportunities in order to pay back their parents. Informants noted how their parents had to work hard their entire lives, and even harder to move them to the U.S., so that they could enjoy peace and a better tomorrow. Perceptions of emerging opportunities were quickly incorporated into an inner desire to take care of their parents and other relatives.

FAMILY RELATIONSHIPS AND SCHOOLING

Frequently, the stresses of the immigration process and immigrants' marginal status in the new society are manifested within the family system and in schools. Vigil (1988) points out that Hispanic parents contending with economic, social, and psychological hardships are often unable to provide their "children with insights into the subtleties of the cultural ambiguities of their lives" (p. 41). The nuclear group, which typically had been supported by the extended family prior to migration, may now become a more isolated unit requiring a shift in structure, hierarchies, boundaries, roles, and rules (Falicov, 1982; Landau, 1982).

Individuals within the migrant family may respond differently; one family member may idealize the host society and devalue the country of origin (as was the case with Richard Rodriguez) using the school system for self-advancement, or even "passing," and another member may devalue the host country and overvalue the country of origin (Falicov, 1982). This split within the family may be characterized as the difference between the "outward-oriented member" (who develops adaptive strategies and a social support network in the new setting) and the "inward-oriented member" (who remains relatively isolated and unacculturated) (Sluzki, 1979).

Dieppa and Montiel (1978) contend that there has been "erosion of the [Hispanic] family as other institutions usurp such functions as child rearing and care, transmission of moral and cultural values, and responsibility for emotional growth and development" (p. 1). They cite such family problems as "drug and alcohol use, child abuse, divorce, juvenile delinquency, school drop-out, malnutrition and other physical and mental health conditions" (p. 1).

Often, the developmentally normal generation gap occuring in all families with adolescents is worsened in immigrant families by a "cultural gap." As Vega (1990) succinctly puts it, ". . . differences in cultural orientation exacerbate normal intergenerational strains to produce unique parenting problems and family vulnerability . . ." (p. 1021). Such family problems are clearly related to school dynamics.

The crisis of cultural adjustment often "creeps into the family through the offspring" (Sluzki, 1979, p. 384) as they tend to acculturate "much more rapidly then their parents do, unleashing a clash of values and styles that strikes at the core of the family" (p. 384). All too often, a pattern emerges whereby Hispanic immigrant parents become "frozen in time," rigidifying some worldview and value orientations (Karrer, 1987). Hispanic immigrant parents may attempt to increase their authority and control at the same point that the children turn more to their peers and to an "American" value orientation. This leaves the family in a situation where "the children are accusing their parents of being 'too Mexican' and the parents fearing that their children have become 'too American'" (Karrer, 1987, pp. 229–230). Hence, a "parent-child cultural dissonance" (Falicov,

1982) may be acted out in children in the form of delinquency, gang membership, and drug abuse (Falicov, 1982).

It may be argued that immigrants, in some respects, have it easier than their children. Immigrants typically set out with a relatively clear set of objectives. They want to do better than they did before, actively using the host society's institutions (including the school system) as avenues for upward mobility. Although they may freely navigate cultural borders between the old and new worlds, immigrants are typically firmly anchored in terms of their identity: they have a sense of security about who they are—outsiders hoping to move up.

The children of immigrants, on the other hand, face some very different issues. Perhaps even more than is the case with other (nonimmigrant) children, the children of immigrants become the repository of their parent's expectations. Yet, unlike their parents, their self-identity may be less securely anchored, particularly in situations of marginality and ethnic conflict (see Vigil, 1988).

The school, perhaps more than any other social institution, is an arena in which many of the problems facing first- and second-generation Hispanics are played out. Educators exposed to Hispanic immigrant children are often surprised to see how vigorously the new arrivals pursue their dream of a better tomorrow through education. These same educators seem puzzled to see how, contrary to commonsense expectations rooted in a simplistic notion of assimilation, too many second- and third-generation children of Hispanic descent grow disaffected with the school system. Educators watch as large numbers of these youths fail to thrive in school environments, turning to gangs or dropping out.

Educators working with Hispanic youths should understand that there are class, gender, and generational factors that shape experience and expectations differently across groups. They should consider the burdens (affective losses, psychological disorientation, cultural discontinuities, and so on) that immigrant children carry. Sensitive educators may emerge as "cultural brokers," bridging some of the generational discontinuities between immigrant children and their parents as well as between immigrants and the dominant culture.

With respect to newly arrived immigrant children, educators are placed in a strategically important position to capitalize on their dynamic of positivism, hope, and desire to succeed. Understanding motivation is at the heart of pedagogy. Yet the assumptions that have, to date, guided pedagogical practice and curriculum strategies are based on an understanding of motivation relevant largely to white, middle-class students from the dominant culture. As we discussed above, the cultural paradigm of individualism that defines and patterns motivation among members of the dominant culture does not apply to Hispanic students. Hispanic students, we have argued, typically achieve in the context of family and peer obligation, not in the context of individualistic self-advancement.

CONCLUSION

It is important for educators to understand that there are important differences within Hispanic groups. As we have noted, there are distinct intergenerational vicisitudes facing first- and second-generation individuals.

It is clear that the Hispanic immigrant experience is a rich and diverse tapestry. Gender, country-of-origin, socioeconomic status, documentation, level of acculturation, generational differences, and psychological resources must all be taken into account when considering Hispanic immigrant responses to change. Only when such issues are considered can we begin to understand, and be of service to, the various Hispanic groups in the U.S.

ACKNOWLEDGMENTS

We dedicate this essay to Henry T. Trueba: Para Don Henry, muy afectuosamente. We thank Pat Phelan for her many helpful editorial suggestions.

REFERENCES

Bernal, G. (1982). Cuban families. In M. McGoldrick & J. Giordano (Eds.), *Ethnicity & family therapy* (pp. 187–207). New York: Guilford Press.

Bettelheim, B. (1980). *Surviving and other essays*. New York: Vintage Books.

Brown, C. (Ed.). (1985). *With friends like these: The Americas watch report on human rights & U.S. policy in Latin America*. New York: Pantheon.

Buckley, T. (1984). *Violent neighbors: El Salvador, Central America and the United States*. New York: Times Books.

Carter, T. P., & Segura, R. D. (1979). *Mexican Americans in school: A decade of change*. New York: College Entrance Examination.

Dayley, J. (1991). One big happy family. *San Diego Reader, 20*(17), 5–8.

De Vos, G. A. (1973). *Socialization for achievement: Essays on the cultural psychology of the Japanese*. Berkeley: University of California Press.

De Vos, G. A. (1980). Ethnic adaptation and minority status. *Journal of Cross-Cultural Psychology, 11*(1), 101–125.

De Vos, G. A. (1983). Achievement motivation and intra-family attitudes in immigrant Koreans. *Journal of Psychoanalytic Anthropology, 6*(1), 25–71.

De Vos, G. A., & Suarez-Orozco, M. M. (1990). *Status inequality: The self in culture.* Newbury Park, CA: Sage.

Dieppa, I., & Montiel, M. (1978). Hispanic families: An exploration. In M. Montiel (Ed.), *Hispanic families: Critical issues for policy programs in human services* (pp. 1–8). Washington, DC: National Coalition of Hispanic Mental Health and Human Service Organizations.

Erickson, E. (1963). *Childhood and society.* New York: W. W. Norton.

Falicov, C. J. (1982). Mexican families. In J. K. Pearce & J. Giordano (Eds.), *Ethnicity and family therapy* (pp. 134–163). New York: Guilford Press.

Grinberg, L., & Grinberg, R. (1989). *Psychoanalytic Perspectives on Migration and Exile.* New Haven, CT: Yale University Press.

Heller, C. (1966). *Mexican-American youth: The forgotten youth at the crossroads.* New York: Random House.

Horowitz, R. (1983). *Honor and the American dream: Culture and identity in a Chicano community.* New Brunswick, NJ: Rutgers University Press.

Karrer, B. (1987). Families of Mexican descent: A contextual approach. In R. B. Birrer (Ed.), *Urban family medicine* (pp. 228–232). New York: Springer-Verlag.

LaFeber, W. (1984). *Inevitable revolutions: The United States in Central America.* New York: W. W. Norton.

Landau, J. (1982). Therapy with families in cultural transition. In M. McGoldrick, J. K. Pearce, & J. Giordano (Eds.), *Ethnicity and family therapy* (pp. 552–572). New York: Guilford Press.

McClelland, D. C. (1984). *Motives, personality and society: Selected papers.* New York: Praeger.

McClelland, D. C., Atkinson, J., Clark, R., & Lowell, E. (1953). *The achievement motive.* New York: Appleton-Century-Crofts.

Murray, H. A. (1943). *Thematic apperception test manual.* Cambridge, MA: Harvard University Press.

Ogbu, J. U. (1978). *Minority education and caste: The American system in cross-cultural perspective.* Orlando, FL: Academic Press.

Piaget, J. (1930). *The child's conception of physical causality.* London: Paul, Trench, Trubner.

Ready, T. (1991). *Latino immigrant youth: Passages from adolescence to adulthood.* New York: Garland.

Rodriguez, R. (1982). *Hunger of memory, the education of Richard Rodriguez: An autobiography.* Boston: Godine.

Rogler, L., Cortes, D., & Malgady, R. G. (1991). Acculturation and mental health status among Hispanics. *American Psychologist, 46*(6), 585–597.

Rogler, L., Malgady, R. G., & Rodriguez, O. (1989). *Hispanics and mental health: A framework for research.* Malabar, FL: Krieger.

Sluzki, C. E. (1979). Migration and family conflict. *Family Process, 18*(4), 379–390.

Stonequist, E. V. (1937). *The marginal man.* New York: Scribner & Sons.

Suarez-Orozco, M. M. (1989). *Central American refugees and U.S. high schools: A psychosocial study of motivation and achievement.* Stanford, CA: Stanford University Press.

Suarez-Orozco, M. M. (1990). Speaking of the unspeakable: Toward a psychosocial understanding of responses to terror. *Ethos, 18*(3), 353–383.

Vega, W. A. (1990). Hispanic families in the 1980's: A decade of research. *Journal of Marriage and the Family, 52*(11), 1015–1024.

Vigil, J. D. (1988). *Barrio gangs: Street life and identity in Southern California.* Austin: University of Texas Press.

Villareal, J. A. (1959). *Pocho.* New York: Anchor Books.

Vlach, N. S. J. (1984). *America y el Alma: A study of families and adolescents who are recent immigrants from Guatemala.* Unpublished doctoral dissertation, Department of Medical Anthropology, University of California, San Francisco.

CHAPTER 5

RESEARCH AND POLICY
IN RECONCEPTUALIZING
FAMILY-SCHOOL RELATIONSHIPS

Concha Delgado-Gaitan

The failure of schools to adequately and equitably reach all children—particularly those from poor and ethnically different families—is increasingly visible to large numbers of people within the society. Questions and debate about what should be done and how it should be done abound, as people in a variety of institutions search for answers and solutions to the complex problems that exist in America's schools. Central among the issues currently discussed are considerations about the appropriate role of parents in their children's education. Although many researchers, policy makers, and educators believe that parent involvement is desirable, there is tremendous variation in the types of programs and strategies that are believed best suited to accomplish optimal parent-school collaboration. Further, the underlying assumptions that prompt educators and others to involve parents in the education of their children affect tremendously the types and quality of programs developed.

In this chapter, I argue that researchers, policy makers, and educators concerned with promoting parental involvement in schools need to examine the ideological premises and underpinnings that guide their endeavors. It is my contention that strategies for parent involvement have historically been based on deficit conceptions of cultures and families and have thus been aimed at remedying perceived family deficiencies. As a result, the opportunity to build upon familial and cultural strengths has, for the most part, gone untapped. My own research in Latino communities in California supports the work of other researchers and educators who challenge the premises upon which deficit conceptions of families are based. The following propositions provide a basis for considering alternative approaches to parent involvement:

1. The knowledge required to participate in schools is socioculturally bound and transmitted in socially constructed settings. Thus, organized efforts are necessary in order to provide parents with explicit knowlege about schools and how the educational system operates, for example, parent education workshops, classes, and parent-school meetings. If this information is not made available to all parents, parent participation is limited to those who have the means to gain access.
2. Parent involvement is a long-term process that occurs over the life span of children; thus, home and school connectedness needs to be understood in the historical, socioeconomic, and sociocultural contexts of communities.
3. When parental involvement efforts focus on the strength of families and promote strategies that enable parents to participate as decision makers, benefits extend beyond improved academic achievement of students to improved parent-community support of the school as well as improved social conditions of families. The latter benefits derive from the organized social networks that develop when families are empowered to work together as decision makers in their children's lives.

These new conceptions challenge existing assumptions and provide an opportunity to build parent involvement strategies and interventions that more fully utilize the strengths and energies of people concerned with the education of their children. In short, parents' involvement in schools needs to be considered in a context that allows us to understand not only why schools need parents to participate, but also how families interpret and play out their relationship to schools. This chapter is organized to address these issues in the following four sections: (1) Why Parental Involvement? (2) Bringing Education to Families: A Historical Overview, (3) Current Conceptions of Parental Involvement: Traditional and Alternative Approaches, and (4) Implications for Reconceptualizing Family-School Linkages.

WHY PARENTAL INVOLVEMENT?

Almost all parents are concerned about their children's education and want to be involved in helping them succeed (Dauber & Epstein, 1989; Phelan, Cao, & Davidson, 1992). For the most part, however, parents do not participate at school sites and few are involved as decision makers in matters pertaining to the education of their children (Dauber & Epstein, 1989; Dornbusch & Ritter, 1988; Leitch & Tangri, 1988). Particularly striking is the conspicuous absence of poor and culturally different parents in schools. Variance in parental participation has been explained in terms of parents' lack of cultural knowledge and political power, language differences between home and school, and the historical experiences of underrepresented groups in a given community (Comer, 1980; Delgado-Gaitan & Trueba, 1991; Laosa, 1983). This research points to the need for equity and access to resources for parents at all levels, including day-to-day interactions with teachers and other school personnel, participation in school events, school-level decision making and district-level committees.

Related to issues of access and equity is that fact that almost all parents report that they not only want specific information regarding their children's academic progress and an understanding of what they are learning, but that they also want to know how they can help their children succeed. In fact, in instances where teachers take a proactive role in involving parents, parent attitudes are significantly more positive than in cases where parents are disregarded (Epstein, 1985, 1986). Interestingly, teacher's perceptions of parents—particularly those from low-income and ethnically different families—are that they are uninterested in participating in their children's education (Davies, 1989). These differences in teacher and parent perceptions not only create barriers to home-school collaborations but also provide an excuse for educators unwilling to expend energy on building relationships between home and school. Most importantly, research on parent attitudes and orientations underscores the fact that, given the opportunity, parents very much want to participate as partners in their children's education.

Equally important is the fact that learning environments in the home matter significantly in children's academic success and sociocultural adjustment (Bronfenbrenner, 1978, 1979; Cochran & Dean, 1991; Comer & Haynes, 1991; Delgado-Gaitan, 1990; Dauber & Epstein, 1989; Karraker, 1972; Lareau, 1987, Leichter, 1979; Leler, 1983). In fact, family practices have been shown to be more important than parent education, race, marital status, or family size in affecting children's academic success. Further, there is increasing evidence that parents' involvement with their children in their educational endeavors may well have important implications for students' academic achievement, attitudes towards school, and ability to adjust. For example, a study of 552 4th-grade Latino students in six of California's largest elementary school districts found that parent involvement makes a difference in Latino students' reading achievement for both high and low achievers. Further, by assisting their children in academic matters, parents became more informed about academic progress (Garcia, 1991). Other studies report similar positive results. For example, the Family Matters Program in Syracuse, New York (which was initiated by Cornell University faculty and local school districts and communities) notes significant academic gains for Latino and Black children whose parents become systematically involved in their schooling. In this study, children's academic performance in the 1st grade was higher than that of children from similar backgrounds in a comparison group (Cochran & Dean, 1991).

Although evidence is accumulating on the relationship between parent involvement and student academic achievement, a great deal of work remains to be done. To date, many studies fail to make direct connections and others are confounded by intervening variables. For example, a student's grades may fluctuate, regardless of parental involvement, due to the difficulty of courses being taken, the pedagogical practices of a particular teacher, or relationships with peers. Even more difficult to document is the relationship between parent attitudes resulting from their involvement in school (i.e., increased emotional support of their children's efforts), and students' overall decisions about their education (i.e., to remain in school instead of dropping out). However, regardless of the difficulties, there is increasing evidence of a positive relationship between parent involvement and students' school-related behaviors, including academic performance, attitudes, and motivation.

Overall, research on parent involvement in education continues to point out the many positive results that accrue when parents participate as active partners in efforts to involve their children in schools and learning. Why parent involvement? Because we know that parent involvement can result in improved linkages between home, school, and community; improved family functioning and communications; more effective schools; and more positive community settings—all desirable outcomes.

BRINGING EDUCATION TO FAMILIES: A HISTORICAL OVERVIEW

The conditions that encourage or constrain the participation of parents in schools reflect historic shifts in the economic, political, and social purposes of public schooling in the U.S. (Spring, 1991). Beginning with the initial proposal made by Horace Mann for public schools in 1837, the common school (later known as the "public school") had as its mission the socialization of children to a common value system (Cremin, 1964). Mann's idea for preventing the tensions that can grow out of religious, political, and social class differences was to socialize children for the political system in which they lived (Cremin, 1964; Spring, 1991). Mann's hope was that a common education would create political consensus and make it possible for a republican society to function. This intent, to school all social classes and ethnic groups in a common philosophy, has prevailed over the century and a half of public education and continues to have a significant impact on the praxis of parent involvement in the schools.

Beginning in the 1880s and continuing into the early 1920s, waves of immigrants from Southern and Eastern Europe to growing East Coast cities raised fears about social disorder and the potential undermining of dominant white, Anglo-Saxon Protestant (WASP) values. Although a small group of intellectuals argued for cultural pluralism, the dominant emphasis was on assimilation. In its most extreme form, immigrants were to be stripped completely of their ethnic character and inculcated with the dominant Anglo-Saxon morality (Cremin, 1964). Around the same time, G. Stanley Hall, pointing out that early public education placed too much emphasis on the content of what children were taught, began to argue successfully for centering education around the natural developmental patterns of the child. Up to this point, educators had assumed that students must adapt themselves to the demands of the school; Hall convinced many that schools should adapt themselves to childrens' backgrounds and perceived needs.

With "Americanization" a burning national issue and a new belief in the importance of ministering to children's needs, immigrants became the focus of social, physical, and moral interventions. Operating primarily out of the belief that immigrant youth and their parents lacked not only academic but moral training, lessons on manners, cleanliness, and dress as well as the English language became a part of many classrooms (Cremin, 1964). For example, in Calvinist churches, where child care for toddlers and older children was offered, obedience to authority, cleanliness, and order were emphasized (Fein, 1980; Florin & Dokecki, 1983). In many cities, immigrant adults were taught the laws, language, and customs of the U.S. These early conceptions of underrepresented and immigrant groups as untamed territory to be tamed and reshaped by teachers and schooling are still held by many in America today.

The civil rights movement and the liberal politics of the 1960s brought a new awareness of unequal opportunities for poor and immigrant youth. As a result, compensatory education for the poor became a prominent national goal, buttressed by the belief that impoverished family environments could be, at least in part, compensated for by early educational enrichment programs for children (Dokecki, Hargrove, & Sandler, 1983). This new consciousness spurred the development of government programs aimed at providing poor and ethnically different children with equal opportunities for education (Florin & Dokecki, 1983). Head Start and other compensatory education programs—many of which contained parent involvement components—focused efforts on training parents in child-rearing practices congruent with those of mainstream Anglo families. Power and authority to instruct parents about improving home learning environments were placed in the hands of the school, with the hope that poor and ethnically different children would enter school academically on a par with their mainstream counterparts.

The orientation to change parental socialization practices was rooted both in assimilation ideals and cultural deficit theory. Further, the assumption of social and cultural inferiority was tied closely to the economic conditions of families. For example, in the early 1960s, Bernstein (1961) concluded that middle-class families are superior to poor and ethnic families because they verbalize more with their children—a practice believed to assist children in developing superior abstract-reasoning skills. Further, the frequent absence of fathers was viewed as negatively impacting children's psychosocial development. Other studies also compared families and reached the conclusion that poor families were inferior because they did not provide their children with the language skills and values prevalent in middle-class European-American mainstream families (Dunn, 1987; Hess & Shipman, 1965; Holtzman, Diaz-Guerrero, & Swartz, 1975). As comparisons were made, theories based on cultural-deficit models became prevalent (Bee, Van Egeren, Streissguth, Nyman, & Leckie, 1969; Hess & Shipman, 1965) and bolstered the belief that parents with low incomes were indeed in need of training for child rearing.

CURRENT CONCEPTIONS OF PARENT INVOLVEMENT: TRADITIONAL AND ALTERNATIVE APPROACHES

Since the 1960s, varieties of parent involvement programs have been developed to solve myriad problems in the schools. Many current efforts continue to be oriented toward changing families to conform to schools' expectations (Delgado-Gaitan, 1991). Programs for parents of poor children, of low-achieving children, of children with special medical or psychological difficulties, and of handicapped children are often based on the premise that parents are inadequately equipped for child rearing and must be trained to assist their children in meeting school goals. This deficit perspective requires that communities and families demonstrate inadequacy and incompetence in order to become eligible for programs and support.

California State Policy: A Case In Point

One of the most visible examples of a well-intentioned policy that falls short of redefining a deficit view of families is California's Assembly Bill 322, signed by the Governor in September 1990. This and other state policies for parental involvement exemplify how difficult it is to execute programs that support family-school relationships and parent roles that move beyond a cultural-deficit perspective. For example, in chapter 16 of Bill 322, the legislature recommends the following to schools:

1. Inform parents that they can directly affect the success of their children's learning by providing parents with techniques and strategies that they may utilize to improve their children's academic success and assist their children with learning at home.
2. Build consistent and effective communication between the home and the school so that parents may know when and how to assist their children in support of classroom learning activities.
3. Train teachers and administrators to communicate effectively with parents.
4. Provide regular and periodic programs throughout the school year that provide for training, instruction, and information on all of the following:

   —Parental ability to affect the success of their children's learning.
   —Parental ability to develop consistent and effective communications between themselves and the school, especially over matters concerning the progress of their children in school.
   —Home activities, strategies, and material that can be used to assist and enhance the learning of children.
   —Parenting skills that assist parents in understanding the developmental needs of their children and in understanding how to provide positive discipline and develop healthy relationships with their children. (Paraphrased from Bill 322)

In Bill 322, the school is recognized as the sole authority for determining how families are to be trained to support the school's educational agenda. Further, interpretation and implementation of this legislation is left to local school districts, where it is not unusual for programs to be developed that are considerably removed from intended state policy. Finally, in California, support from the State Department of Education is lacking, making school districts less motivated to ensure parent participation. In general, the orientation of many districts and schools is to act on what is expedient and manageable in order to be within compliance of the law.

It is my contention that California Assembly Bill 322, as well as other programs aimed at changing family values and modifying behaviors, undermine the strengths of families and communities and place the school as the sole authority in child development. Further, such programs perpetuate a deficit and biased view of particular cultural and socioeconomic groups. The point is not that schools should not work with parents to help their children, but that changes in family systems must begin with family members acknowledging their situation and deciding how they want to change. To impose values and beliefs on families and communities without their participation is to relegate them to an inferior position and to ignore their strengths.

An Alternative Approach: Empowering Parents to Make Decisions in Schools

An alternative way to conceptualize parental involvement focuses on empowering parents to participate as decision makers in schools. Premises underlying empowerment theory as discussed in the literature on educational change and family socialization recognize that the family does not exist in isolation (Barr & Cochran, 1991; Bronfenbrenner, 1979; Cochran & Woolever, 1983; Delgado-Gaitan, 1990; Freire, 1973). Rather, the family is part of a structural system, which includes both an informal social network (extended family, friends) and more formal systems, such as work places, schools, social service agencies, and governing bodies. Further, cultural values, beliefs, and expectations provide the blueprints for actions and interactions among family members, as well as within broader community networks and societal institutions. Whether a family has parents, grandparents, aunts, uncles, and cousins together, for example, affects child-rearing practices and parental self-concepts. Other factors such as employment status, mobility, economic circumstances, child-care availability, and so forth also impact the quality of parental relations with children. Each one of these forces influences family dynamics, both separately and by way of interaction. Indeed, it may be obsolete to want to change the family as an isolated agency, just as it may be futile to expect the schools to change without the participation of families.

Numerous other principles underlie empowerment theory, which stresses the importance of family and community strengths as a starting point in considering educational intervention affecting the home. Central to its tenets is rejection of the deficit model and promotion of the notion that child socialization must rest in the hands of family members closest to children. The belief is that a particular group's worldview—

derived from cultural folkways, traditions, history, and language—cross-cuts generations and contains knowledge about children that should, in fact, supersede that of institutional experts, school personnel, and academicians. Although it may appear naive to attribute such expertise to the collective consciousness of a particular group, we know that worldview and cultural knowledge frequently remain intact even in communities where urban isolation has also meant alienation between family members and families.

Still another principle of educational empowerment is that diverse family forms are valid and need to be promoted. To expect conformity to a monolithic model of the European-American family flies in the face of the reality in every city in the U.S. Research by Hoffman (1974) and Kriesberg (1970) shows that successful child rearing is not dependent on static characteristics such as marital status, place of employment, race, or ethnicity. More important is the ability of parents to marshal the material resources necessary to operate as effective care givers (Cochran & Woolever, 1983). Empowerment theory advances the proposition that it is the people who need resources who must make the decisions about what it is they need. Similar is Freire's (1973) view that those who need to learn how to read can best determine for what reason they most need literacy.

COPLA: An Avenue for Sharing Power

An alternative perspective on ways to cultivate parent involvement is exemplified by an organization of Latino parents in Carpenteria, California. COPLA (Comite de Padres Latinos/Committee for Latino Parents) has existed for three years and began when parents organized to support one another in interactions with the school district. COPLA is an example of the manner in which families who join forces can accomplish a variety of goals and, in the process, become empowered in relation to school. Parents involved in COPLA have essentially transformed the status of Spanish-speaking Latino families from isolation to activism and empowerment.

Carpinteria, a small residential community of 12,000, lies 15 miles south of Santa Barbara. Persons of Mexican descent constitute about 35% of the population; almost 50% are limited English speaking. The Mexican-descent families in Carpinteria emigrated from both urban and rural areas of Mexico and most have lived in the town more than 10 years. Many have children who were born in the community. The average size of the Mexican working-class family is six, including parents and children.

Agriculture, fishing, an aluminum factory, small private businesses, and the public school district comprise the primary places of employment, although some people work out of town in Santa Barbara or Ventura. Census data reveal that Carpinteria's Mexican population is overrepresented in the fields of farming, fishing, and the resort industry (restaurant and hotel employment) when compared to their Anglo counterparts. In contrast, 30% of employed Anglos are managers or professionals, whereas less than 5% of the Mexican group occupy comparable positions. Approximately 48% of Carpinteria's bilingual and Spanish-only residents are employed in service jobs or as laborers. They are largely the immigrant Mexican group. Despite the seasonal nature of employment, Mexican families believe they can readily find work.

Soaring rents in the area have created a devastating financial burden for Mexicans as well as other renters in the Carpinteria community. In 1987, the average yearly family income was less than $13,000 (despite the fact that often two or more adults in the home worked full-time). The high rents have forced many extended families to live together in small one- or two-bedroom apartments. A few live in small homes or on their own ranches on the outskirts of town; others have bought small mobile homes as an alternative to paying exorbitant rents.

Four elementary schools, one junior high school, and one high school comprise the Carpinteria School District, which serves just over 2,000 students. Approximately 35% of the district's students are Hispanic and of that, 40% are limited English-proficient. In contrast, the central school district administration is primarily Anglo, with the exception of one Mexican-American male who coordinates the Migrant Program and one Mexican-American principal. Each school deals with specific requirements from the following state and federal programs: Chapter I, Economic Impact Aid (EIA), State preschool, School Improvement Program, Special Education, and Migrant Education.

Historically, Latino parents in Carpinteria have had little direct involvement with their schools. In the last 3 years, things have changed. Parents have organized themselves around issues that they believe are relevant to helping their children succeed academically. COPLA, the organization they have formed, was initiated when one parent became convinced that it was important to involve more Spanish-speaking parents in school activities. Further, he was very much aware that many parents are extremely knowledgeable about effective ways to help their children academically. Approaching the Migrant Program Director for a list of parents, his intent was to form a group of Spanish-speaking parents who could help each other by exchanging ideas. The first meeting brought together parents who had been active in a number of community settings. Almost immediately they realized that they could benefit from training that would help them communicate with the school as well as strategies to help their children with schoolwork at home. This collective realization—to understand the school system as well as their rights and responsibilities as parents—was the basis upon which COPLA was founded.

Within a short time, four strong advocates in the school district reached out to assist this group of parents—two teachers, a special project director, and the migrant education coordinator (Cummins, 1986; Delgado-Gaitan, 1990). In addition to organizing conferences and workshops, parents shared experiences that they had found successful in improving educational conditions for their children. Further, by working closely with school and district personnel, COPLA members succeeded in negotiating a number of agreed-upon goals aimed at building home-school relationships:

1. School people will work to reach the community in the language of the home.
2. The district will support teachers, through release time, to interact closely with parents as part of the daily curriculum.
3. Parents will be taught specifically about school operations.
4. Parents will maximize home learning environments to help children achieve.
5. Parents will be involved in decisions about their children's education.
6. Parents will train other parents about community and school leadership.
7. School site teams of Spanish-speaking parents, teachers, and administrators will be organized to negotiate common concerns about Latino students.
8. Cooperative dialogue between educators and parents will be developed in an effort to maintain the open conversation necessary to resolve issues as they emerge.

COPLA's accomplishments represent important feats for Carpinteria's Latino families and schools and the achievements of this organization have been praised by all sectors in the community. The following comment by an Anglo community member exemplifies the types of attitudes that have been fostered:

> I think that [Latino] parents feel good about helping their children, they'll help participate in the schools, and when they do

that, they'll participate in the community business and that way they're participating in the development of the community.

The message here is that the entire community benefits when the chain of isolation is broken.

School personnel have also noted positive benefits at both the classroom and school levels as a result of improved communication between families and schools. A statement by "Linda Evans," principal of "Hacienda Elementary School," conveys this point:

> In *Gates to Excellence* it states that there is rage and frustration when you are starving for words. Many times I was starving for words and rather than trying to do anything about it I avoided it. I ignored it and just went on my way and did not really attempt to deal with Latino parents. I was actually afraid that I could not meet their needs since they spoke a different language. Now I'm talking about the fact that Latino parents are almost 50% of the parents. As time went on and the parents approached me and we began to work together, I realized that they didn't want anything different than any other parent—for example, [they wanted] to know about discipline polices in our school and how they could help their children in their homes. I could no longer ignore it. We have now decided that everything should be in two languages so that we value both languages, both cultures, both ethnicities, and that's a very important thing.

Major changes have been made at Hacienda school during the last few years as a result of Mrs. Evans' administration and the dedication of teachers to making their school exemplary in its programs and services for all children.

Perhaps most important, Latino parents note improvements in their children's education as a result of the open communication between Latino families and educators. In his speech to a group of Latino parents at a high school meeting, "Mr. Luis Alcaraz," president of the COPLA organization, represented the views, beliefs, and intentions of the Latino parents active in the organization:

> We are a group of parents in the district that has organized to support ourselves and other parents to help our children through cooperation with teachers and administrators. . . . None of us have any formal education in this country but our life experience is the basis of our unity. It is that experience that we communicate to our children. . . . What we give our children is much more than

information—it is values like responsibility. [For example] we always know where our children are at night and [that] if they are not home early, they cannot be rested to work at school. It is possible to teach them the importance of studying and insist on strict hours for them to be home and prepare for school. . . . As a parent committee we exist to meet and stay in communication with each other and with teachers who also know what our children need at school and can work with us in guiding our children to stay in school. . . . One simple way that we can help our children is to get them to school. Latino students have the highest . . . absenteeism and when the school communicates with the home, oftentimes the student is the person who answers the phone because the parents work. The parents never receive the message. So we need to find a way that the school and the parents can communicate with each other about this and many other questions. I know that what Jaime Escalante says he did in Garfield School in Los Angeles to communicate with the parents was to send letters home to the parents in envelopes with "Sears" as the sending address. It worked. Only then did parents open the mail, and the school and the parents began to talk about things, which before had been . . . [impossible] due to bureaucratic ignorance on the part of the school of how to reach the parents. (Translated from Spanish)

Parents in COPLA have become empowered by modeling how to learn from one another, by respecting each other as leaders who can act on behalf of their children, and by initiating meaningful dialogue between school and district personnel. This process is exemplified by the types of interactions that occur at COPLA meetings. For example, a recent gathering of parents and educators (ten Latino parents, two teachers, the high school principal, and the district's Director for Special Projects) was organized by parents to discuss their adolescent sons' and daughters' lack of interest in school. Like other parents of teenagers, these parents were aware that junior and senior high school students face a variety of difficult challenges. Typically, however, Latino parents feel inadequate in dealing with their young adults whose academic subjects are often too advanced for their parents and whose peer group pressures demand behavior that families often cannot understand or condone. These parents are all too aware that social and academic problems frequently increase during adolescent years. The COPLA meeting began with Latino parents discussing what to do about their sons and daughters, whom they perceived as without interest in school. The meeting also provided an opportunity for parents to share their fears, for instance, that their children would become involved in gang activity or would drop out of school. As people talked, ideas emerged about how parents could support each other as well as their children. Suggestions were also made about how school personnel might be able to help.

> *Female parent:* I don't want my son to get involved with negative elements, yet I feel like nothing I do makes any difference. Maybe some of you [other parents] here have sons and daughters who do well and maybe you can help some of us who are having this type of problem.
>
> *Male parent:* My daughter is in high school and her mother and I have always helped her to get a good education. This year we see that she has changed a lot. She doesn't like school and complains about the teachers because they don't help her understand her work. We've had to come to meet with teachers to see what we can do and we have had to agree with my daughter after talking with them because some of those teachers don't think it's their job to help the student understand. So then we had to go to Mr. Baca, the Migrant Education director, to see what else he could do to help our daughter with her classes. He did help us quite a bit. He helped her get a tutor and we think our daughter may be feeling more confident.
>
> *Female parent:* Yes, I understand. But there is a problem here if our children are turned off to school and the teachers don't care.

As the meeting progressed, the teachers and principal became involved in the discussion. For example, one of the teachers talked about feeling overwhelmed by trying to meet the needs of so many students with special needs. Although the parents were empathetic, they felt that there was more that could be done by the teachers and the school. Requests for additional assistance to help Latino students deal with academic demands were directed to the high school principal. The dialogue that ensued not only informed parents of constraints but also set the stage for the initiation of new strategies within the high school for addressing adolescents' needs. For example, the principal reflected on the possibility of reallocating counselors' time so that they would be able to provide additional academic support to Latino students. He also informed parents about available peer and bilingual tutoring services. Parents listened and commented "Well it seems that if these services are available, students should be directed to them before they get so discouraged that it affects their academic standing." Another parent added, "Why should I as a parent have to come out to ask what to do about my daughter's difficult course work if these services are available? Why aren't the students told about these services and why don't teachers know about these services . . . [where] students can go to receive some support?"

The teachers and the principal addressed these questions, explaining that students are told about available services at orientation. However, because of parent input they also acknowledged that these messages should probably be reinforced throughout the year by teachers. The idea of organizing a group of students to inform their peers about available services was also suggested.

Other information was also new to parents. For example, the principal explained that the Chicano Student Organization (MECHA), originally organized to support unity of Mexican-American students through social and academic activities, currently lacked leadership. In this case parents had suggestions. For example, one person commented that the administration could specifically support a bilingual teacher to help the students organize and to advocate for the services they needed. The COPLA parents also offered their assistance. For example, one parent suggested that they revive MECHA with a family dinner night. As the meeting progressed the need for extra resources—not only for students but also for teachers—was isolated as a problem. Although the suggestion to sponsor a MECHA meeting did not mean a quick solution to students' academic problems, it opened dialogue about the ways in which students could learn more about accessing the system.

As parents listened to each other, the teachers, and the principal they came to realize that they were not alone in their concerns for their adolescent youth. Their despair at not knowing how to motivate their children and their general frustration at their teenagers were transformed into a more differentiated view of the situation and a more constructive attempt to solve the problems they faced. Further, they realized that responsibility for motivating youth lay not only with themselves but also with the school. As the discussion unfolded, both teachers' and parents' perceptions changed—the parents began to understand more fully the extent of teachers' workloads and pressures and the teachers and principal gained a new appreciation of the contributions and responsiveness of parents. Even more important, ideas for assisting Latino youth were generated in an atmosphere where everyone's ideas were valued.

Overall, the 6-year Carpinteria parent empowerment study has shown gains in the following areas of praxis:

1. Social isolation has been reduced for Latino parents as they share information about resources and knowledge about the school culture.
2. Parents have felt validated for their expertise in raising children.

3. Latino parents have worked collectively and systematically with school personnel to resolve children's educational concerns.
4. Latino parents have significantly improved their communication with school personnel.
5. Programs and services for Latino children have improved as a result of parent advocacy.
6. Latino children have shown academic gains as a result of parental advocacy in both the school and the home.

Over and above these results, families in COPLA, despite language and cultural barriers, have assumed responsibility for breaking their cycle of isolation. This in itself represents a form of empowerment. Further, that school personnel have listened with care to the Latino community and have made significant changes to benefit Latino children from kindergarten through high school indicates a major restructuring in expectations about Latino children. Indeed, changes have been important not only for families, but also for the schools and the wider community of which they are a part. Contrary to the ways in which many schools impose remedies on family systems, this community of parents reached out to the school district to establish a dialogue for the purpose of enhancing the possibility for their children's academic success.

The parent-involvement model in Carpenteria also has important policy implications. First, it supports a growing body of research that documents the fact that ethnically and linguistically different parents and those who are poor are very much concerned about their children's learning. This type of information must be used to advocate for interventions that actively involve parents in decisions that affect their lives and the lives of their children. Second, efforts in Carpenteria clearly indicate that policies, programs, and interventions designed to positively impact children and youth are most effective when parents, as well as school people, have a voice in the decisions that are made.

IMPLICATIONS FOR RECONCEPTUALIZING FAMILY-SCHOOL LINKAGES

Library shelves are packed with how-to books on how to improve home-school relationships in general and how to accomplish the goal of parent involvement in particular. Geared toward an audience "in the trenches," struggling to make sense of and improve home-school partnerships, these directives provide step-by-step instructions detailing strategies to link families with schools. An explication of the underlying purposes and premises on which programs and interventions are based is frequently missing, however. Although there is no single answer or approach to cultivating the conditions that lead to parental involvement, the question as to whether proposed solutions will actually create change must be asked. Unfortunately, many current initiatives are designed to perpetuate the very system that created the problems in the first place. However, there are also examples of policies that have the possibility of creating meaningful change.

For example, California Senate Bill 997 represents a current effort on the part of the legislature to make structural changes in the coordination of children's services (Chang, Gardner, Watahara, Brown, & Robles, 1991). The intent of the bill is that a service plan, comprehensible to families and children, will be developed. This bill mandates counties to involve various agencies in planning services for children. The interagency councils include a presiding juvenile court judge, the county superintendent, at least one superintendent of a unified district within the county, county staff persons who manage alcohol and drug programs, children's services, housing and redevelopment, mental health services, public health services and welfare programs, a city or county prosecuting attorney, a nonprofit representative, a member of the board of supervisors, a law enforcement representative, and a local child abuse council representative. Senate Bill 997, which has received little attention to date, is a bureaucratic response to the need for family support. Its innovation lies in the fact that it specifically calls for interagency collaboration in efforts to serve children and families. Although the significance of this legislative policy has not yet been tested, theoretically, collaboration resulting from Bill 997 will serve to help coordinate services for children and families. Further, it is possible that improvement in coordination will also create positive changes in agency procedures and operations.

Another, less formal example of collaboration is exemplified by the efforts of "Mrs. Martinez," an elementary school principal in "Montevideo" California. The majority of Martinez's students are low-income Latino and Southeast-Asian refugees. In an attempt to coalesce local, state, and federal policies, Mrs. Martinez and her staff are working toward the accomplishment of a number of explicit goals: to implement national ideals of multicultural education, to carry out California state recommendations to promote home-school relationships, and to respond to local school policies that expect teachers to perform their jobs in the most effective way.

Mrs. Martinez speaks proudly of the work she and her staff have done to make the school more relevant to the student populations they serve:

Yes, our teachers have made outstanding gains with the children because we have become social workers and parents before beginning to teach. They check to see where the children are. Did they have breakfast? Did they get enough sleep? Do they even have a home? I have five foster children myself who attend my school, and I drive to and from "Langston" because that is the only place I can afford to live with a family that size. The truth is, however, that the State has let us down. We are making all of these changes in our school out of our [own] time and personal resources. ("February Open Town Meeting," 1991)

Although the energy and dedication of people like Mrs. Martinez and the teachers at Montevideo Elementary School are admirable, their experience continues to point to the obstacles faced by those at the local level.

CONCLUSION

In this chapter, I have argued that the educational system works best when schools, families, and communities work together. Regardless of what type of collaborative efforts are developed, continuing education of teachers, administrators, and parents is in order. We cannot expect educational restructuring to succeed without additional training of key personnel to play new roles in the schools and communities in which they work. It is my belief that an empowerment approach to restructuring family-school relationships is critical for the types of changes that are needed to make schools more viable and responsive institutions. Beyond the tightly designed formulas that have governed reforms in family-school relationships in the past, restructuring must be tailored to recognize the continuous social and cultural changes that families experience, as well as the historical and economic contexts of which they are a part. Most important, parents must be included meaningfully in the decisions that affect their lives and the lives of their children.

REFERENCES

Barr, D., & Cochran, M. (1991). Preparation for the empowerment process: Identifying competencies and developing skills. *Networking Bulletin, 2*(1), 26.

Bee, H. L., Van Egeren, L. F., Streissguth, A. P., Nyman, B. A., & Leckie, M. S. (1969). Social class differences in maternal teaching strategies and speech patterns. *Developmental Psychology, 1,* 726–734.

Bernstein, B. (1961). Social class and linguistic development: A theory of social learning. In A. H. Halsey, J. Floud, & C. A. Anderson (Eds.), *Education, economy, and society* (pp. 288–314). New York: Free Press.

Bronfenbrenner, U. (1978). Who needs parent education? *Teachers College Record, 79,* 767–787.

Bronfenbrenner, U. (1979). Beyond the deficit model in child and family policy. *Teachers College Record, 81*(1), 95–104.

Chang, H. N., Gardner, S. L., Watahara, A., Brown, C. G., & Robles, R. (1991). *Fighting fragmentation: Collaborative efforts to serve children and families in California's counties.* San Francisco: California Tomorrow and Children and Youth Policy Project.

Cochran, M., & Dean, C. (1991). Home–school relations and the empowerment process. *Elementary School Journal, 91*(3), 261–269.

Cochran, M., & Woolever, F. (1983). Beyond the deficit model: The empowerment of parents with information and informal supports. In I. E. Sigel & L. Laosa (Eds.), *Changing families* (pp. 225–247). New York: Plenum Press.

Comer, J. P. (1980). *School power: Implications of an intervention project.* New York: Free Press.

Comer, J. P., & Haynes, N. (1991). Parent involvement in schools: An ecological approach. *Elementary School Journal, 91*(3), 271–277.

Cremin, L. A. (1964). *The transformation of the school: Progressivism in American education, 1876–1957.* New York: Vintage Books.

Cummins, J. (1986). Empowering minority students: A framework for intervention. *Harvard Educational Review, 56,* 18–36.

Dauber, S. L., & Epstein, J. L. (1989). *Parents' attitudes and practices of involvement in inner-city elementary and middle schools* (Report 33). Baltimore, MD: Johns Hopkins University Center for Research on Elementary and Middle Schools.

Davies, D. (1989). *Poor parents, teachers, and the schools: Comments about practice, policy and research.* Paper presented at the Annual Meeting of the American Educational Research Association, San Francisco.

Delgado-Gaitan, C. (1990). *Literacy for empowerment: The role of parents in children's education.* London: Falmer Press.

Delgado-Gaitan, C. (1991). Linkages between home and school: A process of change for involving parents. *American Educational Journal, 100*(1), 20–46.

Delgado-Gaitan, C., & Trueba, H. (1991). *Crossing cultural borders: Education for immigrant families in America.* London: Falmer Press.

Dokecki, P. R., Hargrove, E. C., & Sandler, H. M. (1983). An overview of the parent child development center social experiment. In R. Haskins & D. Adams (Eds.), *Parent education and public policy* (pp. 80–112). Norwood, NJ: Ablex.

Dornbusch, S. M., & Ritter, P. L. (1988). Parents of high school students: A neglected resource. *Educational Horizons, 66,* 75–77.

Dunn, L. (1987). *Bilingual Hispanic children on the US mainland: A review of research on their cognitive, linguistic and scholastic development* (Monograph). American Guidance Service. Minnesota Circle Pines.

Epstein, J. L. (1985). A question of merit: Principals' and parents' evaluations of teachers. *Educational Researcher, 14*(7), 3–10.

Epstein, J. L. (1986). Parents' reactions to teacher practices of parent involvement. *Elementary School Journal, 86,* 277–294.

February open town meeting. (1991) Oakland, CA: Public Broadcasting Service.

Fein, G. G. (1980). The informed parent. In S. Kilmer (Ed.), *Advances in early education and day care, 1.* Greenwich, CT: JAI Press.

Florin, R. R., & Dokecki, P. R. (1983). Changing families through parent and family education: Review and analysis. In I. E. Sigel & L. M. Laosa (Eds.), *Changing families* (pp. 23–64). New York: Plenum Press.

Freire, P. (1973). *Education for critical consciousness.* New York: Continuum.

Garcia, A. (1991). *Hispanic parent involvement: A study of the relationship between school achievement and parental attitudes and involvement.* Paper presented at the Annual Meeting of the American Educational Research Association, Chicago.

Hess, R. D., & Shipman, V. (1965). Maternal influences upon early learning: The cognitive environment of urban pre-school children. In R. D. Hess & R. M. Bear (Eds.), *Early education: Current theory, research, and action* (pp. 869–885). Chicago: Aldine.

Hoffman, L. W. (1974). Effects of maternal employment on the child: Review of the research. *Developmental Psychology, 10,* 204–228.

Holtzman, W., Diaz-Guerrero, R., & Swartz, J. (1975). *Personality development in two cultures: A cross-cultural longitudinal study of school children in Mexico and the United States.* Austin: University of Texas Press.

Karraker, R. J. (1972). Increasing academic performance through home-managed contingency programs. *Journal of School Psychology, 10,* 173–179.

Kriesberg, L. (1970). *Mothers in poverty: A study of fatherless families.* Chicago: Aldine.

Laosa, L. M. (1983). Parent education, cultural pluralism, and public policy: The uncertain connection. In R. Haskins & D. Adams (Eds.), *Parent education and public policy* (pp. 331–341). Norwood, NJ: Ablex.

Lareau, A. (1987). Social class differences in family-school relationships: The importance of cultural capital. *Sociology of Education, 60,* 73–85.

Leichter, H. J. (1979). Families and communities as educators: Some concepts of relationships. In H. J. Leichter (Ed.), *Families and communities as educators* (pp. 11–23). New York: Teachers College Press.

Leitch, M. L., & Tangri, S. S. (1988). Barriers to home–school collaboration. *Educational Horizons, 66,* 70–74.

Leler, H. (1983). Parent education and involvement in relation to the schools and to parents of school-aged Children. In R. Haskins & D. Adams (Eds.), *Parent education and public policy* (pp. 114–180). Norwood, NJ: Ablex.

Phelan, P., Cao, H. T., & Davidson, A. L. (1992). *Navigating the psycho-social pressures of adolescence: The voices and experience of high school youth* (Report P92–144). Stanford, CA: Stanford University, Center for the Context of Secondary School Teaching.

Spring, J. (1991). *American education: An introduction to social and political aspects.* New York: Longman.

CHAPTER 6

FOR TEACHERS:
SOME SKETCHES OF CURRICULUM

Reba Page

Somewhat more than a year ago, Athol Fugard's (1989) wrenching tragedy, *My Children! My Africa!*, was produced by the Los Angeles Theater Center. Eloquently bespeaking conditions in South Africa and the differences that schooling can (and cannot) make in that war-torn country, the play also prompts reflection on the import of ordinary school lessons here and how U.S. schools use curriculum to respond to diverse students.

Fugard's play juxtaposes old-fashioned and revolutionary ideas about school knowledge and social change. A black teacher, Mr. M., urges his most promising student, Thami, to see his own acumen as illustration that "the inferior education" the white government forces on blacks "to keep us permanently suppressed" can be "sabotaged" to "liberate your mind" and, nonviolently, the country:

> If the struggle [against apartheid] needs weapons, give it words. Stones and petrol bombs can't get inside those armored cars. Words can. They can do something even more devastating than that . . . they can get inside the heads of those inside the armored cars. (p. 59)

Thami's head, however, is "rebellious" and Mr. M.'s world is no longer his because he has looked at the adults around him who were once just as promising and, imagining "the Future," he can see only misery and humiliation. Therefore,

> [I]t is not as easy as it used to be to sit behind that desk and learn only what [the Government Inspector for Bantu Education] has decided I must know. . . . My head refuses now to remember when the Dutch landed, and

159

the Huguenots landed, and the British landed. It has already forgotten when
the Old Union became the proud young Republic. But it does know what
happened in Kliptown in 1955, in Sharpeville on twenty-first March 1960
and in Soweto on the sixteenth of June 1976. Do you? Better find out
because those are dates your children will have to learn one day. (p. 50)

Thami has found "another school" and what some might call a relevant
curriculum. In it, "the people meet and whisper names we have been told
to forget, the dates of events they try to tell us never happened, and the
speeches they try to say were never made. Those are the lessons we are
eager and proud to learn, because they are lessons about *our* history, about
our heroes" (p. 50).

Tragedy strikes when Thami and Mr. M. act according to these ideologies. Even though Isabel, who attends a secondary school for white
girls, sees that the student and teacher love each other and urges them
to talk to each other, in these circumstances, neither can yield. First,
Thami, with Isabel as his partner, backs out of participation in a scholastic contest that, for Mr. M., would have demonstrated the "lunancy" of
apartheid, which has produced so many "wasted lives," black and white.
Instead, Thami, with "the comrades," calls a boycott. When bloody riots
follow, Mr. M. informs on the strikers to save his pupils and his Africa.
However, his action is deemed treachery and the teacher is killed by the
people. In turn, Thami is forced to flee to the north and exile. At the
play's end, it is too late for either the traditionalist or the revolutionary.
Only Isabel remains on stage, thinking of Thami, remembering Mr. M.,
and promising that because she too is one of Mr. M.'s "children," she
will work hard not to "waste" her life.

Thami, Mr. M., and Isabel are characters in a play. Their inspired
discourse about curriculum and the part it plays in present and future
relations between the generations, races, and sexes in South Africa is high
drama. LATC performed it to packed audiences and rave reviews.

Although less dramatic, the role of school knowledge is no less critical in the real-life dialectic of differentiation and integration that teachers and students perform in everyday school lessons. In U.S. schools, as
in South Africa, curriculum and culture conjoin so that students learn
about their places in life as they learn their lessons.

Yet we in the U.S. seldom scrutinize the scholastic and sociocultural
dramas enacted in school lessons. Unlike Fugard's characters, we infre-
quently acknowledge the compulsion to learn and the power of knowledge, we disregard the brutality that may limit the significance of schooling, or we fail to see that a perverse consequence of being open to all

knowledge may be cynicism about the value of any knowledge. Instead, we take school knowledge for granted, expecting public schools to somehow be all things to all children.

Fugard's play also points to the importance of developing an intelligent, sophisticated, public discourse for addressing curriculum and culture and the relationship between them. Like Thami and Mr. M., we presently rely on commonsensical dichotomies to describe the distribution of knowledge among diverse students: Lessons are college prep (or vocational), high status (or low status), elite (or average), academic (or experiential), abstract (or relevant), high track (or low track), bookish (or practical), headed (or handed), mental (or manual), or the common heritage of all (or the distinctive construction of each).

Although merely symbolic, characterizations such as these come to life and have consequences in concrete programs: As Fugard's characters show us, people act on ideas, and, persuading or coercing others to acknowledge them, they enact them. With words, then, the school world and the social world are carved into domains and relationships: groups of students, forms of knowledge, tracks, types of schools, relations of reciprocity, asymmetry, and hierarchy, and so forth. In this chapter I sketch some of the processes and circumstances through which this happens and describe its import.

My focus is curriculum, and particularly the differentiated lessons in tracked classes that schools produce in the name of diversity but which also generate deep suspicions. I examine the "curriculum in action" (Schwab, 1969/1977) that teachers and students construct together and use as they negotiate roles and knowledge. Playing on a related, Geertzian (1982a) concept as well, I consider curriculum as "local school knowledge." Accordingly, I explore various types of school lessons, looking particularly at their variations across and within tracks and schools; the curricular "sensibility" (Geertz, 1982a, p. 18), particularly of teachers, that undergirds decisions about what to teach and why; and how knowledge is represented in school lessons to convey not only academic information but its socially normative appropriateness, so that, however tacitly, lessons exhibit a commingling of local and larger precepts about what the interconnections between diverse participants, classrooms, and communities are and about what they ought to be.

I write about the use of school knowledge to mean and make scholastic and social differences for educators, and particularly for teachers who, consciously or otherwise, are the artisans of curriculum. I select examples from the world of classrooms, representing in sketches some lower-track lessons that two teachers, in two high schools, provided for students they deemed different and academically unsuccessful. Such sketches may seem too parochial in focus or limited in scope to be of use to other teachers, in different settings, facing other students. However, the sketches are not a generic model of tracked lessons but a comparative case. Because I have made them thick with specifics and principled in analysis, I hope that teachers anywhere may recognize how things are in these two schools and, by comparison, how they may appropriate the sketches to reflect on their own curricular prerogatives and responsibilities and the purposes to which knowledge is put in their schools.

Furthermore, I suggest that this kind of sustained explication of school stories, although apparently only abstract talk about academic research, is preeminently practical. It is a medium and means with which we may grapple with what and who schools are for (Sarason, 1971) and the kind of world in which we want to live. By contrast, other responses to the issue of valued knowledge and its proper distribution mask disagreements by seeking to forge a prior consensus for a national curriculum and a national test; technicize curricular decision making through "realistic" measuring and matching of different kinds of knowledge with different kinds of students; or reduce curricular judgment to demographic formulae, polls of interest groups, or manpower assessments, thereby rendering education synonymous with social structure, politics, or vocationalism.

In short, explicating school stories, curricularly and culturally (the Spindlers might say therapeutically), may illumine the "distinctive way of imagining the real" (Geertz, 1982a, p. 173) that education and here, curriculum, contributes to formulations of human society such as America. Curriculum studies offer a way of thinking. Like other human endeavors and disciplines such as law, religion, art, and politics, to all of which it is related without however being equivalent, it poses fundamental questions such as what we shall teach and why, and a special world, today most often the school, with the pragmatic aim of designing defensibly educative experiences. Given this, teachers have something to add to cacophonous school debates as well as something to learn.

THE BIG PICTURE OF THE SCHOOL CURRICULUM

To consider curriculum as a means by which schools respond to diverse students requires that such curriculum be described. However, even if regarded quite simply, as course content or subject matter, curriculum is difficult to specify. This is particularly the case with regard to tracking.

Most descriptions of curriculum from research studies are oversimplified. They itemize such ready data as the credits students earn, the minutes teachers devote (or say they devote) to particular topics and activities, or the most popular texts. When aggregated, and perhaps correlated with learning outcomes, these data yield the big picture of the school curriculum. It, in turn, forms a standard with which to infer what other schools teach and, usually implicitly, what all schools should teach.

Thus, for example, traditional research about tracking in U.S. high schools (Goodlad, 1984; Oakes, 1985, 1990) describes a generic, lower-track curriculum. Different from regular-track knowledge and ways of knowing, it consists of rudimentary content and highly stylized form. Measured most often against students' social characteristics and achievement scores, it is adjudged efficacious and fair, or not.

Although appealingly parsimonious, the big picture provides an inadequate description of curriculum, which, in turn, sustains wrongheaded policies and practices. Put simply, it trifles with the meaning of curriculum. Because curriculum is both a message about how the world makes sense and a medium through which sense is made (Erickson, 1986) most immediately, by teachers and students, we remain in the dark about what any school subject is if we do not know what its study means to the people who experience it directly.

Therefore, in the sketches that follow, I explore the intertwining of curriculum and culture specifically by considering the lower-track lessons of two respected veterans, Mr. Thompson and Mr. Bauer.[1] The men work in two of the well-regarded, public high schools (Southmoor and Marshall) of Maplehurst, a middle-class, medium-sized city in the Midwest. During the 1982–1983 school year when I conducted research on tracking in Maplehurst,[2] they continued long-established schedules in which, in addition to three regular-track history courses, each chooses to teach a lower-track, Additional Needs history course (one is World History, the other is American History).

Maplehurst is an interesting setting because its schools provide resources, such as smaller-sized classes and what the district terms "adaptive" curricula, for students who are at risk of failing regular history and who are ineligible for special education. Furthermore, although the disproportionate representation of poor and minority students in the lower-track classes suggests that the school order corresponds to the socioeconomic order, this is not quite the case in Maplehurst. There, most Additional Needs students are, like their regular-track peers and unlike many of the lower-track students described in other research studies of tracking (Metz, 1978; Oakes, 1985), white and middle class; they also are not as academically unsuccessful as familiar stereotypes suggest, but score, on average, in the third rather than the lowest quartile on standardized achievement tests in reading and math. In other words, the students grouped in Maplehurst's lower-track classes are not notably disadvantaged or different from regular-track students, at least as such things are currently measured (but see Geertz, 1986, for a different view of diversity). It is precisely the homogeneity and averageness of these schools that may allow us to better appreciate the ubiquity of processes of differentiation and integration.[3]

At the same time, a close-up focus on specific lessons and schools may also move us beyond simplistic slogans about curriculum to a better appreciation of the complexities and uses of curriculum. Tracking, in particular, although it is the most common manifestation of curriculum differentiation in U.S. secondary schools, is perennially confusing because it grounds cherished but contradictory values of the common good and individualism. Thus, in the abstract, critics charge that tracked lessons discriminate because the students who come to school already socially and academically disadvantaged are given a lower-status curriculum that only further limits their educational and social opportunities. However, proponents counter that tracked lessons differentiate knowledge and thereby accommodate students' individual educational needs and fairly promote their life chances.

Distinguishing differentiation and discrimination is and will continue to be difficult. Fugard renders this dilemma when he places Isabel and Thami in a debate at the school about whether men and women should be educated differently. When Thami invokes non-Western, African traditions, some of which are patriarchal, to argue the necessity for "different educational syllabuses for the two sexes," Isabel counters with an analogy that evokes apartheid:

> The argument against equality for women, in education or any other field, based on alleged "differences" between the two sexes, is an argument that can very easily be used against any other "different" group. (p. 5)

Teachers also experience this paradox: They are enjoined to individualize curriculum in recognition of each child's unique needs and interests yet they are also to provide the same curriculum to all children so that they all receive equal educational opportunities.

Local sketches of curriculum may modulate instinctive, abstract conjectures about the difference curriculum can (and cannot) make. As apparently simple, singular patterns of tracking shatter into ambiguous signs, involved processes, opaque folklore, and obliquely knotted webs of local and larger circumstances, the views are untenable that curriculum is either

miraculously transformative and able to resolve all the struggles of a pluralistic society or that curriculum is mired in transmission and able only
to reproduce that society. Instead, considered locally, curriculum emerges
as a scholastic and sociocultural translation. Like any literary translation,
lessons are distinctive versions, constructed in schools, of original texts
of the culture and, as such, exhibit both degrees of freedom and definite
constraints. Thus conceived, as an enduring dilemma that constitutes difference and the common good rather than as self-evident truth or a contradiction that can be resolved in a once-and-for-all decision to treat
everyone the same or uniquely, the role of school knowledge in the play
of school and society deserves both serious interest and more modest
expectation.

LOCAL SNAPSHOTS:
CURRICULUM IN TWO LOWER-TRACK CLASSROOMS

One or two visits to Mr. Bauer's and Mr. Thompson's Additional
Needs history classes might suggest that lessons in Maplehurst are easily
described and obvious in significance. The classes would seem to repli-
cate the expected, generic, big-picture pattern for lower-track, remedial
curriculum: knowledge as a list of discrete, noncontroversial facts and
knowing as an independent activity of reading texts and retrieving information called for in short-answer questions drawn from the texts. Such
lessons are presumed to contrast with the more advanced, engaging
requirements of regular-track lessons.

Thus, Mr. Bauer's class at Marshall High School always begins
promptly and proceeds smoothly, with the teacher unobtrusive but steady
at the helm. When the clock hand jerks to 8:03, silence reigns. Immediately, Mr. Bauer asks the 15 9th graders to take out their books and homework. They do so amid some minor bustling. With a smooth "okey-dokey,
here we go,"[4] Mr. Bauer begins the review of questions from the end of
the textbook chapter on which students began work in class the previous
day and which, if necessary, completed at home. The questions, which
require students to retrieve words or phrases from the text, are listed at
the end of each chapter in an old (1956), remedial textbook that has short
chapters (1–2 pages long), large print, simple syntax, and standard, chro-
nologically organized content (the explorers, the 13 colonies, the Revolution, and so on).

The review of questions proceeds steadily through about half the class
period. At its completion, Mr. Bauer asks students to take out their answers
to a set of reading-skill questions. There is again some minor shuffling

and murmuring as students find their papers. This second set of questions, although written by Mr. Bauer, resembles and is reviewed as efficiently as those at the ends of chapters. Then, with the second review completed, Mr. Bauer announces the total points for the homework assignment, students add up their scores, and Mr. Bauer records them, calling students by name for their scores. With somewhat less than half the class period remaining, Mr. Bauer hands out the next day's reading-skill worksheet and assigns the reading of the next chapter in the text, along with the questions at the end of the chapter. Students work independently and quietly on the homework assignment until one or two minutes before the period's end. At 8:53 on the electric clock, they stand and leave, quickly and noisily.

Mr. Bauer directs this routine almost every day of the week. As he once explained to students, they should never have a question about their assignment because "it's always the next chapter in the book." The routine is interrupted only by unit tests, which come about once every four or five weeks; by reviews for unit tests, which proceed from study sheets similar to the homework and reading-skill assignments; or by a film or slides, which are shown on the second and fourth Fridays of the month. Mr. Bauer's lower-track lessons differ from his and other teachers' regular-track lessons at Marshall in the degree to which knowledge is basic, skills-based, routinized, and remote.

Mr. Thompson's 10th-grade World History class at Southmoor High follows a similarly structured, two-part format of individual reading and group recitation. Its first segment begins when the teacher strides into the room as the bell rings. He says, "Lights," and a student near the door turns off the lights. Continuing on his way to the front of the room, Mr. Thompson points to his right and says "Shades" and two or three students jump up to pull down the long, beige windowshades. Then, on reaching the front, Mr. Thompson switches on an overhead projector, a soft glow suffuses the classroom, the daily quiz appears on the screen, and Mr. Thompson intones in a deep bass voice, "Awright, class. Here is today's quiz. You may begin. Good luck and good hunting."

With little ado, students open their copies of *Time* magazine and "begin." First, they are to read independently the four or five articles the teacher designates for the day. Then, they work at finding answers to the 20 short-answer or multiple-choice questions that appear on the overhead and that the teacher has grouped in fours and fives around each article. For about 35 minutes, the class is silent.

During the second part of the lesson, an efficient if occasionally raucous review commences. Mr. Thompson marks its beginning by announcing that "time is up" and starting a box of red pencil stubs around the room. Then he stands ready at the front by the overhead projector while students noisily exchange papers and write their names at the bottom to indicate that they are the "checker." During the recitation, Mr. Thompson proceeds steadily through the list of 20 questions displayed on the overhead. At the end of the period, he calls for grades and collects the papers.

The two-part lesson was standard fare in Mr. Thompson's Additional Needs history class during the 1982–1983 school year. For the most part, the only change was the cover of *Time*. Moderating the routine were occasional short games in the last few minutes of class (a crossword item, a Multiple Mystery Riddle), hour-long films (on hand for Mr. Thompson's regular-track classes), and school news or jokes or songs (during the week before the holidays, accompanying a recording of the song "How'd You Like to Spend Christmas on Christmas Island," Mr. Thompson sang a verse a day). The lower-track curriculum differs from the classically academic content and freewheeling give-and-take of Southmoor's regular-track classes.

The problem with such passing descriptions of curriculum is that what the lower-track "adaptation" is remains in doubt because what it signifies is difficult to ascertain with any confidence. Stereotypes rather than specifics come into play and evidence is construed instinctively. Using the dichotomy of individualism vs. the common good that characterizes American culture, interpretations miss the irreducible paradoxes that emerge because the culture pursues both individualism and community (Bellah, Madsen, Sullivan, Swidler, & Tipton, 1985; Edelman, 1977; Kammen, 1974; Merelman, 1984; Riesman, 1950; Spindler & Spindler, 1990; Varenne, 1977). Thus, some may read the glossies from Maplehurst and conclude that lower-track lessons there are discriminatory: Social control overwhelms educational purpose because teachers, using watered-down content and strict routines to head off the misbehavior they anticipate from poor, minority, and academically unsuccessful students, deny the students access to knowledge with "high exchange value." Indeed, the "adaptation" has an element of conspiratorial deception. How can transcripts be credited with World History when Mr. Thompson teaches *Time* magazine? How can Mr. Bauer's students be credited with History 9 when, instead of concentrating on post–Civil War history as the district framework mandates, they revisit the content they studied the previous year in middle school?

Alternatively, however, the "adaptative," lower-track lessons may be seen by others as providing the basic knowledge and structured activities that are effective with students who have histories of scholastic deficiency and "short attention spans." They are "realistic" prerequisites if students are to think at higher levels or deal with more complex materials. Furthermore, the disproportionate representation of poor and minority students in Additional Needs classes is not discrimination but a statistical artifact because, in Maplehurst, the presence of one minority student in a class may constitute disproportionate representation.

Given these equally plausible but contradictory views (which in their partisan polarity capture 80 years or so of research on tracking), a description of lower-track curriculum remains elusive. To clarify rather than conventionalize it so that lessons become strange rather than all-too-familiar (Spindler & Spindler, 1982) requires a closer and longer look at the Maplehurst courses. The point, however, is not simply to secure more details, or more realistic details, that can flesh out or humanize a static photograph. Rather, looking closely provides a chance to think altogether differently about curriculum: One may begin to see it, like other human activities, as a meaningful, meaning-making endeavor. Then, adequate description requires attention to what teachers and students in the lower-track history classes think they are up to and to the tangled processes and contexts that inform their local translations of school knowledge.

A DIFFERENT "TAKE" ON LOWER TRACK: CURRICULAR AMBIGUITIES

The key assumptions in traditional descriptions of tracking are that there is such a thing as *the* lower-track curriculum, that it is a stable and clear-cut phenomenon, and that its correlates and causes are straightforward. Moreover, because its significance is assumed to be self-evident in such facts, researchers can provide general directives to teachers of remedial classes: Hold high expectations and care about students so that positive prophecies will be fulfilled; spell out expectations because academically unsuccessful students need or like structure; choose relevant topics because poor students' interests and aptitudes are not academic; or, do away with questions of differentiation and discrimination altogether simply by abolishing tracking.

However, as Schwab (1977) put it, local specifics "modulate" abstract generalizations. Looked at curricularly and culturally, "lower-track" is neither a univocal nor an unequivocal sign. As I describe below, extended visits in Mr. Thompson's lessons at Southmoor suggest that they deviate surprisingly from the rule-of-thumb characterization of lower-track curriculum as simple knowledge and straightforward routine. Equally surprising, they also deviate from Mr. Bauer's. Such variations across lower-track lessons suggest the all-too-human complications of curriculum and the insufficiency of tidy formulae for tracking.

Inconsistency in Mr. Thompson's World History Curriculum

Seen over the course of several months, the apparently straightforward, two-part structure of Mr. Thompson's World History class dissolves into a differently constructed order. Beneath the precision of silent reading and 20 Questions about *Time* is an alternative format that parallels and undercuts the formal lesson.

For example, coexisting with the daily routine of individual seatwork and whole-group recitation is an underworld of surreptitious highjinks. In this third format, Mr. Thompson studiously ignores the students as they read *Time*. He sits at his desk at the front of the room, works to prepare the next day's quiz, and, if there is some untoward noise, looks up to monitor the class or check for questions. As long as the classroom is silent, Mr. Thompson does not look up. Meanwhile, although the Additional Needs students are noiseless and almost motionless, the room is in pandemonium. Rather than simply reading or working independently on the quiz, students also share answers, listen discretely to Walkman radios, do other homework, pass around food, pass around notes, gossip, toss spit wads, or gaze at the ceiling.

Students orient implicitly to the alternating structures. They shift instantly away from the underlife to the formal lesson should Mr. Thompson get up to leave the room or should an outsider enter. Some students also describe the rules of the game explicitly:

> Some articles (in *Time*) people don't even read. You take a percentage out of how many people sit there and read the articles, and you won't get much. You will not get very much at all. 'Cause most of the time, you know, all you have to do is just skim through, just try to find the letter. Like if it says, what is the percentage, all you do is look for that little percent sign, and then you read the sentence. So you take your percentage out of that class and you won't get very much because *nobody* sits and reads.

If pandemonium undermines initial impressions of Mr. Thompson's masterful management, inconsistency threading through the recitations further complicates description of the Additional Needs curriculum. Interspersed in the routine work of reviewing answers to questions about *Time* is a brisk, playful, personalized patter. The classroom is noisy as students jostle to participate, many voices contribute to an exchange of jokes and quips as well as answers, and the atmosphere is fluid and spontaneous, if sometimes chaotic. A student explained the value of a personable teacher:

> A good class depends on how the teacher talks to you. Being mean is like, totally, it's like *ignoring* you. It's just like being *personally* mean. Because I have teachers that, if you raise your hand, they ignore it. But Mr. Thompson, he smiles and he really is nice and, um, he goes, "You look so nice today."

Even though "Mr. Thompson is not mean," as the student put it, she acknowledges some ambivalence because "in ways he can be." If his direction of exchanges in the recitation can call forth a kind of regular-track camaraderie between teacher and students as well as allow for student contributions to the lesson, it can also provide a platform for demeaning moralizing.

For example, when reviewing questions about an article on higher education, Mr. Thompson comments that college graduates make more money and that their jobs carry "power and status." He then turns to Gloria, a notorious chatterer in the class, and comments offhandedly, "See, Gloria, you can be a schoolteacher and talk all the time in *front* of the class." Similarly ambiguous is the teacher's admonition to students about "talking back" even as the recitation he directs encourages them to talk back: When he explains the vocabulary word, "retaliation," Mr. Thompson says, that "Retaliation is something *you* can never do. If I ever kinda tease you, about your name or something like that, you'd never respond by calling me Bill, or something like that."

Whether such exchanges are compliments or "mean," jokes or sanctions, is difficult to sort out because "relevance" and "personableness" are double-edged swords, not unmitigated pedagogical virtues. For example, relevant materials may insult students by conveying negative judgments of their present lives or bleak forecasts of their futures: If a teacher provides lessons about teen pregnancy, does she imply that she thinks students are at risk of pregnancy? Worse, relevant materials may open students' private lives to public invasion or ridicule: As Jules Henry (1963) once described, classrooms are easily converted into witchhunts. Relevance can also be used to keep students in their places: If teachers choose only materials that students respond to and fail to introduce unfamiliar materials that might expand students' knowledge, curriculum will lack the "direction" (Dewey, 1902/1956) that makes it educative.

In short, curricular truisms—high expectations, high-status knowledge, caring, relevance—are singularly unhelpful in making sense of Mr. Thompson's Additional Needs class where ambiguous encounters confound expectations for a readily interpretable, lower-track pattern. The course content is not clearly rudimentary. If *Time* magazine is not the traditionally academic content in regular World History classes, it also is not mind-numbing basic skills. Indeed, Southmoor's lower-track students may have more access to knowledge than many regular students, if Charlotte Crabtree is correct that 50% of U.S. high schools do not require World History for any students, regular-track or otherwise. On the other hand, the rhetoric of *Time* may exceed the grasp of teens with uncertain reading skills. By the same token, the course format is not clearly stylized: For all the inconsistencies in Mr. Thompson's management, he also personalizes lessons and possibly engages Southmoor's lower-track students more than many regular students are engaged elsewhere. Yet, as I have suggested, personalization exists in more than one way in his classroom.

These data and an interpretation that credits their ambiguity lead us nearer to the veteran teacher and his lower-track students themselves: How does the inconsistent adaptation of World History make sense to them? This question becomes especially pointed when, by contrast, extended observation in Mr. Bauer's classroom confirm its consistent rules and self-evidently schooled content. Compared to Mr. Thompson's course, Mr. Bauer's is the very model of effective, consistent, remedial education that many experts recommend to teachers. However, as we shall see, it contains its own troubling ambiguities and unintended consequences.

Order in Mr. Bauer's American History Course

On the 50th day in Mr. Bauer's class, as on the first, events unfold like clockwork. Students read when they are supposed to read; they listen when they are supposed to listen. There is an economy of content, as Mr. Bauer translates American History into basic skills. There is an economy of interchange as well, so that, for example, the teacher can indicate the activity as well as the question to which he wants an answer simply by stating the page and the number of a question; students, matching their responses to the teacher's questions, can cite a letter of the alphabet as an acceptable answer:

> *Mr. B:* Awright, page twenty, part one, number one.
> *S:* A.
> *Mr. B:* (*reading the question from the text*) "Which area had more railroads?" A. Yes. "The North had more railroads."

Dispassionate efficiency also infuses Mr. Bauer's brief elaborations on topics in minilectures, during which students sit quietly, posing no questions. When Mr. Bauer's minilectures evolve into recitations, his domination of the topic and talk continues. During these recitations, Mr. Bauer, unlike Mr. Thompson, rarely directs personalized remarks to students or invites them from students. Rather, he appeals to students for participation by asking easy questions about commonplace facts, adhering to the basics rather than chancing spontaneity. For example, when reviewing questions about the French and Indian War, Mr. Bauer interrupted the recitation with a prosaic analogy to present-day Canada and bilingualism. He asked how many students had traveled to Canada and when several raised their hands, he continued: "Did you notice anything as you drove along the highway?" A girl said, "It wasn't very exciting." Mr. Bauer frowned slightly and narrowed his question: "I mean the road signs." Then a boy volunteered that the mileage is given in miles and kilometers. Mr. Bauer responded: "Right! I loved going 100 kilometers an hour." The class murmured appreciatively. Mr. Bauer then added that the signs are in two languages.

Although Mr. Bauer's course corresponds to the conventional view of what lower-track curriculum is and, for many, ought to be, dysjunctions in it, as in Mr. Thompson's course, raise questions about how the lower-track adaptation of history makes sense to the teacher and students who experience it. Particularly opaque is whether the necessary but delicate balance between goals of order and goals of education is overwhelmed in pursuit of time, training, and the basics. Lower-track curriculum teachers at Marshall raise the query when they complain that the remedial curriculum "allows too many good students to be underachievers" and "enables" poor students to maintain inadequate learning behaviors yet still graduate. Students also ask the question, at least implicitly. After about two weeks of school, as Mr. Bauer passed out the usual homework questions, a boy asked him, "Will we get through this *whole* book this year?" Mr. Bauer replied, rather proudly, "The whole thing, I promise you." Then a girl chimed in, somewhat plaintively, with her own question: "Won't we have no filmstrips, or anything?" Phlegmatically, Mr. Bauer promised to "work in some of those every other Friday or so."

These descriptions of Maplehurst contradict traditional research assumptions that lower-track curriculum is a uniform organizational practice. Surface similarities in the content and form of knowledge, visible after one or two observations, belie important differences that emerge with extended scrutiny. Curriculum differentiation is a more complicated business than the big-picture description conveys: Significant differentiation of curriculum occurs across schools as well as within them, such that differences among lower-track classes may deserve as much scrutiny as differences between lower- and regular-track classes. Equally important, such diversity suggests that tracking is what people make it, rather than what it, in some mechanical fashion, makes them. The critical questions, therefore, are not whether tracking, in general, works or is good or bad, but what people think they are up to in lower-track lessons and how particular, local circumstances affect variations in people's constructions of the meaning of school knowledge.

ADDING A WIDE-ANGLE LENS: TRACKING IN SCHOOL CONTEXTS

That lower-track classes can differ from each other as well as from regular-track classes may come as a surprise only to those of us who have spent too much time reading the research literature on tracking! Teachers in high schools expect differences between classes. Sometimes they are considered problematic. Usually, they are attributed to characteristics of individual teachers (personality, training, management skills), characteristics of students (race, ability, attitude, socioeconomic status), or to flukes in scheduling or events in communities.

Such features explain the differences in lower-track curriculum; in Maplehurst, the longer I observed, the more prominent the distinctive cultures of the two high schools became. Put simply, dissimilarities in Mr. Thompson's and Mr. Bauer's curricula draw on and frame the different milieux in which the men teach.

The differences in organizational milieux, because they are cultural, reflect how people in the two schools represent their situations. Their significance of these differences is not given by or inherent in the facts of the situation nor is it, strictly speaking, a logical or rational construction.

Indeed, if we surveyed Southmoor and Marshall using some typical measures, we might group them together as one type of school. They are virtually equivalent in size, budgets, faculty-student ratios, faculty characteristics, formal administrative procedures, and physical resources. Both schools serve student bodies that are preponderantly white and middle class. However, even though the schools share a quite similar structural reality, they bestow different meanings on that reality.[5] The symbolic constructions are consequential because, to paraphrase Geertz (1973), individuals in both regular- and lower-track classes spin and are suspended in a school's web of meaning when they describe, justify, and enact curriculum.

In brief,[6] Southmoor defines itself as a "nearly perfect," if not "heavenly," institution. Regular-track students are "easy-to-teach" because, as teachers explain, they are "from middle- and upper-middle-class, largely professional families." At the same time, teachers are powerful, knowledgeable "professionals" and "no one is running around, checking up on you." In interaction, these local, institutionally acknowledged definitions of students and faculty reflect and provide for a relaxed, "college-campus atmosphere." Intellectual achievement, pursued with elan and considerable success, is the school's preeminent goal. Accordingly, regular-track lessons provide classically academic content that is deemed important both in its own right and as a base from which students join with teachers to think divergently, "make connections" between diverse ideas, and probe issues with "creativity" and "spontaneity." Coupled with the academic enthusiasm is a liberal disciplinary policy so that, both in and out of regular-track classes, relations between and among teachers and students exhibit a spirited, almost playful camaraderie.

By contrast, Marshall High, just 20 minutes across town, makes something different of the structures that, objectively measured, are so similar to Southmoor's. As several teachers put it, the school is guided by a "nothing-out-of-the-ordinary" ethos. Intent on producing credentials for students whom teachers see as "typical blue-collar kid[s]," the school presents the "practical," skills-based curriculum that a working-class community, given a "consumer economy," will buy. To the "no-nonsense," scholastic regimen is affixed a "tradition of discipline" that emphasizes punctuality, attendance, and obedience. Therefore, distance and good order mark relations between adults and adolescents. They also determine the role of teachers on Marshall's bureaucratic "team," so that teaching is a job, performed competently if perfunctorily. As a teacher who had taught at both Marshall and "heavenly" Southmoor noted, "You don't have to believe in your job at Marshall."

These descriptions may suggest that Southmoor and Marshall teachers, wittingly or unwittingly, transmit knowledge that corresponds to two, socioculturally different communities: college-preparatory lessons to Southmoor's middle- and upper-middle-class students, practical skills to Marshall's blue-collar students. However, the match is not quite so straightforward because schools mediate scholastic and sociocultural facts. They represent them.

This subtlety is of crucial importance in understanding how schools do and may respond to diverse students. People in schools develop and acknowledge[7] designations of who a school's students are by selecting as important particular sociocultural and scholastic features. Their selections are reasonable in the sense that they reflect what people know, explicitly and tacitly, about the requirements of their situations (Spindler, 1982). People characterize the features of students so that difference among students is variously meaningful—a rich resource in one context but a cause for distress in another, for example. They also represent the knowledge that such students "need" and that "the community wants," providing thereby for the concrete manifestation and re-creation of symbolic difference. Accordingly, Marshall provides a skills-based curriculum to the regular-track students it characterizes as "blue-collar kids" even though more than 40% of its seniors will go on to college, just as Southmoor provides classical academics even though more than 35% of its regular-track seniors will not go directly to college.

Similarly oblique are the processes of internal differentiation in a school. Lower-track lessons are not direct responses, whether positive or prejudiced, to remedial students themselves. They are relational, cultural responses. A lower-track curriculum can be thought of as a version of a school's regular curriculum, provided to students who are designated as "different" from regular students (and, often lost sight of, similar to each other). Because the meaning of "difference" can vary, lower-track lessons may be parallel to regular lessons in some schools (Valli, 1990), but gross caricatures of those lessons in others (Page, 1991). In other words, the distribution of school knowledge as a response to diverse students is not readily predictable. Teachers do consider cognitive and cultural differences among students in devising lessons, but the influence of difference is filtered symbolically within multilayered contexts of classroom, school, local community, and American culture.

Thus, because schools have distinctive characters, curriculum is always *local school knowledge*. Lessons are not the idiosyncratic construction of an individual teacher, a standardized technology imposed by a district bureaucracy or by textbooks, or a mindless, autonomic replication of social categories such as race or social class. Lessons are scholastic and sociocultural constructions in which teachers, with students, translate the ethos, history, locale, and larger contexts of a school. With curriculum, a school can make a difference: It uses school knowledge to define difference. In Maplehurst, for example, the precepts that organize Mr. Bauer's and Mr. Thompson's lessons resonate with institutionally acknowledged rationales for regular-track lessons, so that lower-track lessons are, simultaneously, both similar to and different from regular lessons within a school. The cultures of the schools similarly inform lessons of other lower-track curriculum teachers at Southmoor and at Marshall. They mark students' responses to lessons as well. Teachers and students in daily school lessons, within and across tracks, contribute to and "drink from [a school's] cultural stream" (Waller, 1932, p. 106).

I introduce the concept, school culture, to clarify further what lower-track curriculum is and how it varies between Mr. Bauer's and

Mr. Thompson's Additional Needs history classes. To it I add a focus on the teachers' curricular sensibilities. Moving back and forth between curriculum and culture, I attend to the two teachers' descriptions and justifications of lower-track lessons and to the circumstances that make what they say about them understandable. This uncovers another strata of the meaning of curriculum and clarifies further the significance of its differentiation in school lessons.[8]

ZOOMING IN: A TEACHER TALKS ABOUT CURRICULUM

Mr. Thompson uses the word "relevant" to describe the curriculum in Additional Needs World History when I ask him about it in an interview, and in the process, he resolves many of the inconsistencies that can be observed in the course's content, format, and teacher-student relationships. Using "relevance" colloquially, he gives it substance in ways that are sensible within Southmoor's culture. The term resonates as well with a long, progressive tradition in curriculum that, also adapted in schemes for remedial education, stresses the child's needs and interests as the starting point for selecting worthy knowledge (for the history of this tradition, see Kliebard, 1986).

In describing the course, Mr. Thompson begins with the formal, district rationale for Additional Needs courses: adaptive curriculum for at-risk students. Mr. Thompson explains that he means for lower-track World History to be different from regular-track World History. It would be "criminal" as well as inefficient to expect the Additional Needs student to deal with the "familiar" academic curriculum at Southmoor, "which the kid has failed already":

> The kids you get there are almost all remedial. They've, this is a required course, World History, and if they flunk it they have to make it up. And so, ah, you know, the teacher is under some pressure to design some kind of a curriculum that is going to be as different from the familiar environment in which the kid has failed already as you possibly can.

Given these ground rules, Mr. Thompson takes responsibility for providing "as *different* [a curriculum as he] possibly can." At the same time, however, he minimizes the considerable prerogatives that he, like all Maplehurst teachers, has to determine curriculum, recalling instead that he merely "came up with" the two-part, read-and-recall innovation:

And, one of the things I came up with, ultimately, was, well, I started using newspapers. Then I wanted to switch to a news magazine. So, I just get a copy [of *Time* magazine] for every kid enrolled, and I just make out a hunt-up-the-answer type of quiz for them. And that has really worked out sensationally. I just have a very good accomplishment of arousing the kids' interest, keeping the rate of attrition down, and, I think really accomplishing something.

Mr. Thompson notes that the curriculum is both "relevant" to lower-track students and different from the familiar regular-track curriculum because it presents materials that remedial students are used to. The contents of *Time*, he implies, is germane to academically unsuccessful students whereas history is far beyond their ken:

I think . . . it's fundamental to a kid's daily existence. Most people have a newspaper or *Time* magazine in their home, and they're familiar with their parents reading it, and things like that. And so, it's something that . . . the kids grow up with. And of course a lot of the things that these kids are interested in [are] nothing but the comics page or the sports section or the people section or something like that. But they're used to reading it. And so it isn't really much of a bridge to cross, really. They just move to the new sections, or to the editorial sections, or something like that.

The course is different in format as well, and diverges from the extended, often freewheeling and provocative units that develop in regular classes at Southmoor:

These kids just *look* for something different in a class, I think. Rather than just the old format of homework and . . . recitation of some kind. Here, they're under the gun, they have to do something in 45 minutes, it can't be put off til tomorrow, it's gotta be done today.

Although short term, the regularized activities carry over from day to day: "Kids think, 'It's third period and I'm going to history and, boy, there's something prepared there for me to do and, you know, I might not get into it *fully*, but that's going to be my choice if I don't.'" Mr. Thompson adds that the provision of 20 questions about articles in *Time* indicates that he has met his responsibilities as well: "The kids see I've done my job (by preparing the daily quiz) and they have to do theirs. It's not a free-air day of some kind (like some lower-track classes)."

Notable by its absence from the teacher's description of curriculum is school knowledge itself. The nature of history, or of remedial history, and its apt translation for adolescents is not deemed problematic by Mr. Thompson the way it was, for instance, to Keddie's (1971) teachers of social studies in England during the heyday of curriculum reform. For example, Mr. Thompson justifies using *Time* because it is a familiar object that students have lying around the house; he does not defend it as world-history-in-the-making, as he might have were the nature of school knowledge his concern. Similarly, he mentions that school lessons are valuable for credentialing purposes but he does not assert that they carry knowledge about current events that can inform and empower lower-track students.

Indeed, *Time* recommends itself as lower-track content virtually by default. Given the tacit precepts at Southmoor that militate even in lower-track classes against knowledge that is technicist or skills based, the magazine, with its hip slang and wide distribution, is both substantial, at least compared to the mundane drills that infuse many remedial texts, and distinguished from the familiar, classical canon. In short, Southmoor's lower-track curriculum, emergent in the play between its differences from and similarities to the regular curriculum, is fundamentally ambiguous. For example, the course is not easily judged discriminatory because, even though Mr. Thompson is moralizing, he is also right that "all of us could do a better job of paying attention to what is going on in the world."

If course content is irrelevant in Mr. Thompson's curricular sensibilities, student character is not: Remedial students *are* problematic at Southmoor and the curriculum must accommodate their "difference from other students." However, the problem that such students pose is obscured. Mr. Thompson characterizes students contrarily by loosely amalgamating local and larger notions about remedial and regular students' academic ability, social backgrounds, and deportment. For example, lower-track students are deemed able and willing to read the "sophisticated rhetoric" of *Time* because they are from homes with enough capital, cultural (Bourdieu & Passeron, 1977) and otherwise, to buy, read, and value the news magazine. Alternatively, however, Mr. Thompson also characterizes students as "poor," both in ability and "where they come from." Additional Needs students also have bad "attitudes" so that they are deemed recalcitrant as well as remedial.

Further exacerbating the confusion, Mr. Thompson's portrayal of lower-track students draws less on who they are and more on who they are not: Additional Needs students are not "easy-to-teach," regular-track

students "from middle- and upper-middle-class, mostly professional families." Regardless of Additional Needs students' considerable social and
academic advantages, they are said to be "miles apart" from the ideal pupil
(Keddie, 1971) in the school order at Southmoor:

> Kids are a lot more individual than we realize. I think as I acquire
> more experience in this profession, I realize that just where kids
> come from and, boy, the difference, just as a good student and a
> poor student are many more miles apart than we really dream that
> they are.

Yet even this dichotomy and its terms oscillate in Mr. Thompson's descriptions. As I noted earlier, the place of regular students in the culture of a
school is a complicated refraction of both scholastic and demographic facts
rather than their mimetic reproduction. Hence, a sizeable number of
Southmoor's seniors—about 35% if plans for college is the criterion—may
not be middle class, even though the school defines its students as middle
class, provides them what some would call a middle-class curriculum, and
differentiates a lower-track curriculum from it.

Mr. Thompson's inattention to course content combines with his
ambiguous characterization of students when he justifies Additional Needs
World History. The adaptive curriculum "has worked out sensationally"
because, in Mr. Thompson's book, what is relevant about and for remedial students is their "attitude." If *Time* does not contribute to students'
knowledge about World History, that is not of much consequence because
the magazine does get students to "try":

> The one kid, for example, who, for whom very definitely *Time*
> magazine is just too sophisticated rhetoric is Joe Wilson. He's the
> black boy, he sits right there in front. And yet of all the kids that
> come in and just try, and, who really, I think, have gotten some-
> thing out of the whole course, I would say that it's Joe.

"Just try[ing]" is what Joe and others have gotten out of the "whole course."
Even when students cannot read *Time* and have not been instructed in
history, current events, or reading skills that might, be a "bridge" to such
knowledge, students "just get wrapped up in it." Mr. Thompson would
"sell" the course on the basis of Joe's compliance "under the gun":

> If I just had to sell this class and what it's doing on the basis of
> one person, his performance, I bet it would be Joe. Because he
> really goes at it. But . . . his grades are poor, and . . . I suppose I'll

have to give him a D, as a semester grade. But he really doesn't expect any more, and just from the standpoint of how he's functioned, and how he's improved in some ways, his attitude, he would deserve even better than that, you know, if you were grading on, ah, process rather than product . . . He just comes in and take his magazine, and just goes and sits down and just gets wrapped up in it for 40 or 45 minutes.

Throughout his representation of Additional Needs history, Mr. Thompson's tone is genial, relaxed, and matter-of-fact. This is no burned-out misanthrope, mindless bureaucrat, or inarticulate incompetent. Instead, in what he says and how, Mr. Thompson represents the description and justification of adaptive lessons as straightforward. Additional Needs World History is what it is because it is what the situation requires and everyone with good sense knows it. In a word, curriculum is reckoned commonsensical.

Geertz (1982b) explains that common sense, although informal and colloquial in expression, is an ordered cultural system, or ideology. Metaphorically, it is an older suburb, close to the tangled core of traditions, untutored emotions, and received wisdom of the ancient city of culture, while simultaneously somewhat distant from the logistical theories and methods of disciplinary knowledge in rationally planned suburban communities. Accordingly, like modern, formally structured systems of thought such as art or religion, common sense purports to explain the world as it really is. Unlike them, however, common sense denies its own constructedness. Its tone conveys a "maddening air of simple wisdom" (Geertz, 1982b, p. 85); its style is axiomatic rather than explicative. It is a cultural genre whose authority rests on appeals to nature, practicality, literalness, ad hoc decisions, and unspecialized, sometimes anti-intellectual ways of knowing.

Seen through this lens, Mr. Thompson construes curriculum as a kind of unassailable, pedagogical folklore (Schwab, 1977, p. 36). Using a homely vernacular of education to talk about Additional Needs World History, he asserts that differences in intellect exist in the nature of the human condition. Conversationally, he implies that any practical person has the good sense to understand the importance of "keeping the rate of attrition down." Speaking colloquially, curriculum is simple if necessarily contradictory: Just "start where the kids are" (wherever that is) but "give them what they have not failed already" (whether or not it has value). There is no need to discuss or investigate these issues further, his confidential tone conveys, because they are what "everyone knows."

Now, the notion that curriculum is an unspecialized rather than a disciplined endeavor is not peculiar to Mr. Thompson. It is institutionalized. The structure of schooling is such that teachers' days provide no time for considered reflection on curriculum; few teachers are taught in schools of education to question, curricularly or culturally, the production and distribution of school knowledge; resources to design curriculum have declined; and accountability measures (curriculum frameworks and tests) further limit teachers' traditional curricular responsibilities and prerogatives (McNeil, 1986; Wise, 1979).

In addition, these structures revivify and support concretely the defining ethos of the school. According to Sarason (1971), a school is an institution whose culture silences discussion of its chief principles and activities, rendering them unmentionables. Accordingly, other teachers, like Mr. Thompson, seldom inquire into what is taught, how knowledge is distributed, or how learning is evaluated because they take the issues at face value. The unwritten rule in school is that questioning knowledge or teaching contravenes the norms. Questioners risk being deemed fools, childishly naive, or pariahs. (I suspect that this is even more the case with curriculum than it is with such topics as teaching and learning.)

From this perspective, the ambiguity that distinguishes Mr. Thompson's description of relevant curriculum stems from and constitutes the commonsensical manner with which he and others at preeminently academic Southmoor speak about student "difference." As a public, comprehensive high school, Southmoor has diverse students it cannot ignore. However, as a high school that defines itself and is seen by the community as preeminently academic, it hears few constituents demanding curricular resources for "different" students who are academically unsuccessful. Indeed, Additional Needs classes are sometimes characterized as "a waste" that inequitably drains off scarce school resources from "regular students who could really benefit from them."

Therefore, in the culture of Southmoor, remedial students, even though they have considerable advantages, are deemed so many "miles apart" from regular students—so much "the basic bottom" or "the dregs," as other teachers put it—that no one expects them to return to regular-track classes. Consequently, World History can be about *Time*, any topic, or no subject at all, as when, with Joe, "trying" is the criterion of success. Respected professionals can treat remedial lessons commonsensically.

At the same time, the Southmoor case demonstrates the strong but subtle independence with which a local school responds to diverse students. A school has a distinctive ethos, with some autonomy to define and differentiate teaching, students, and knowledge, even as it is also bound by some constraints. Students who in other contexts might be seen as average can be marginalized—symbolically and concretely—with relevant lessons provided by personable and knowledgeable professionals because their academic progress is only occasionally consequential in a "heavenly" school where the heights of academic accomplishment are everything. Bending equivocal facts about students, knowledge, schooling, and society to its own purposes, the school makes a difference.

REVERSE IMAGES: ANOTHER TEACHER'S TALK ABOUT CURRICULUM

To some extent, common sense is a contradiction in terms. Sense, if it is ever common, is only so within a culture. Therefore, if one moves across town from Southmoor's "nearly perfect" environs to Marshall's pedestrian grounds, common sense about lower-track knowledge shifts. Teachers at both schools portray Additional Needs lessons as self-evident, but each school construes its own, local version of what is commonsensical. Whereas Mr. Thompson represents relevant curriculum as a matter that requires little reflection or expertise, Mr. Bauer, in addition, presents a lower-track curriculum *in* common sense. In contrast to the "sophisticated rhetoric" of *Time*, Additional Needs American History is neither mysterious, cerebral, or specialized. As Mr. Bauer reassures his 9th graders, lower-track history is practical, predictable, and available to all.

Mr. Bauer's regularized, skills-based lessons correspond closely to the prevailing remedial model. Borrowing elements of a long-established theory of direct instruction (see Bloom, 1981, for a recent incarnation and Kliebard, 1986, for the history), the theory holds that if students are told explicitly what to perform and if they are provided unambiguous, step-by-step tasks, they will be able to concentrate without confusion on academic mastery.

During the first week of the school year, therefore, Mr. Bauer paints Additional Needs American History as common sense. With straight strokes, he delineates his expectations, depicts the reasonableness of classroom routines, matter-of-factly provides the structure that academically unsuccessful students presumably require, and renders "bookish" history a practical skill. His "no-nonsense" orientation to "the basics" reflects the dominant thinking about lower-track curriculum within the "tradition of discipline" at "working-class" Marshall.

"Good work habits" are what Mr. Bauer expects, he tells the 9th-grade Additional Needs students on their first day of high school. One of the most important habits is punctuality; a second is attendance. Mr. Bauer drives home his message about the importance of such clock-related work habits by telling a fable, one of his low-key devices for inculcating procedures:

> You know, I play tennis, and at the club, the bartender had a job opening. He was getting six or seven calls an hour about that job. That's the kind of times we live in. Now, suppose an employer called me about some students. Say, one student, student A, has been absent 50 times and tardy, 60 times. (He makes a chart of the students on the blackboard.) Student B, never absent or tardy. Student C, oh, absent 4 times and tardy 7 [times]. Student D, 45 and 30. Student E, 13 and 23. Now, who's not going to get my recommendation? (He begins to draw lines through students A, D, and E.) And, kids, I'm not even talking about educational qualifications, just about work habits, about showing up and being dependable. As young people going out into the world, I hope the unemployment rate will get better, but as young people moving into the world of work, it's important for you to get into good work habits now.

"Good work habits," which will pay off functionally as good job habits, are instilled through the assignment and assessment of daily, individual schoolwork, Mr. Bauer lectures. Therefore, the teacher provides time for work in class, just as many jobs require no extra at-home hours. Daily points and periodic test scores, like wages, are earned individually. By the end of the first class period, Mr. Bauer has "not even talked about educational qualifications" because, as he describes curriculum, school success hinges on adherence to routine.

By the end of the second period, Mr. Bauer has redefined history. He reduces an academic discipline that frames and clarifies multivocal, often controversial accounts of the past to grist for developing reading skills:

> Now, I want to talk this hour about history . . . [I]n this particular 9th-grade history class, we're less concerned about history and more concerned about improving your reading skills, graph skills, and your map reading skills. Would you believe, last year I had a student who had trouble remembering that the top of the map is North?! So we are going to learn geography, too. And I hope we are going to see some reading test improvement. We're going to start with U.S. history from the beginning. From a historical viewpoint, we'll move rapidly. But from a reading standpoint, we'll

take our time. You know, I like to think if we give you a bit every day, you'll get better over the long haul. But it takes patience and practice.

In the same lecture, the teacher also demystifies learning by rendering mind building as transparent as body building (on mental discipline, see Kliebard, 1986). Just as he worked determinedly to improve his tennis game over the summer, Mr. Bauer soliloquizes, so students should persevere in improving their reading skills through daily "bits" of practice on worksheet assignments. Reassuringly, Mr. Bauer's requirements are straightforward and within the reach of all: School success follows "patience and practice."

So important is patient practice that Mr. Bauer's "talk this hour about history" renders *what* students read less important than *how*. Like Mr. Thompson, Mr. Bauer minimizes the content of lower-track lessons. However, unlike Mr. Thompson, he promises a sure-fire method for success: SQRRR.

Letter by letter, the teacher describes and justifies "practical" reading. Before students read the daily chapter in the history textbook, Mr. Bauer intones, they should warm up by *Surveying* the selection. Noticing chapter titles and headings of sections, pictures, or charts "helps you figure out what you are going to read about." Students should also ask themselves *Questions* about the reading selection. As Mr. Bauer explains, this means looking at the questions at the end of the chapter: "If you don't have anything to look for when you're reading, if you're not set, you won't find anything." After these preparations, students actually *Read*, albeit always in a directed manner: "What do you read *for* when you read? For the answers to the questions you or the book or your teacher [have] created."

The last two letters of SQRRR, *Recite* and *Review*, emphasize that repetition is the heart of learning, as it is in physical training and good work habits. After Reading, students Recite or "say again," the answers to the questions in the text. In Additional Needs history, reciting is done by "writing the answers, it's the same thing as reciting." A third round of recitation is provided in the oral review of worksheet items, a fourth in a reading skills worksheet, and a fifth in its review.

Not surprisingly, then, the last "R," Review, is given the most importance in Mr. Bauer's explication. Turning again to a fable, the teacher justifies the elementary content and routines in Additional Needs history by reiterating the connection between physical exercises and doing the "exercises" at the end of the chapter:

Back in the sixties, kids came to school saying, "Oh, American History, we've done that before. I did geography in 8th grade. I did it once." Now, if you are on a baseball team, you'll do a lot of reviewing during batting practice. You've heard of Ted Williams, the "greatest natural hitter in baseball"? It's his last game, he's batting .400. Doesn't have to play the doubleheader, so he can go out with a lifetime average of .400. But he *wants* to play anyway. What happens? He gets seven hits with nine times at bat and goes out with .406. "Greatest natural hitter?" Talent? If you mean by that he went out for batting practice one-half hour early and stayed one-half hour late! Talent? Naw, he *worked* at it. You gotta review. Your brain works like this. You get an idea, it triggers some cells, if you never get that idea again, it goes away. If you hit that brain cell over and over again, it doesn't disappear. You may never be as good a reader as Ted Williams was a hitter, but you will get better.

Mr. Bauer's description and justification of the adaptive curriculum at Marshall, like Mr. Thompson's at Southmoor, rests on an ambiguous, socially acknowledged definition of lower-track students, portrayed in relation to the school's regular-track students. More than the school's "typical blue-collar kids" who, as "materialistic . . . consumers," are "anti-intellectual," interested in school but only for the "job ticket," and unimpressed with the knowledge teachers have and value, Additional Needs students are "unsocialized . . . even uncivilized." Mr. Bauer opines that they "are like puppy dogs. They're likeable, and I like to see them grow up over the year, but they've got to be trained." Training in school is important because students, "coming from families where both parents work and don't have time to supervise the kid," can be "behavior problems." More than a few have "an attitude" and that leads teachers to anticipate "explosions" if lessons "set students off."

The curriculum in common sense acknowledges and, paradoxically, provides for the re-creation of this mixed view of students. On the one hand, Mr. Bauer reasons that "working-class" students cannot quarrel with a "practical" content of "basic skills," whereas they might resist an abstract subject such as history; that even Additional Needs students recognize the direct usefulness of reading in a technological society, although they might object to literature; and that because reading skills require no specialized techniques or ambiguous processes but can be mastered by all through simple drill and practice, students will "buy in" to the routine.

In this way, Mr. Bauer uses knowledge to assuage ambivalent students'

doubts about school, assuring them that all can succeed if only they practice. Simultaneously, he controls behavior unobtrusively by controlling
knowledge. In other words, the curriculum in common sense provides
the training that students with "attitudes" and skill deficits need and it
protects against "explosions" from the "uncivilized." Thus, in practice,
Mr. Bauer limits inquiry and controversial topics that might prompt
disagreements by focusing on neutral facts and skill development. For
example, he transforms the open-ended question "Do you agree that the
U.S. is a melting pot?" to a safe one by remarking: "Everybody gets two
points for that one. Any answer you have is right, because this is an 'agree'
question." Mr. Bauer also takes few chances with student spontaneity,
opting instead for a routine so regular that students never have to ask
what the next assignment will be. In contrast to the supremely self-confi-
dent, personalized note struck by Mr. Thompson at Southmoor, Mr. Bauer
provides remote control teaching on automatic pilot.

On the other hand, no matter how user friendly, the curriculum in
common sense exacerbates students' ambivalence about schooling and,
paradoxically, distances students from knowledge so that even greater
control measures appear sensible. First, school knowledge is so simplified
that students wonder whether learning it is worthwhile. The repetitive
worksheets render knowledge about American history or reading skills
trivial and, even though the exercises count, students undertake them
lackadaisically.

Furthermore, although Mr. Bauer's curriculum in common sense
appears self-evidently useful and reassuringly simple, a contradiction lies
at its center: School knowledge is *not* common sense. Drawn from the
disciplines, school knowledge presents (or is supposed to present) distinctive, systematic efforts to confront and sort out the perplexities of the
world. It is not supposed to work, as common sense does, to close such
questions down. In the same way, knowing in schools is not a commonplace; it requires specialized talents, interests, and aspirations, not to
mention luck.

Mr. Bauer and his students experience the paradoxes of a commonsensical curriculum in ordinary lessons. The first instance occurs on the
fifth day of the school year. Mr. Bauer announces, somewhat surprisingly
in the Marshall milieu, that he wants students to become "active readers:
readers who ask questions as they read." Reasoning that if students generate their own questions their comprehension scores will improve, he
adds a reading exercise to the daily homework: Before reading and answering questions, students will skim the chapter, creating one question of
their own for each of its paragraphs.

"Active reading" and "creativity" are curricular buzzwords. They are given local meaning when Mr. Bauer translates them, drawing on Marshall's "tradition of discipline." Thus, he begins by directing students to the chapter for the next day: "Look at the first paragraph of the chapter and read the first sentence, *just the first sentence*, of the paragraph, and create a question. Who can make a question based on that first sentence?" (The chapter concerns Cortez's conquest of Mexico; the first sentence reads, "The central and eastern parts of Mexico were ruled by an Indian people called the Aztecs.") A boy volunteers: "What are Aztecs?" Mr. Bauer accepts this response, saying to the whole class, "Okay, write that down, 'What are Aztecs?'"

This auspicious beginning in creating questions is short-lived, however, as students' questions for subsequent paragraphs prove unacceptable. "Now, read the first sentence of paragraph two. To yourself. Now, can somebody create a question for me?" (The sentence in the text is: "Many young men came from Spain to the New World to seek their fortunes.") This time the student's suggestion, "What kind of fortunes were they looking for?" is negatively evaluated: "I would have asked a different question." Mr. Bauer then points the "active readers" in the right direction by reminding them of a handy, question-making formula: "Let's remember, what are the five basic questions?" In unison students chorus "who, what, where, when, and how." "What kind," not being in the refrain, is not the right kind of question. With no further discussion, Mr. Bauer asks: "Who can make another question?" A girl volunteers: "Who are these explorers?"

Then, however, even with the question-making formula, students run into further difficulties. The third paragraph, beginning with "Cortez had been able to conquer the powerful Aztecs with only 600 men," presents trouble. Using one of the "five basic questions," a student asks: "Who was Cortez?" But Mr. Bauer objects, saying, "Now look at that sentence again . . . Anybody want to take another one of the five?" With no discussion as to how one selects from among the five interrogatives, a second student randomly takes another: "When did Cortez do this?" Again, this is not the answer Mr. Bauer has in mind. Dissatisfied, he hints: "I've got a feeling the author wants you to ask that hard question, you know the one I mean?" With this prompt, a third attempt is successful. Mr. Bauer comments: "Good. 'How did Cortez conquer them?' I would suggest you use the 'how.'"

As Mr. Bauer and the class continue through the paragraphs, the "active" routine becomes increasingly daunting. Told to create questions, students find that they are to use preformulated questions. When the formulae fail, as they must, effort wanes. Promised certain success, students become testy when it is not forthcoming. In time, they refuse altogether to be "active" in reading. Confronting a deepening silence, Mr. Bauer begins to provide the answers. Within three days, he gives up on requiring students to create their own questions, explaining that he is dissatisfied with them: "They don't know how to ask good questions, and it's less chancy if I do it. If the students practice answering my questions, some of it (generating questions) will seep into their heads."

Hitting a baseball "over and over again" may have worked for Ted Williams, but "hitting a brain cell over and over again" has mixed effects for Mr. Bauer's 9th graders. It affects students' "batting averages" on history quizzes and report cards inconsistently. Because lessons in common sense are both simple and mindless, they invite yet discourage students' willingness to "come out for extra practice." Over the course of the school year, students' patience and willingness to practice in Additional Needs American History fluctuates, prompting an ever more controlling regimen.

At both Southmoor and Marshall, Additional Needs students present "different," and problematic, characters. Accordingly, in both schools, students' academic progress is less important than whether they try. In both Mr. Bauer's and Mr. Thompson's descriptions of lower-track curriculum, school knowledge receives passing attention at best.

For all the similarities in the two schools, however, the nature of the problem that diverse students pose, the curricular response to it, and students' responses to school lessons are dramatically different. At Southmoor, personable "professionals" assume responsibility for providing relevant lessons and an indulgent atmosphere for students who are "the dregs" of the academic hierarchy. Because Additional Needs students "drink from the cultural stream" of the school, they agree the school is "heavenly," they characterize teachers as "nice" adults who are on their side, and they say Additional Needs World History and *Time* have some "relevance." With a positive view of the school, they blame themselves when they fail to make academic progress in lower-track classes. Lower-track placement and school failure are stigmatizing at Southmoor. Lower-track students, despite considerable advantages, resolve the problem by dropping out at an astonishing rate of about 50%. Ironically, their absence serves to confirm Southmoor's reputation as a preeminently academic institution.

At "nothing-out-of-the-ordinary" Marshall, students who are as advantaged as Southmoor's drink from a different "cultural stream" and make something rather different of lower-track lessons, schooling, and self. There, remote taskmasters oversee dispassionate training in practical, basic skills for students who, not yet "socialized to the school," threaten it. In this milieu, students agree that schooling is unexceptional, lessons are work, knowledge should be utilitarian, and the teacher is "the boss," if not "the enemy." Accordingly, playing the system makes sense. As one student put it, choosing to "drop down" to an "easier," lower-track class is a "smart con" because schooling is not very consequential anyway. At the same time, when students experience trouble in Additional Needs classes, they blame "the system," thereby regenerating the disdain for school that teachers attribute to them. Nevertheless, fewer lower-track students at Marshall drop out than at Southmoor. The pedestrian school responds commonsensically to their difficulties by providing further differentiated, "low-low" classes.

CONCLUSION

These sketches of curriculum take two directions. The first traces descriptions of curriculum, notably lower-track curriculum, to argue the complexity and subtle power of ordinary school lessons. If curriculum is a meaningful, meaning-making enterprise, it is particularly worthy of consideration as a resource that schools may use to respond to diverse students. Worthy lessons are the least we can expect of schools (even though they are most difficult to get right). Lessons cannot rearrange the world, abolish poverty, secure the future, or generate love, but they can provide children, and teachers, with an experience of themselves among others (Geertz, 1986). With that, like Thami and Isabel in Athol Fugard's play, youth may appropriate knowledge, know themselves by knowing others, and, in relation, play meaningful parts.

Seen thus—with modest expectation—curriculum nevertheless requires our thoughtful attention, and particularly that of teachers. Relying on truisms, whether about "difference," "relevance," "basic skills," or any other curricular idea, we risk lessons that lack direction and go awry in irony, and sometimes brutality. Planning ordinary lessons requires sustained attention to commonplace, often ambiguous, assumptions: about the bases on which we group students together and, simultaneously, set them apart (for example, ability, age, race, class, gender, appearance, behavior, illness, disability, language, drugs, pregnancy, single-parent family); about what does, does not, and might go on in that most intimate of public places, the classroom; about the relationship that does and should exist between processes of curricular and cultural differentiation; and about the worlds we educators bring into view using the language, and perhaps more often, the vernacular of education.

Because curriculum is "local school knowledge," people in and associated with local schools must pay attention to it. This is what makes curriculum so complicated. It cannot be managed from afar, standardized with mandates, or leveraged with testing (or funds associated with test scores); not, at least, without such unintended consequences as driving careful teachers out of the profession or securing small and unstable test gains at great cost to children. Neither can curriculum be wrought by valiant individuals, notwithstanding inspirational appeals in one-day workshops or bully-pulpit reports that encourage everyone to do their best despite a bad system (or in a good-enough one). Curriculum is a social construction, wrought within the semibounded cultures of distinctive schools. To define and clarify school knowledge requires continuing, deliberative discourse among a school's local publics.

Following in this direction, I can imagine and hope that scholars in education might be invited to contribute to local deliberations over curriculum. We might provide university classes that acknowledge the process. We might furnish knowledge about other instances of schooling and analytic constructs from curricular and sociocultural studies, so that, through comparisons, local teachers might meaningfully comprehend their own practices. Overall, we have resources that teachers, in re-structured schools, can use to move beyond a commonsensical curricular sensibility.

The second direction these sketches take grows out of the first to consider the value of research about diverse students and schools for teachers. This tack has diverged unexpectedly, as I follow it with Geertz's notion of common sense and Mr. Bauer's and Mr. Thompson's talk about lower-track lessons close at hand. I find, with not a little irony and chagrin, that I have not managed to put my money altogether where my mouth is.

I assume that teachers, like most people, read little educational research. This may reflect the predominance of the big-picture perspective that, passing over life where most teachers live it, fails to inform teachers about their concerns. It may also be that school structures allow teachers little time to do the reading and thinking that professionalism requires. It may be that there are better things to read or to do.

However, I became suspicious that something else may be going on as well when, in rereading the interviews with the two teachers, I felt as though a student was running a fingernail down the black board. I have had this sensation before, but in the past, I have always passed over it, regarding it as a personal predilection for reflection and empathy with lower-track students. This time around, however, I wondered if it might signal the unequal power relations that any encounter between researcher-from-the-university and practitioner-from-the-school can engender. And I wonder if *this* "difference" figures in whether research about diverse students influences teachers.

In a researcher-interviewing-practitioner context, common sense may be an apt way for teachers to represent curriculum because it is a perfect assault on and defense against "high IQ morons" (Geertz, 1982b, p. 76) from the university who have lots of good ideas for how teachers can do better. It challenges scholars, who come defined by their specializations in formal disciplines, but in its very nature, it is unassailable.

Considering this, I suspect I did not and have not understood, sympathetically, teachers' commonsensical portrayals of curriculum. Instead, I regard them as *merely* commonsensical, as not *my* common sense, and as something to correct and move past (the first direction taken by these sketches). This means two things: First, I am not engaging much in inquiry; second, I am looking down my nose, treating the teachers as disrespectfully as I often saw them treating lower-track students.

In reconsidering this, therefore, I formulate an agenda for myself, to go along with that for practitioners. It begins with taking teachers' commonsensical curricular sensibility on its own terms. What is its source? How does it arise in schools to form the "musculature of everyday life" (Geertz, 1982a)? What is the potentially positive value of curricular common sense? For example, if Geertz is right that common sense is one of the first efforts to give the world shape, does pedagogical lore, like folklore or herbal lore, carry information that the science and the art of education, in rationalizing schooling, have somehow elided? In what instances, specifically, do teachers use common sense and when do they turn to more formal systems, and what does each open to view? How do teachers sustain faith in common sense, an important question when so many studies of schooling and recommendations from policymakers assault teachers' traditionalism yet, as Sarason (1971) notes, "the more things change, the more they stay the same."

The second agenda item concerns doing some hard thinking about my own, presumably less colloquial, reasoning about curriculum. Understanding "the temper" and "turn of mind" (Geertz, 1982b, p. 84) of commonsensical reasoning, I may clarify the differences and similarities between scholars' "worked-up shapes of studied culture" and teachers' "rough-cast shapes of colloquial culture" (Geertz, 1982b, p. 74).

Finally, I may contemplate that teachers' commonsensical portraits of curriculum are fundamental to theorizing better about what a school is, what kinds there are, what school knowledge is, and how schools translate and distribute knowledge among diverse students. This is not to suggest that teachers' common sense about curriculum is correct and that if scholars would only credit it, the mysteries of education would dissolve. When teachers do not reflect on the lessons they teach, curriculum goes awry in unintended consequences, as we see happening in the good schools, with good teachers and good students, in Maplehurst. Instead, it is a focus on Geertz' hypothesis that common sense is an older, mediating suburb in the metropolis of culture, not as straightly laid out as the remote suburbs of art, religion, science, or law, but not as twisted as the walled city. With this perspective, explicating the vernacular of education may be a means of connecting education as a fundamental sociocultural process, educational studies as a discipline, and education as a schooled practice. As I understand a bit better, getting these into closer proximity with each other is, at least in part, what forging a relationship between research and practice is all about.

NOTES

1. All names are pseudonyms.

2. The two cases are drawn from a larger educational ethnography (Page, 1991) that probes the meaning of lower-track placement for teachers, students, and curriculum; how meaning is constructed; and how classroom constructions are related to wider institutional and sociocultural circumstances such as age, ability, race, or social class. Conducted during the 1982–1983 school year, it entailed regular observation and participation in the lower-track classes of nine teachers of English and social studies and, less regularly, in their regular-track classes. Interviews were conducted with the teachers and many of the lower-track students as well as with other faculty members in the schools and the district; documents were collected; and selected lower-track lessons were audiotaped. Taken together, these strategies furnish data about participants' curricular and cultural knowledge.

3. George Spindler has long urged anthropologists and other scholars to study ordinary high schools.

4. Quotation marks designate the words of people in Maplehurst, unless otherwise specified. I also indicate characteristics of talk using the following symbols: emphasis by italics and greater emphasis by CAPITAL LETTERS; ellipsis by . . . ; and descriptions or explanations of the situation by (parentheses). The quotations have been slightly edited to remove indications of pauses and elongated proununciation.

5. I follow Waller (1932) and Schlechty (1976) in conceptualizing the culture of a school as arising in the interaction between its definition of students and its definition of faculty modes of operation. For empirical studies of structurally similar but culturally different schools, see Lightfoot (1983), Metz (1978; 1986), and Page (1989).

6. For an extended account of the cultures of Southmoor and Marshall and their relationship to lower-track curriculum, see Page (1991).

7. Varenne (1986) distinguishes culture as shared meaning and as acknowledged meaning to call attention to the coercive power of culture.

8. For descriptions of lower-track students' perspectives on curriculum and other faculty members', see Page (1991).

REFERENCES

Bellah, R., Madsen, R., Sullivan, W., Swidler, A., & Tipton, S. (1985). *Habits of the heart: Individualism and commitment in American life.* New York: Harper & Row.

Bloom, B. (1981). *All our children learning.* New York: McGraw-Hill.

Bourdieu, P., & Passeron, J. (1977). *Reproduction: In education, society, and culture.* Beverly Hills, CA: Sage.

Dewey, J. (1956). *The child and the curriculum.* Chicago: University of Chicago Press. (Original work published 1902)

Edelman, M. (1977). *Political language: Words that succeed and policies that fail.* New York: Academic Press.

Erickson, F. (1986). Qualitative methods in research on-teaching. In M. Wittrock (Ed.), *Handbook of research on teaching* (3rd ed., pp. 119–161). New York: Macmillan.

Fugard, A. (1989). *My children! My Africa!* New York: Theater Communications Group.

Geertz, C. (1973). *The interpretation of cultures: Selected essays.* New York: Basic Books.

Geertz, C. (1982a). Local knowledge: Fact and law in comparative perspective. In C. Geertz, *Local knowledge: Further essays in interpretive anthropology* (pp. 167–234). New York: Basic Books.

Geertz, C. (1982b). Common sense as a cultural system. In C. Geertz, *Local knowledge: Further essays in interpretive anthropology* (pp. 73–93). New York: Basic Books.

Geertz, C. (1986). The uses of diversity. In *The Tanner lectures on human values* (pp. 253–275). Salt Lake City UT: University of Utah Press.

Goodlad, J. (1984). *A place called school: Prospects for the future.* New York: McGraw-Hill.

Henry, J. (1963). *Culture against man.* New York: Random House.

Kammen, M. (1974). *People of paradox: An inquiry concerning the origins of American civilization.* New York: Knopf.

Keddie, N. (1971). Classroom knowledge. In M.F.D. Young (Ed.), *Knowledge and control: New directions for the sociology of education* (pp. 133–150). London: Collier-Macmillan.

Kliebard, H. (1986). *The struggle for the American curriculum: 1893–1958.* London: Routledge and Kegan Paul.

Lightfoot, S. (1983). *The good high school: Portraits of character and culture.* New York: Basic Books.

McNeil, L. (1986). *Contradictions of control: School structure and school knowledge.* London: Routledge and Kegan Paul.

Merelman, R. (1984). *Making something of ourselves: On culture and politics in the United States.* Berkeley: University of California Press.

Metz, M. (1978). *Classrooms and corridors: The crisis of authority in desegregated secondary schools.* Berkeley: University of California Press.

Metz, M. (1986). *Different by design: the context and character of three magnet schools.* London: Routledge and Kegan Paul.

Oakes, J. (1985). *Keeping track: How schools structure inequality.* New Haven, CT: Yale University Press.

Oakes, J. (1990). *Multiplying inequalities: The effects of race, social class, and tracking on opportunities to learn math and science.* Santa Monica, CA: The RAND Corporation.

Page, R. (1989). Cultures and curricula: Differences between and within schools. *Educational Foundations, 4,* 49–76.

Page, R. (1991). *Lower-track classrooms: A curricular and cultural perspective.* New York: Teachers College Press.

Riesman, D., with Glazer, N., & Denny, R. (1950). *The lonely crowd: A study of the changing American character.* New Haven, CT: Yale University Press.

Sarason, S. (1971). *The culture of the school and the problem of change.* Boston: Allyn & Bacon.

Schlechty, P. (1976). *Teaching and social behavior: Towards an organizational theory of instruction.* Boston: Allyn & Bacon.

Schwab, J. (1977). The practical: A language for curriculum. In A. Bellack & H. Kliebard (Eds.), *Curriculum and evaluation* (pp. 26–44). Berkeley, CA: McCutchan. (Original work published 1969)

Spindler, G. (Ed.). (1982). *Doing the ethnography of schooling: Educational anthropology in action.* New York: Holt, Rinehart & Winston.

Spindler, G., & Spindler, L. (1982). Roger Harker and Schonhausen: From familiar to strange and back again. In G. Spindler (Ed.), *Doing the ethnography of schooling* (pp. 20–46). New York: Holt, Rinehart & Winston.

Spindler, G., & Spindler, L., with Trueba, H., & Williams, M. (1990). *The American cultural dialogue and its transmission.* London: Falmer Press.

Valli, L. (1990). A curriculum of effort: Tracking students in a Catholic high school. In R. Page & L. Valli (Eds.), *Curriculum differentiation: Interpretive studies in U.S. secondary schools* (pp. 45–66). Albany: State University of New York Press.

Varenne, H. (1977). *Americans together: Structured diversity in a midwestern town.* New York: Teachers College Press.

Varenne, H. (Ed.). (1986). *Symbolizing America.* Lincoln: University of Nebraska Press.

Waller, W. (1932). *The sociology of teaching.* New York: John Wiley & Sons.

Wise, A. (1979). *Legislated learning: The bureaucratization of the American classroom.* Berkeley: University of California Press.

CHAPTER 7

CULTURAL DIVERSITY AND CONFLICT: THE ROLE OF EDUCATIONAL ANTHROPOLOGY IN HEALING MULTICULTURAL AMERICA

Henry T. Trueba

It is a common belief that traditional democratic principles led this country to open its doors to immigrant groups from all over the world, and to create the conditions that permitted these individuals to succeed precisely because, as citizens, they had rights equal to those of U.S.-born Americans. Members of ethnic group after ethnic group managed, over time, to become integral and successful participants in American social institutions. The civil rights struggles of the mid-20th century strengthened and further clarified this interpretation of democratic principles.

As American society becomes more complex, both socially and culturally, it is becoming increasingly polarized along economic and ideological lines. Economists alert us to the increasing gap between the rich and the poor, the media alert us to the rising number of hate groups. The fear of ethnics has motivated neo-Nazis to organize vigilante raids and Ku Klux Klan members to infiltrate political parties. We argue bitterly over how our schools should be organized for cultural diversity, with conservatives advocating monolingualism and monocultural policies (through the English-only Movement) and others, such as the scholars in this volume, arguing for a multicultural approach, including bilingual education.

All this comes at a time in our history when many Americans from all socioeconomic quarters and ethnic backgrounds feel victimized, disenfranchised, angry, displaced, and unhappy about the prospects for their, and their children's, futures. The rise in unemployment, particularly among certain minority groups, and the decaying quality of life in urban

America signal to the public that "something is very wrong in America." Senior citizens are warehoused in larger numbers or are seen homeless and sick in our streets. Young families—ethnic and nonethnic—find themselves in poverty despite their continued efforts to escape their misery. And American cultural values are changing in ways previously unforeseen.

The main reason to make these points is that both social scientists and the general public see a relationship between crises in modern American society (i.e., unemployment, interethnic conflict, alienated youth) and schooling. America has experienced poverty, cultural conflict, and intolerance of linguistic and racial diversity in previous decades. However, what is unique about America's sociopolitical climate today is that the public blames schools for not assimilating ethnics quickly enough. Citizens, assuming that academic decay is the result of cultural diversity, are bringing a sense of urgency to questions about the impact of cultural diversity on achievement and the quality of learning environments. Schools, blamed and scapegoated for the incompetence of the labor force and the overall decay of American technological and economic infrastructures, are also asked to address many social ills, including ethnic conflict and the low academic achievement of children from various ethnic groups. However, citizens do not often talk of investing additional resources; they want discipline and competence with a minimum dollar investment.

Today's educators are not sure whether or how they might begin to control the damage that families are inflicting on their own children or how to heal a society that fosters anger and racial hatred. The purpose of this chapter is to present and analyze some current anthropological thinking about the role of schools in healing America's wounds and preparing our children to face the challenges of the next century. Educational anthropology attempts to identify the schooling experience of children and the role of the family in children's education from the perspective of the home culture, and to examine school problems in their cultural context. More concretely, this chapter asks the following questions:

1. Are the problems faced by schools part of larger systemic problems in American society? Are current national attempts to rectify the problems in schools merely *reformist*, thus ultimately doomed because they only address symptoms and not the root causes of our educational problems? Can we blame schools for racism, intolerance of cultural diversity, and the isolation of ethnic communities?
2. What are some of the current theoretical explanations of underachievement, disempowerment, and disenfranchisment? Are these explanations adequate?

3. Can anthropological research provide a starting point from which to think about these problems? Is "cultural therapy," for example, part of the solution?

THE PROBLEM IN ITS SOCIAL CONTEXT

Perhaps the overall feeling of hopelessness expressed by educators working in low-income and ethnic neighborhood schools that are often plagued by drugs, homicide, prostitution, gang warfare, pollution, and hunger is only the tip of an iceberg, the iceberg of a new America that has changed radically. For example, in 1980 there were 34.6 million speakers (15% of the total population) of languages other than English in America (Waggoner, 1988, pp. 79–81). The largest group, with 15.5 million people, was Spanish speaking (45% of all language minorities). Groups speaking French, German, Italian, and Polish each numbered at least one million, and 30 other language groups had at least 100,000 persons each. Of these foreign-language speakers, 2.6 million were children under age 5 and 7.9 million were school-age youth.

As 52% of the school-age children living in language minority families, the 4.2 million Spanish-speaking school-age children constitute a particularly important demographic group.[1] Spanish-speaking children in America live in families with incomes that barely permit them to subsist. In the last 10 years, an additional one million Latino (Hispanic) children joined the ranks of the poor (a family of four with an annual income under $10,000). In 1989, a total of 2.6 million Hispanic children (out of 7.2 million total) were poor, and most of them lived in urban and suburban areas. In 1989, 48.4% of all Puerto Rican children were poor, 37.1% of all Mexican children were poor, and 26.1% of Central and South American children were poor. The use of home languages (such as Spanish) and the low socioeconomic status of ethnic groups are important features of their isolation.

To complicate matters, increasing cultural and linguistic diversity comes at a time when America seems to be giving up its commitment to educating these children. The wave of intolerance for the instructional use of languages other than English is reaching its peak, and educational reform is viewed by many as an attempt to disperse funds provided by taxpayers to "immigrant populations." Indeed, many families (particularly African-American families) seem to have been disregarded and forgotten by our society.

Take the following scenario for the purpose of discussion. The details are drawn from the description of East St. Louis in *Savage Inequali-*

ties (1991), a book in which Kozol describes a number of inner-city communities. East St. Louis, whose population is 98% African American, is a city with 75% unemployment and no trash collection. It is a city clouded with toxic fumes from chemical companies, where one third of the population earns less than $7,500 per year. The city attracted a number of industries in the first two decades of this century. However, in 1917, in an attempt to break white unions, employers brought many blacks from the South and, during the depression, most of these companies left town, leaving thousands of unemployed black parents behind. A short-lived bonanza during World War II resulted in a peak population of 80,000 residents, which by 1970 had decreased to less than 50,000. Today, chemical companies have purchased entire blocks of homes to prevent potential lawsuits that could arise from frequent toxic spills. Occasionally, sirens call for mass evacuations, the closing of schools, and the hospitalization of residents. Two years ago, some 450 residents were taken to the hospital after 300 gallons of phosphorous trichloride were spilled. Upon release, each resident received $400 to exonerate the company from any liability.

East St. Louis has very sick children and ranks among the cities in Illinois with the highest premature birth and fetal death rates. The average daily food expenditure for children is only $2.40, and many children are not immunized for polio, diphtheria, measles, or whooping cough. East St. Louis is crowded with filth (backed up raw sewage often inundates school buildings), and it has become the theater of violent death, with one of the highest rates of homicide in Illinois. Within this environment, pathos and misery are everyday experiences.

As if the city's unhealthy environment was not enough, these children come to schools in deplorable condition. East St. Louis schools are not only dilapidated and grossly underfunded, but a risk to children's health. The science labs at East St. Louis High, for example, are 30 to 50 years outdated. Kozol (1991) writes: "John McMillan, a soft-spoken man, teaches physics at the school. He shows me the lab. The six lab stations in the room have empty holes where pipes were once attached. 'It would be great if we had water,' says McMillan" (p. 27). Kozol summarizes his visit to a school as follows:

> Before I leave the school, I take a final stroll along the halls. In a number
> of classrooms, groups of children seem to be involved in doing nothing.
> Sometimes there's a teacher present, doing something at his desk. Some-
> times there's no adult in the room. . . . In one of the unattended classrooms
> on the second floor, seven students stand around a piano. When I stick my
> head into the room, they smile and invite me to come in. . . . One of the

students, a heavyset young woman, steps out just before the others. When she sings, her pure soprano voice transforms the room. "Sometimes I feel like a motherless child," she begins. The pianist gazes up at her with an attentive look of admiration. (p. 33)

Kozol pauses to reflect on what is happening as he tours one of the most depressed school environments he ever encountered. He writes:

> The loveliness and aesthetic isolation of the singer in the squalor of the school and city bring to my mind the words of Dr. Lillian Parks, the super-intendent of the East St. Louis schools. Dr. Parks says: "Gifted children are everywhere in East St. Louis, but their gifts are lost to poverty and turmoil and the damage done by knowing they are written off by their society. Many of these children have no sense of something they belong to. They have no feeling of belonging to America. . . . There is a terrible beauty in some of these girls—terrible, I mean, because it is ephemeral, foredoomed." (pp. 33–34)

Kozol is talking about survival and societal factors that create disenchanted and disenfranchised youth. How typical, how generalizable are the observations made by Kozol in East St. Louis and other cities (Chicago, New York, and San Antonio)? The "terrible beauty" of many children in America has yet to be discovered in many other places in the country. However, even without encountering the extreme situations described by Kozol, many of our nation's educators voice similar despair.

In light of Kozol's graphic and disturbing images, today's government-sponsored reports on educational reform seem hopelessly naive and un-realistic. For example, in *What Work Requires of Schools: A SCANS Report for America 2000*, the Secretary's Commission on Achieving Necessary Skills (SCANS) (U.S. Department of Labor, June 1991) recommends the follow-ing:

1. Define the skills needed for employment.
2. Propose acceptable levels of proficiency.
3. Suggest effective ways to assess proficiency.
4. Develop a dissemination strategy for the nation's schools, busi-nesses, and homes.

The report also stresses the notion that "good jobs will increasingly depend on people who can put knowledge to work" and that "more than half of our young people leave school without the knowledge or founda-tion required to find and hold a good job" (pp. xv–xvi). The report talks about the need to improve reading, writing, mathematical reasoning, and computational skills, as well as to improve the interpersonal skills necessary for working as a team member in work settings and the cognitive skills necessary to search for, evaluate, and organize information, and to handle complex systems (social, technological, and financial). However, even assuming that teachers possess the background to teach these required skills, it is doubtful that they can convince youth of the worth of such knowledge in urban schools plagued with the problems outlined by Kozol.

The reason for raising these issues is to point out that the "problem" of schools is described in entirely different terms by different groups of educators and analysts. In other words, there is no consensus as to the roots of the problem. It may be the teachers, but it may also be that cultural disenfranchisement has segregated minority-student populations and communities from American institutions.

CURRENT ANTHROPOLOGICAL EXPLANATIONS OF THE PROBLEM

Many of the students who seem to lack higher-order thinking skills and the personal qualities to succeed in school share a common characteristic: they are socially marginal, isolated, and neglected. These youngsters are victims of the new American society. How do we explain this widespread phenomenon? Is this a serious social structural problem (i.e., stemming from the government or the organization of educational institutions)? Is there a social disease leading to general neglect and abandonment of school children and youth? Does America need healing?

Explanations of minority school children's failure (academic and socioeconomic) have been discussed by educational anthropologists for the last 20 years. More recently, the debate over these explanations has focused on a number of theories, including "cultural ecological" theories of school failure and success (DeVos, 1973, 1983; Gibson 1987, 1988; Ogbu, 1974, 1978, 1987, 1989; Suarez-Orozco, 1989, 1990, 1991; Suarez-Orozco & Suarez-Orozco, 1991; Wagatsuma & DeVos, 1984). The cultural ecological perspective focuses specifically on castification, a process whereby ethnolinguistic, low-income, or racial groups find themselves disempowered to function in American society (especially in schools). This process is explained both in terms of the macrosociological factors that determine the status of these groups and their relative access to resources and other means of participation in mainstream institutions, and in terms of psychosocial mechanisms for the development of castelike ethnic identities. Concretely, the development of an ethnic identity that is defined in opposition to that of mainstream persons creates a castelike person. The conflict embedded in such a definition results from viewing successful participation in mainstream society (especially school achievement) as "selling out," or giving away one's own identity.

Although cultural ecological explanations have been very instrumental in understanding the failure of some groups, they have been criticized for not explaining the success of other groups, or differential performance within groups, either synchronically or diachronically. Many scholars view the application of the castelike ethnic identity as stereotypic and problematic, particularly because castelike attributes vary within groups and even within families of the same group. The reservations about the application of this model, however, should not overshadow the central contributions of cultural ecologists to our understanding of the role of macrosocial factors (organizational structural features) that are used in a given culture to prevent full and successful participation of some individuals in social institutions.

Other educational anthropologists have emphasized cultural explanations of the problem. George and Louise Spindler, central figures in the founding of educational anthropology, first stated a basic premise that they articulate in this volume in the mid-1950s: culture is "in process, in everything that we do, say or think, in or out of school" (Spindler, 1987). The Spindlers see school as "a mandated cultural process" in which the teacher is a cultural agent. This, of course, assumes that the role of teachers is to socialize children to American cultural values, that is, to "transmit" American culture (Spindler & Spindler, 1990). If my interpretation is correct, the Spindlers view today's schools as institutions that are systematically alienating children and creating cultural conflicts. These conflicts ultimately result in irreversible (permanent) marginalization of students in society.

The central theoretical premises that the Spindlers present are built around concepts of self-identity. They distinguish between the "enduring self" and "situated self" in this volume and in other writings (1992). The enduring self is built during the early socialization stages and is retained by the individual for life. For George Spindler, for example, the enduring self is founded in the lakes, forests, and landscapes of Wisconsin, where he spent his childhood, and in the midwest, where German and Scandinavian cultures shaped the land, minds, and lifestyle of many Americans (Spindler & Spindler, 1989).

The situated self reflects the changes that we are forced to make in new settings with diverse cultural values and life-styles. It is constructed as an effort to adjust to new settings, that is, to the immediate realities of modern life. George Spindler's situated self at Stanford took reality as he became a high-achieving intellectual who played key roles in the American Anthropological Association, published many books and articles, guided the form and content of hundreds of publications, participated in public forums and professional conferences, and taught thousands of students during his career. In some sense, Spindler was uprooted from the rural Midwest. In a similar sense, many children have been uprooted from their culture of origin. As these children attempt to adjust to new sociocultural (and linguistic) school settings, many face intense feelings of marginality. These feelings, generated out of the conflicts that can arise between the home cultural environment that nourishes the enduring self and the new environment that requires a situated self, are deeply embedded. The crises these children confront have been addressed in the anthropological literature under many rubrics. But ultimately, as George Spindler suggests, they can result in the development of an "endangered self." This term, I believe, means that the essential cohesiveness of the personality is in danger, for the individual cannot establish a healthy relationship between the enduring and situated selves. Further, the alienation caused by schooling seems to suggest that many children can never successfully develop a situated self that permits them to participate effectively in American institutions.

In their chapter in this volume, the Spindlers explore the differential adjustment patterns of ethnolinguistic, racial, and other minority groups to mainstream American culture. They describe four basic types of responses to cultural conflict (i.e., the conflict resulting from cultural contact with persons from other cultural groups), especially contact associated with oppression. Although the typology presented by the Spindlers (1984) is drawn from data collected during the years they spent with the Menominee Indians of Wisconsin, it also applies to the adjustment of other ethnic minority groups.

1. *Nativistic:* A nativistic response is the rejection of foreign cultural values because they are seen as incompatible with recognized and accepted home cultural values. This position is often accompanied by profound commitment to the maintenance of the home language and culture.
2. *Transitional:* A transitional response is suspended support for any cultural values—a noncommittal position with respect to both the cultural values associated with the home culture and the new cultural values associated with mainstream society.
3. *Assimilationist:* An assimilationist response is a rejection of home values (including language and culture) and acceptance of new mainstream cultural values.

4. *Multicultural:* A multicultural response accepts in principle the compatibility of cultural values from both the home and mainstream cultures. It is characterized by willingness to acquire the language of mainstream members of society without giving up one's home language.

By implication, the nativistic, transitional, and assimilationist responses of some minority children may be guided by lack of grounding in their home language and culture for the period necessary to develop a strong enduring self. The uprooting of these children may interrupt the process of self-identity. In the context of cultural contact between mainstream persons and those from different linguistic and cultural backgrounds, I believe that the least conflictive position is taken by those persons who adopt a multicultural response. The psychological justification for retaining one's enduring self, a personal framework for self-understanding and for self-acceptance, the setting to which we feel attached as children, the quintessence of what we are in our own eyes, remains unchanged, regardless of other adjustments. The enduring self is the basis of deeper emotional peace and stability. If forced to abandon this inner frame of reference, a child is isolated from the world of his dreams and the world of his affection. Sooner or later a child will comprehend that the rejection of one's own language and culture is ultimately the rejection of one's own self. How can a child deal with two different worlds and transfer information from one to the other if the bridge between the two (the language) is broken? How can a child retain a measure of psychological integrity if he or she is not allowed to reconcile conflicting values from home and school? How can a child be enriched by his home learning environment if going home is seen as degrading? How can a child seek emotional and cognitive support from parents who are seen as unworthy and despicable?

In their chapter, the Spindlers advance the notion of cultural therapy[2] as a means to compare and contrast cultural values and understandings, enhance communication, and resolve conflicts arising from misunderstandings in interethnic or intercultural exchanges. I take the concept of cultural therapy advanced by the Spindlers to mean the healing that can result from understanding one's own culture and the culture of those with whom one interacts. A strong personal cultural or ethnic identity is obtained by legitimizing and recognizing an individual's enduring self. From my perspective, there are at least two ways in which cultural therapy can help. First, it can help people to develop a strong personal identity based on a better known and better understood cultural background. Second, cultural therapy can also increase an individual's ability to identify areas of value conflict, differences in interpretation of messages and expectations, and the range of acceptable etiquette, preferential protocol, and other expected behavioral responses.

One of the premises embedded in the notion of cultural therapy is that it can enhance our ability to make appropriate adjustments during cultural contact, and thus permit us to develop a new situated self. A strong cultural self-identity is, by implication, viewed as necessary in order to adjust to new settings demanding a new behavioral repertoire and a lifestyle different from the lifestyle associated with our enduring self. In other words, we are better able to adapt and change when there is something that remains consistent and that will always be part of our identity or survival kit. Perhaps the development of instrumental competencies[3] is linked to the strength of our enduring self and our ability to adopt new situated selves as required. One could speculate that the development of these competencies is deeply linked to the opportunity children have to develop a strong enduring self and strong situated selves during their various cultural transitions.

REFLECTIONS ON THE CONTRIBUTIONS IN THIS VOLUME

The authors in this volume help us look more closely at the lives and psyches of children. All have produced work aimed at understanding the dilemmas we face as a nation and addressing the challenges we face as educators in a multicultural world. As these authors describe the experiences of youth in family, peer, and school settings, they help illustrate the demands and conflicts that can arise for children as they work to develop their youth and adolescent selves.

The Suarez-Orozcos' chapter provides a penetrating analysis of the dilemmas that face immigrants. As they point out, the nature of the disempowerment of ethnolinguistic and racial minorities is very complex and requires a multilevel analytical approach. If we examine the problem of academic low achievement as a sign of cultural maladjustment and disempowerment and look at high achievement as a sign of adjustment and empowerment, we may be ignoring other more eloquent signs of relative failure or relative success. In other words, school failure may, from the perspective of students, be the price of ultimate success. It may be rational to drop out of school, to reject assimilation, or to retain one's language and culture in the face of pressure to reject them.

In thinking about this chapter, I believe it is important to point out that disempowerment occurs for immigrant, refugee, and other minority children in the context of rapid social, cultural, and linguistic change because many of them experience a rapid loss of their home language. Language is an essential instrument in the acquisition of self-identity and learning and in adjustment to new situations. Sociolinguistic research and research on the ethnography of communication emphatically argue for the significance of language in the communicative process, in the construction of new knowledge, and in the transmission of cultural values (Cook-Gumperz, 1986; Gumperz, 1971, 1982; Gumperz & Hymes, 1964, 1972; Heath, 1983; Hornberger, 1988a, 1988b; Skutnabb-Kangas, 1984). We live in concrete linguistic and cultural environments created within family, community, and social institutions. As we acquire language, we acquire the means to transfer our thoughts, values, and attitudes. Speech communities (Gumperz & Hymes, 1964, 1972), families, and peer groups create settings that contextualize linguistic communication in such a way that we can make sense of messages. When those contexts are changed, we cannot communicate until we build new contexts. We are forced to reconstruct these contexts by facing continuous miscommunication and cultural misunderstandings. New knowledge is not acquired until we bridge previous knowledge through equivalent contexts that permit us to make sense of the content of communication. In a very real sense, the home language and culture is the "survival kit" for minority children. It is through language that they understand different scenarios and settings, different participation structures, the various uses and purposes of language, different forms of communication (for example, text or face-to-face), diverse genres (poetry, prayer, lecture, etc.) and the norms of communication associated with various forms and usages.

The loss of the mother tongue before a new language is acquired can cause serious cognitive and emotional problems, as the case of Richard Rodriguez, described by the Suarez-Orozcos, demonstrates. The authors are most insightful when they remark that Rodriguez, angry when his mother stopped using Spanish in the home (after being advised to do so by a teacher), retaliated by hurting his parents in the way he corrected their English. Rodriguez's anger was replaced by guilt and shame; "I was not proud of my mother and father" (Rodriguez, 1982, p. 52). The irony of these confessions, as the Suarez-Orozcos point out, is that Rodriguez became so isolated and lonely that he sought intimacy with unknown readers by sharing his most personal thoughts. Alienated from his family, his peers, and his community, he attacks the use of home languages and views self-rejection as the means to become accepted by American society: "To give up Spanish to acquire English represents a symbolic act of ethnic renunciation: it is giving up the mother tongue for the instrumental tongue of the dominant group" (Suarez-Orozco & Suarez-Orozco, Chapter 4).

Is Rodriguez a failure or a success? Is becoming upper middle–class, fluent in English, and educated a clear sign of success? Did Rodriguez have a choice? Probably he did not. The choices open to many who retain the home language and acquire a second, third, and fourth language, thus being enriched culturally, were never open to him. Yet Rodriguez is persuaded that self-rejection (via the rejection of the home language and culture) is the only way to succeed in American society. Is Rodriguez empowered to participate in American social institutions? The psychological scars resulting from self-rejection and his break with his family and community are crippling factors that he will have to face for life.

Delgado-Gaitan's contribution to this volume, based on the literature on empowerment derived from ethnic community and family relationships, is consistent with her previous contributions to the field (Delgado-Gaitan, 1990; Delgado-Gaitan & Trueba, 1991). For ethnic children to succeed, they must do so without losing their home values and their family relationships. Consequently, Delgado-Gaitan suggests that schools invest in efforts to organize ethnic parents and draw on parents' ability to act as a positive force vis-à-vis school through socializing their children to achieve. Such socialization has at least two important dimensions. First, children must understand the culture of the school, in particular its organization and power structure and the best means to obtain support and recognition from teachers and the principal. Parents must know the school culture well enough for them to provide their children with this knowledge. Second, children must be socialized in the means to acquire new knowledge. This dimension is enhanced by parents modeling several cognitive strategies for learning: inquiry, critical analysis, generation and testing of hypotheses, and recapitulation of knowledge obtained. For parents to learn how to train their children in the acquisition of new knowledge, they must learn how to interact with their children around academic topics, even when they (the parents) do not have the empirical knowledge to offer.

Delgado-Gaitan's advocacy of partnerships between parents-community and school is clearly a logical extension of her theoretical perspectives and an excellent suggestion. Moreover, her basic approach to parental empowerment is congruent with both the Spindlers' work on cultural therapy and the Suarez-Orozcos' conception of the high cost of self-rejection that stems from the rejection of the home language and culture. However, she does not delve into the problems of rescuing parents from various stages of castification, nor into the role they must play in socializing each other to the role of school partners.

Phelan, Davidson, and Yu specifically focus on the emergence of "multiple worlds" and the types of adjustments high school students from diverse backgrounds must make as they move from home to school, from school to peer group, and from peer group to home. In particular, cultural differences and the need to make the transition from one world to another raise important concerns about the isolation of ethnic youngsters trapped between two or more conflicting worlds. The ethnographic data and analysis in this chapter provide excellent insight into the mechanisms used by some youngsters to make the transition between worlds as they face anxiety, depression, fear, and lack of self-confidence (psychosocial borders); unexpected cultural norms and expectations (sociocultural borders); poverty and the resulting constraints of hunger, desperation, and anger (socioeconomic borders); difficulties in communication (linguistic borders); or school organizational factors that effectively isolate, segregate, or reject them (structural borders).

Similar to the Spindlers, Phelan and associates describe four patterns high school students fall into as they work to resolve the conflicts they confront when crossing borders. For some students, transitions are smooth. However, for others, whose worlds are different, transitions can be manageable, very difficult, or impossible. The specific ethnographic descriptions of these typologies are extremely helpful for understanding the differences among these four types. Can students move from one typology to another as time passes and they acquire the linguistic and cultural knowledge they need to function in schools? What are the characteristics of students who find transitions easy in contrast with those who find them impossible? These are questions the authors discuss. Another important observation I would like to make about the research by Phelan and associates is that students also play a key role in cultural changes occurring in the home; in other words, they can become change agents in their own home. Thus, we deal with moving targets: home, school, and peer worlds are all changing at a different pace and influences can be reciprocal. I also believe that a final important factor is whether the student sees himself or herself as primarily affiliated with the home, school, or peer worlds. The point of reference, and the dominant cultural values of those worlds, affect children's choices of adaption strategies and their tolerance for culture shock in their transition from one world to another.

Pease-Alvarez and Hakuta pursue issues related to language choice and the maintenance of Spanish as the home language. Their underlying assumption is that home-language maintenance (bilingualism) depends on the early linguistic acquisition and maintenance of the home language. Their observations of the intimate relationship between home-language maintenance and attitudes towards ethnicity (self-identity in terms of ethnic affiliation) are very important and congruent with the work of the Suarez-

Orozcos and of Phelan and associates. They also raise questions about the role of parents in the early linguistic socialization of children. This role for parents is most compatible with the roles advocated by Delgado-Gaitan that result when parents become effective advocates for their children's education. Pease-Alvarez and Hakuta analyze two school programs for enhancing the maintenance of Spanish as the home language and provide interesting information about the relationship between teachers and parents, as well as the community and school. For a school home-language maintenance program to be effective, it must have strong support from the community and continued support in the form of linguistic and cultural resources for teachers. This is an important contribution to our understanding of the role of home-language maintenance, for languages do not exist in a vacuum. Ultimately, the loss or maintenance of home languages reflect both macro- and micro-sociological forces and structures. Social sanctions and pressures that result in language loss have been felt by many generations of immigrants (including European immigrants). Until American society comes to view languages as a treasured and integral part of our multicultural heritage, the support for home-language maintenance will be a function of the strength and commitment of ethnic communities.

The chapter by Page brings one of the most controversial and difficult issues of our time to the fore. American society, with a democratic infrastructure that at times pursues contradictory goals and defends somewhat opposing values (e.g., individualism and conformity), has been extremely unclear about what it views as reprehensible "tracking" and what it sees as sensible ability grouping. The debate over how to define tracking and how to deal with school structures that result in differential allocation of resources and differential learning is very contentious. Page provides a wealth of ethnographic information to shed light on this complex issue and notes that there can be marked differentiation of curriculum within schools and across schools. Consequently, curriculum differentiation (even when it becomes a flagrant case of tracking) does not provide the entire picture of the distribution of knowledge. One needs to examine curriculum by considering the ethnic composition of schools, the quality of instruction, and the preparation of entering students.

Although Page does not address these issues, the following questions occur to me. Are we a society that permits one group to hold power over the mechanisms used to transfer knowledge to different groups in such a way that the concentration of economic and political power continues to be in the hands of a single group? To what extent can we argue with Apple (1989, 1990) and Popkewitz (1991) that there is a vested interest in tracking, that is, in transferring knowledge differentially? Relevant knowledge may be a pretext for dividing students in such a way that a transition to the world of college (drawing on the language of Phelan and associates) will become impossible or most difficult because of curricular differentiation. In short, I believe that we can not examine a single element of tracking or curriculum differentiation unless we look at the entire social and political context of instruction. Indeed, there are special cultural values attached to theories used to perpetuate certain instructional practices, such as academic tracking:

> The cultural values that drive the construction of institutional practices contribute significantly to current reform proposals. Possessive individualism and instrumental rationality establish a belief in a meritocracy and a consensus of goals in a society that is, in fact, culturally, ethnically, and economically differentiated. . . . The reform reports legitimate the transformation occurring and are involved in the processes related to production. The policy formulations articulate particular interest-bound responses to social and economic transformations. (Popkewitz, 1991, pp. 164–165)

An interpretation of the previous statement could mean that to the extent that school reform promises to bring about positive outcomes for the economy and technology, it will receive public support. There is a symbiotic relationship between institutional practices (e.g., tracking, or "ethnically relevant" curriculum) and the public support for such practices, which depends on the extent to which the public interprets such practices as functionally contributing to the strength of our economy.

CONCLUSION

Current social theories are not only used to create consensus and perpetuate the social order, but also to perpetuate institutional pedagogical practices. Talking about ideology and the social formation of teachers, Popkewitz (1987) writes:

> Theories relate individuals to the social order of the occupation. Images are created that can deflect attention from the actual priorities, values and patterns of social control. . . . The theories dull critical reasoning by creating illusions of a world already made, devoid of social interests and unyielding to human interventions. (p. 19)

Departure from such practices would depend on a shift in cultural values. It is precisely when changes in cultural values demand significant reform that reform becomes a priority. Meaningful school reform can be understood as a cultural change that affects political and social institutions first and educational institutions later:

> policy formulations articulate particular interest-bound responses to social and economic transformations. The resulting practices are neither neutral, disinterested, nor without social consequences. (Popkewitz, 1991, p. 165)

University faculty and administrators have the unavoidable responsibility of creating the knowledge necessary to face the various historical challenges that are transforming American society and culture. Universities that pursue excellence and ignore equity are not fulfilling their national responsibilities. The future of American society as a vigorous, powerful, democratic society depends on all its democratic institutions to ensure its future. Whereas past social efforts were supposed to be politically nonpartisan (Popkewitz, 1991), I argue that educational researchers can no longer hide under the pretext of being only "scientists" and "objective," for research on educational equity is not neutral. As Michael Apple (1990) eloquently argues:

> [M]y position has embodied a political commitment. Implicit in my exploration of some aspects of the ways schools and intellectuals function in the cultural and economic reproduction of class relations is a claim that it is very difficult for educational and social theory to be neutral. Thus ... curricular and more general educational research needs to have its roots in a theory of economic and social justice, one which has as its prime focus increasing the advantage and power of the least advantaged. (p. 158)

Research genuinely supportive of democratic educational policies and practices, according to Apple, has two fundamental characteristics:

> First, it aims at illuminating the tendencies for unwarranted and often unconscious domination, alienation, and repression within certain existing cultural, political, educational, and economic institutions. Second, through exploring the negative effects and contradictions of much that unquestioningly goes on in these institutions, it seeks to promote conscious [individual and collective] emancipatory activity. (p. 133)

Educational research, especially if inspired by the anthropological principles of cross-cultural comparative research, can be highly instrumental in the interpretation of democracy in the U.S. and in providing us with a better understanding of cultural conflict and ethnic controversies.

Philosophers of science, in full agreement with educational anthropologists, argue eloquently for an educational system predicated on democratic principles. One of these principles requires us to recognize the importance of a "social epistemology," which views the acquisition of knowledge and power as being intimately related to the instructional process. For cultural therapy to function as an instrument of educational empowerment for all children and their teachers, we all need to take an active role as advocates of children's education. Indeed, teachers must redefine their role as advocates of minority children and change agents along the lines suggested by Cummins (1986, 1989). The role of teachers in cultural therapy is essential, for teachers who are familiar with the cultures of ethnic children and have a strong ethnic identity can find ways to draw on the cultural capital of their students for pedagogical purposes. Instructional effectiveness requires high expectations for minority children, as well as the ability to inspire them to work cooperatively in both the acquisition of knowledge and the strengthening of their linguistic and cultural resources.[4] Educational researchers and administrators should help schools create learning environments in which teachers can develop and strengthen their self-identities and become role models for their students, as well as support students' linguistic abilities, self-respect, and ethnic pride. Schools can become genuinely exciting learning environments in which students become the primary engineers of their learning experience and make a full commitment to learn as much as possible. Moreover, schools can help prevent cycles of racism, intolerance for diversity, and even violence against ethnic and other disenfranchised groups such as low-income women, gays, the homeless, senior citizens, the poor, the sick, and the handicapped.

Cultural diversity and respect for our democratic society go hand in hand. Controversy, conflict, and open discussion about reform is congruent with our form of government. Reform movements are often accompanied by profound reflection and healing. However, whether today's reform efforts will truly focus on the achievement of ethnic and racial minorities or the interests of other groups is still in question. America should take pride in its ethnic diversity and commit resources to the education of all its children. For America to reform, it will be necessary first to heal, that is, to recognize the destructive environments in which many of its children live. We Americans must invest additional resources in the proper education of America's diverse children, especially those who suffer poverty and isolation. In past years, it was the conscious commitment of both immigrant and mainstream communities to educational equity that resulted in strategies for collective, quiet action that changed schools and society. Today the interpretation of our democratic American society demands that we learn to live in pluralistic, multicultural settings and respect cultural and linguistic differences.

NOTES

1. Since 1980, at least 824,000 legal Spanish-speaking immigrants have come to the U.S. to join the 15.5 million who were already here (Waggoner, 1988, p. 105), and it is possible that by 1995 the total Spanish-speaking population (including both documented and undocumented immigrants based on estimates of the undercount of previous censuses) will exceed 20 million.

2. The notion of "cultural therapy" has encountered some resistance, but is now beginning to gain attention. Some of the problems with using "therapy" language is that people assume there is something personally wrong with those in need of cultural therapy. The medical therapy model is, for example, very narrow. (Particularly, as it has been applied to special education.) Yet, in some very real sense, the acceptance of cultural therapy will make us recognize that there is something that Americans must address: our need to better understand American culture and to appreciate the cultural and linguistic resources of the U.S.

3. The Spindlers' "instrumental competencies" may be interpreted basically as the knowledge, skills, and experiences necessary to participate actively and effectively in social institutions of industrial societies, especially in school settings.

4. The requirements of such learning environments have been studied by a number of scholars using Vygotsky's sociohistorical perspective on cognitive development (Moll, 1990; Trueba, 1991a, 1991b, 1991c, 1991d; Trueba, Jacobs, & Kirton, 1990; Vygotsky, 1962, 1978; Wertsch, 1981).

REFERENCES

Apple, M. (1989). *Teachers and texts: A political economy of class and gender relations in education.* New York: Routledge, Chapman & Hall.

Apple, M. (1990). *Ideology and curriculum.* New York: Routledge, Chapman & Hall.

Cook-Gumperz, J. (Ed.). (1986). *The social construction of literacy.* New York: Cambridge University Press.

Cummins, J. (1986). Empowering minority students: A framework for intervention. *Harvard Educational Review, 56*(1), 18–35.

Cummins, J. (1989). *The empowerment of minority students.* Los Angeles: California Association for Bilingual Education.

Delgado-Gaitan, C. (1990). *Literacy for empowerment: The role of parents in children's education.* Philadelphia: Falmer Press.

Delgado-Gaitan, C., & Treuba, H. (1991). *Crossing cultural borders: Education for immigrant families in America.* Philadelphia: Falmer Press.

DeVos, G. (1973). Japan's outcastes: The problem of the Burakumin. In B. Whitaker (Ed.), *The fourth world: Victims of group oppression* (pp. 307–327). New York: Schocken Books.

DeVos, G. (1983). Ethnic identity and minority status: Some psycho-cultural considerations. In A. Jacobson-Widding (Ed.), *Identity: Personal and socio-cultural* (pp. 90–113). Uppsala, Sweden: Almquist & Wiksell Tryckeri AB.

Gibson, M. (1987). The school performance of immigrant minorities: A comparative view. *Anthropology and Education Quarterly, 18*(4), 262–275.

Gibson, M. (1988). *Accommodation without assimilation: Sikh immigrants in an American high school.* Ithaca, NY: Cornell University Press.

Gumperz, J. (1971). *Language in social groups.* Stanford, CA: Stanford University Press.

Gumperz, J. (Ed.). (1982). *Language and social identity.* New York: Cambridge University Press.

Gumperz, J., & Hymes, D. (Eds.). (1964). The ethnography of communication. *American Anthropologists, 66*(6).

Gumperz, J., & Hymes, D. (1972). *Directions in sociolinguistics: The ethnography of communication.* New York: Holt, Rinehart & Winston.

Heath, S. B. (1983). *Ways with words: Language, life and work in communities and classrooms.* New York: Cambridge University Press.

Hornberger, N. (1988a). *Bilingual education and language maintenance: A southern Peruvian Quechua case.* Providence, RI: Foris.

Hornberger, N. (1988b). Iman Chay?: Quechua children in Peru's schools. In H. Trueba & C. Delgado-Gaitan (Eds.), *School and society: Teaching content through culture* (pp. 99–117). New York: Praeger.

Kozol, J. (1991). *Savage inequalities: Children in America's schools.* New York: Crown.

Moll, L. (1990). *Vygotsky and education: Instructional implications and applications of sociohistorical psychology.* New York: Cambridge University Press.

Ogbu, J. (1974). *The next generation: An ethnography of education in an urban neighborhood.* New York: Academic Press.

Ogbu, J. (1978). *Minority education and caste: The American system in cross-cultural perspective.* New York: Academic Press.

Ogbu, J. (1987). Variability in minority responses to schooling: Nonimmigrants vs. immigrants. In G. Spindler & L. Spindler (Eds.), *Interpretive ethnography of education: At home and abroad* (pp. 255–278). Hillsdale, NJ: Lawrence Erlbaum.

Ogbu, J. (1989). The individual in collective adaptation: A framework for focusing on academic underperformance and dropping out among involuntary minorities. In L. Weis, E. Farrar, & H. Petrie (Eds.), *Dropouts from school: Issues, dilemmas, and solutions* (pp. 181–204). Albany: State University of New York Press.

Popkewitz, T. S. (1987). Ideology and social formation in teacher education. In T. S. Popkewitz (Ed.), *Critical studies in teacher education: Its folklore, theory and practice* (pp. 2–33). London: Falmer Press.

Popkewitz, T. S. (1991). *A political sociology of educational reform: Power/knowledge in teaching, teacher education, and research.* New York: Teachers College Press.

Rodriguez, R. (1982). *Hunger of memory: The education of Richard Rodriguez, an autobiography.* Boston: David R. Godine.

Skutnabb-Kangas, T. (1984). *Bilingualism or not: The education of minorities.* Clevendon, England: Multilingual Matters.

Spindler, G. (1987). *Education and cultural process: Anthropological approaches.* Prospect Heights, IL: Waveland Press.

Spindler, G., & Spindler, L. (1984). *Dreamers with power: The Menomini Indians.* Prospect Heights, IL: Waveland Press.

Spindler, G., & Spindler, L. (1989). Instrumental competence, self-efficacy, linguistic minorities and cultural therapy: A preliminary attempt at integration. *Anthropology and Education Quarterly, 20*(1), 36–50.

Spindler, G., & Spindler, L. (1992). The enduring, situated, and endangered self in fieldwork: A personal account. In B. Boyer (Ed.), *The psychoanalytic study of society.* Hillsdale, NJ: Analytic Press.

Spindler, G., & Spindler, L., with Trueba, H., & Williams, M. (1990). *The American cultural dialogue and its transmission.* London: Falmer Press.

Suarez-Orozco, M. M. (1989). *Central American refugees and U.S. high schools: A psychosocial study of motivation and achievement.* Stanford, CA: Stanford University Press.

Suarez-Orozco, M. M. (1990). Speaking of the unspeakable: Toward a psychosocial understanding of responses to terror. *Ethos, 18*(3), 353–383.

Suarez-Orozco, M. M. (1991). Migration, minority status, and education: European dilemmas and responses in the 1990's. *Anthropology and Education Quarterly, 22*(2), 99–120.

Suarez-Orozco, M. M., & Suarez-Orozco, C. (1991, October). *The cultural psychology of Hispanic immigrants: Implications for education research.* Paper presented at the Cultural Diversity Working Conference, Center for Research on the Context of Secondary School Teaching, Stanford University, Stanford, CA.

Trueba, H. T. (1991a). The role of culture in bilingual instruction: Linking linguistic and cognitive development to cultural knowledge. In O. Garcia (Ed.), *Festshcrift in honor of Joshua A. Fishman* (pp. 43–55). Amsterdam: John Benjamins.

Trueba, H. T. (1991b). Learning needs of minority children: Contributions of ethnography to educational research. In L. M. Malave & G. Duquette (Eds.), *Language, culture and cognition* (pp. 137–158). Philadelphia: Multilingual Matters.

Trueba, H. T. (1991c). Linkages of macro-micro analytical levels. *Journal of Psychohistory, 18*(4), 457–468.

Trueba, H. T. (1991d). From failure to success: The roles of culture and cultural conflict in the academic achievement of Chicano students. In R. R. Valencia (Ed.), *Chicano school failure: An analysis through many windows* (pp. 151–163). London: Falmer Press.

Trueba, H. T., Jacobs, L., & Kirton, E. (1990). *Cultural conflict and adaptation: The case of the Hmong children in American society.* London: Falmer Press.

U.S. Department of Labor. (1991). What work requires of schools: A SCANS Report for America. Washington, DC: United States Government Printing Office.

Vygotsky, L. S. (1962). *Thought and language.* Cambridge, MA: MIT Press.

Vygotsky, L. S. (1978). *Mind in society: The development of higher psychological processes*. In M. Cole, V. John-Teiner, S. Scribner, & E. Souberman (Eds.). Cambridge, MA: Harvard University Press.

Wagatsuma, H., & DeVos, G. (1984). *Heritage of endurance: Family patterns and delinquency formation in urban Japan*. Berkeley: University of California Press.

Waggoner, D. (1988). Language minorities in the United States in the 1980's: The evidence from the 1980 Census. In S. L. McKay & S. C. Wong (Eds.), *Language diversity, problem or resource: A social and educational perspective on language minorities in the United States* (pp. 69–108). New York: Newbury House.

Wertsch, J. (1981). The concept of activity in Soviet psychology. Armonk, NY: M. E. Sharpe.

CONCLUSION

THE VOICES OF PROFESSIONAL EDUCATORS

Harry Handler, Don Hill, Richard P. Mesa, Laurie Olsen, and Arlando Smith

... often the frameworks educational researchers use, especially within the social science disciplines, screen out certain complex problems that don't fit existing ways of thinking. We ask questions for which we know how to find answers. Many educational researchers, imbued with the ethos of a science, often overlook unwittingly (or perhaps wisely) the enduring tension-ridden dilemmas that practitioners and policy makers must manage in their organizations. (Cuban, 1992, p. 7)

INTRODUCTION *by Patricia Phelan*

This chapter presents the reflections of professional educators with respect to the substance and process of the Cultural Diversity Conference at Stanford. We include the discussants' comments and thoughts in an attempt to take into account (rather than overlook) persons who, for the most part, will ultimately determine the practicality of the research presented in this volume. These practitioners and others have the primary responsibility for translating the ideas from research into their own work in schools.

Although we do not assume that the forum of the Stanford conference (which included researchers and practitioners in a dialogue about current ideas and issues related to cultural diversity) is the only, or necessarily the best, way to bridge the worlds of research and practice, it did provide an opportunity to bring people together. After 3 years of working in urban high schools, it was our feeling that forums must be created where a variety of voices can be heard. In the case of the working conference at Stanford, we did not want to, in Cuban's words, "unwittingly overlook the enduring tension-ridden dilemmas that practitioners and policy makers must manage in their organizations," particularly when such management often includes responsibility for the distillation and transformation of research into practice.

The conference discussants are people who have all contributed to our own research in schools. Harry Handler, Pete Mesa, Don Hill, and Arlando Smith have spent innumerable hours discussing ideas, sharing their thoughts, and helping us to resolve dilemmas, and Laurie Olsen's policy reports have provided us with invaluable information. Repeatedly, we have asked our colleagues, "Does the information we are gathering provide new insights?" "In what ways can it be translated for use by teachers and administrators?" "What implications does it have for policy, practice, curriculum, and pedagogy?" We find that these "practitioners," as well as many others, are not only interested in what we are doing (and what we can tell them about what other researchers are doing), they also provide a perspective that broadens our view and adds complexity to our work. Our own experience of soliciting input from people "in the field" convinced us that other researchers could benefit as well. It did not seem reasonable, to us, to mount a conference about the implications of cultural diversity in educational settings without including those most intimately involved in the day-to-day operation of schools. The decision to include at least some of the people who have assisted us throughout the tenure of our own study was not a difficult one to make. We were not disappointed. The diverse perspectives represented by the discussants were instrumental in creating the lively and thought-provoking 2-day conversation which ensued. In addition, each individual discussant brought a wealth of experience gleaned from their own histories in a multitude of educational settings.

Dr. Harry Handler, former Superintendent of Los Angeles Unified School District and currently Adjunct Professor, and Assistant Dean of Relations with Schools, University of California, Los Angeles, has participated as a member of the Board of Directors for the Center for the Context of Secondary School Teaching for the past 5 years. Known as one of the most intellectual of superintendents, issues of cultural diversity are not new to Dr. Handler. Growing up in East Los Angeles and teaching in inner-city schools were only precursors to his spearheading one of the country's most massive and complex urban desegregation programs. Dr. Handler's renowned leadership in Los Angeles, his hands-

on participation in a wide variety of ethnically diverse community organizations, his years as a classroom teacher, his involvement in almost all
levels of public school administration, and his current role as a university
professor enabled him to bring a wealth of experience (from a variety of
perspectives) to issues raised at the conference. As a member of the
Center's Board of Directors, Handler frequently reminds us of our obligation to the field. Our own work has benefited greatly from his consistently discerning comments and relentlessly probing questions. Handler's
reputation as a skilled mediator, facilitator, and expeditor of ideas was
borne out in his role as facilitator at the Stanford conference.

Don Hill, also a discussant, is a 27-year veteran high school social
studies teacher and currently Director of the Professional Development
Center of the Stanford/Schools Collaborative. We knew that Hill would
be well aware of the teachers' perspectives. Hill became interested in education while working in a community education project as a law student
at Harvard. "Ultimately," he says, "working in schools was just more engaging than the field of law." Four years ago, with some reluctance, Hill
left the classroom to become the first Director of the Professional Development Center, a partnership between Stanford University and four local
school districts. In his role as Director, Hill works with teachers, administrators, and university scholars to build bridges between the worlds of
research and practice. Hill, too, is a member of the Center's Board of
Directors and, like Dr. Handler, has consistently pushed us to explore the
policy and practical implications of our research—particularly as it applies
to teachers and students. As a result of the conference at Stanford, Hill
initiated a project that involved us collaboratively with a counselor, teacher,
and an ethnically diverse group of 12 students in a 7-week class to
explore the relevance and applicability of ideas generated from the
Students' Multiple Worlds study (see Phelan & Davidson, in press). This
project, a direct result of the Stan-ford conference, expands even further
our vision of what can occur when diverse voices are brought together.
Hill's idea of "testing" a research model in the field is an illustration of
the benefits that can result when researchers and practitioners unite.

Also bringing a wealth of experience to bear on issues of diversity in
school settings was Pete Mesa, Superintendent of Oakland Unified, which
is believed by many to be one of the most complex and troubled inner-
city school districts in the country. Issues of cultural diversity have marked
every aspect of Mesa's career—managing sometimes explosive racial conflicts as principal of San Jose High School in the 1960s; building and
implementing community involvement strategies in 25 ethnically diverse
poverty sites throughout the country as Executive Director of the Urban/
Rural School Development Program at Stanford in the 1970s; develop-

ing programs and policies affecting schools and school districts throughout California as Chief, Deputy Superintendent, State Department of Education in the 1980s; and now, perhaps most demanding of all, building a school system that can respond positively to large numbers of minority children and youth who deal daily with the devastation of poverty and life in an inner-city infected with drugs and violence. Mesa's participation as a conference discussant is only one example of the numerous ways in which he consistently maintains strong ties with the academic community. While committed to keeping abreast of current educational research, Mesa, like many practitioners, expresses frustration at the lack of connection between the contributions of research to improved learning and what is actually practiced in classrooms. Mesa's contributions at the conference, as well as his consistent interest and discerning reflections on our work for the past 3 years, have been invaluable.

Laurie Olsen, Director of California Tomorrow, also brought both practical and policy perspectives to the conference discussion. Olsen's experience "in the field" is impressive. Assistant to noted anthropologist Margaret Mead, high school social studies teacher, editor and writer at the Clearinghouse on Women's Studies, and Director of the Citizens Policy Center in Oakland are positions that have shaped Olsen's commitment to youth involvement and the access of minorities to public education. Olsen's (1988) ground-breaking work on the immigrant experience in California is portrayed in her highly acclaimed policy report, "Crossing the Schoolhouse Border." As Executive Director of California Tomorrow—a nonprofit research and policy organization committed to California's future as a multicultural, multiracial state—Olsen has been responsible for a variety of publications aimed at informing policy and assisting practitioners in the development of school practices appropriate for diverse student populations. Our own research has benefited greatly from Olsen's powerful depictions of immigrant students' experiences in California schools. As a conference discussant, we knew that Olsen would bring unusual breadth to discussions of diversity as a result of her active involvement with schools and school districts throughout the state. Olsen's orientation toward gathering information and disseminating ideas directed specifically at effecting change make her a prominent figure in policy arenas not only in California, but throughout the nation.

Over the past 2 years we have also had an opportunity to know and work with Arlando Smith, principal of Gunderson High School in San Jose, California. Smith's thoughtful critiques on the dilemmas facing today's students and his explication of the multiple roles and responsibilities of a principal make us increasingly cognizant of the pressures facing those who are responsible for the day-to-day operations of schools. Smith's experience as a social studies teacher for 9 years, and his work in administration both as an assistant principal and as principal in a number of schools and school districts throughout the state, provide him with a variety of lenses through which to consider the ramifications of learning environments for culturally diverse youth. Smith's frequently articulated belief that it is possible to create educational environments where all children can succeed is the foundation upon which his work with teachers and students is based. Deeply committed to building optimal educational circumstances for all youth, Mr. Smith works daily to create the changes necessary to accomplish his goals.

HARRY HANDLER

Perhaps one of the best ways to describe my reactions to the Cultural Diversity Conference at Stanford is to discuss what it was and what it was not. It was not just another 2 days of listening to university scholars reporting on the importance of what has conventionally become known as multicultural education, and practitioners and policy makers defensively presenting a show-and-tell of what they are presently doing. It was a sincere effort on the part of each of the participants to analyze the relationship between cultural diversity and learning in the schools from a number of perspectives.

Although researchers/scholars generally seek review and counsel regarding their work from colleagues, it is *not* common practice to subject one's work, prior to publication, to review by members of the potential audience—in this case practitioners. The authors of the essays were provided with the opportunity to learn if their work was consistent with the expectations of the Center for Research on the Context of Secondary Teaching and to reflect on the different interpretations that surfaced on what they were attempting to communicate. Understanding the importance of Kaplan's (1964) dictate that "Theory is of practice and must stand or fall with its practicality, provided only that the mode and contexts of its application are suitably specified," they were engaged in discussions related to the practical implications of their work with practitioner/scholars, with the recognition that practitioners are scholars or learned persons trained in a special branch of learning. However, it was not 2 days of playing "gotcha" while critiquing the drafts that had been circulated prior to the conference.

It was not another session where one could easily detect the lack of professional respect frequently observed amongst researchers, practi-

tioners, and policy makers. And, it was not 2 days of listening to representatives of each group speaking in their own language, unable to communicate with members of other groups. Given that there are significant
institutional cultural differences amongst the three groups, at times the
discussions and sometimes debates nibbled at perhaps another dimension
of the Spindlers' concept of cultural therapy.

It was not a surprise that there was agreement regarding the complexity of the topic and that some members of the group went through a
phase of attempting to identify who was to blame for the current state of
affairs and who needed to change if progress was to be made. The Conference provided an opportunity for each participant to express his or
her frustrations. Political and philosophical interpretations were challenged
in terms of their relationship to the role of research in the schools.

By the close of the conference most of the participants were close to
agreement on a selected number of key issues and on what might constitute the future research agenda in this area. The majority supported the
position that researchers need to become directly involved in facilitating
the implementation of programs based upon their work and that practitioners and policymakers have a responsibility to make it happen.

The publication of this work is but a next step toward demonstrating the relationship between cultural diversity and learning in the schools.
It is how the content of the chapters in this book is used to stimulate
discussion and to influence both policy and practice that will determine
their value.

DON HILL

I do not find it easy to comment on the presentations and dialogue
of the cultural diversity conference at Stanford. There is so much that
one can say, it is hard to compress my thoughts. I will start with the comment that I believe the Spindlers' essay, "The Processes of Culture and
Person: Cultural Therapy and Culturally Diverse Schools," has tremendous
practical power. First of all, it is an integrator of the other research contributions. The Spindlers' conceptual language provides a means to connect those contributions to each other, as well as a way to relate many of
the ideas to practice. Secondly, I see the central concept of cultural therapy
as a viable way of addressing some of the problems that we face as we
encounter an increasingly diverse school population.

My other preliminary comment is, that as a teacher for 27 years who
knows many creative, wonderful teachers who involve students in exciting ways, it makes me want to cry when I hear researchers say, "In the

classes we observed, 90% of the teachers talked 90% of the time." (This comment was made as a part of the conference discussion.) This really is alarming. It makes me recognize how far we have to go to transform schools so that all students will be *actively* engaged in learning.

At this conference my mind often wandered to what was not being addressed. The Spindlers use the terms "enduring self" and "situational self" to illustrate their analysis of the interaction between the culture and the individual. They emphasize the importance of preserving the enduring self while also building the competence of the situational self. Unfortunately, there are several constraints that make this difficult in schools, some of which are obvious. I think that the society unleashes all kinds of pressures that denigrate the enduring self and undercut the situational self. For example, many students face economic realities that lead them to believe that the development of instrumental competencies does not really matter. Whether you can do things or not, you are not going to get a job, so why bother?

Another issue that I think was hovering in the background of our discussions and not really talked about explicitly—and I think this is very, very crucial—is the way that many things are grouped together with derision as dominant white middle-class values. Unfortunately, when this occurs it is difficult to separate out those skills that are legitimate and that are necessary for the situational self to be able to perform in our society. Clarifying these issues is important. There are a lot of conscientious, talented, knowledgeable teachers who are not making it in today's classroom because what they think they are doing is teaching what needs to be taught to all kids—they feel that changing what and how they teach in response to changes in the student population would be wrong and racist. During the course of their careers these teachers have developed a way of teaching that has worked, and they feel that the incorporation of different strategies will lower standards and thus violate their responsibility.

And as recipients of schooling, there are students who think, "This is not my society, it is not my culture, it has no meaning for me," and they reject, out of hand, everything that is going on in school. I believe an important point is that a part of what is being attempted in "white middle-class schools" is very legitimate. Students need to have a clear sense, supported by parents and teachers, that some school curriculum is important—that what is being taught is what needs to be learned. They must feel "It is important for me to learn this because what I want to do in my life depends on my learning it." This is not possible, however, if teachers lack cultural sensitivity and are pedagogically rigid. Teachers cannot find ways to help students learn if they fail to discern the difference between imposing white middle-class values and teaching the knowledge and skills necessary for young people to navigate effectively in our society.

Conversely, many students and parents reject the value of schooling because they do not discern the difference between values and methods that can and perhaps should be resented and rejected and the knowledge and skills nested in white middle-class values that are crucial for the successful development of the instrumental self. There needs to be, in my judgment, a cross-cultural consensus on those aspects of schooling that are necessary and will empower students to gain the instrumental competencies they need. I believe that issues of culture must be put off center stage for this to occur. I do not say completely off stage—certainly cultural issues are tremendously important—but the present conflicts and debates dominating center stage are contributing to a massive lack of learning in the schools.

Another constraint in the schools, of course, is the enormous pressure on teachers to try to do what society unreasonably expects them to do. Most research and administrative criticism fails to grasp what teaching is like. (I think that school research might have a 75% increase in relevance if researchers were required to teach 2 or 3 days a year in K–12 schools.)

I think there are two dominant teaching models in schools today that might be related to the language introduced at this conference. One focuses on nurturing the enduring self. I see that there are people who think, correctly, that there are valid reasons why children have low self-esteem. Many of these parents and teachers see their role as trying to build self-esteem—which they do by focusing attention on appreciation of the child's culture. They also do it by trying to protect students against having experiences of failure, and they do it by adjusting their standards in an effort to keep students in school. Their goal is to give students a realistic sense that they can make it. There are some wonderful people in this group. They are the people that society often puts highest on the humane scale, and they are, in fact, keeping some seriously at-risk students in school by promoting positive feelings of self-worth.

There is another group of equally committed and caring teachers who see their job almost totally as one of developing instrumental competence. And they work at trying to treat all students the same and keeping their standards very high. They feel that all this self-esteem, culture stuff is irrelevant, if not dangerous, and further, that it has no place in the school. They believe that schools should help students learn, and that teachers should teach. These teachers meet their responsibilities by focusing on skill acquisition.

It is my belief that we need people who can combine both of these approaches. In other words, it should not be an either-or choice. We need people who can nurture the enduring self, and at the same time focus on helping students develop instrumental competencies. Of course, this is a tall order. Unfortunately, we have not provided the kinds of support and help to enable teachers to do this. Maybe we don't know how. It seems to me that many times researchers and administrators find it much easier to criticize either or both approaches than to help teachers learn to combine them.

Secondly, I think we need what might be called a navigational guidance system that embraces teachers, parents, and students. By that I mean we need to help young people understand more explicitly the kinds of choices involved in dealing with family, school, and peer boundaries. Students, and to some extent teachers and parents, are dealing with boundaries every day, but without concepts to help make this a conscious or reflective experience. Students often do what they do without being aware of the implications of their actions. The chapter by Phelan, Davidson, and Yu, "Students' Multiple Worlds: Navigating the Borders of Family, Peer, and School Cultures," organized students into four groups according to the level of difficulty they experience in confronting borders between their family, peer, and school worlds. My guess is that all of the young people described in this chapter lack the conceptual tools to reflect on the implications of the movements they make.

If I am correct, this raises a very interesting question: Would it be useful to explicitly teach students to identify different navigational patterns? If so, one possibility would be to bring together a diverse group of high school students to assess the validity of Phelan and colleagues' theoretical model and to test its potential to help young people deal more effectively with the borders they face. Students might begin by looking at case vignettes drawn from the research and later be encouraged to explore their own patterns so as to increase their insight into what it takes to navigate across boundaries. If the research model proves to be powerful, students could become involved in selecting stories for use with younger children as well as their peers. By making explicit the borders that students face, energy could then be devoted to assisting them in building the instrumental skills necessary for navigation. I am convinced that such student-created knowledge could offer untapped power for change in our schools.

I also think that teachers will find the Phelan, Davidson, and Yu model very useful to their efforts to help students succeed. For the most part, teachers are so overwhelmed by trying to prepare lessons that make sense in terms of their own expectations that they often don't focus specifically on the difficulties in their students' lives. How to make such thinking possible is not an easy question. Teachers have almost no time for reflection within the current educational structure. But I would like to suggest that we could bring some teachers and counselors together with people who are involved in the research and start looking at the implications for school practice. I think it is something that could and should become part of teacher training. To me, Phelan and associates' model is very rich in conceptual power. And I think very exciting.

RICHARD P. MESA

I have been a teacher and educator for over 30 years. I have spent at least 13 of those years as a superintendent of schools responsible for the education of over 60,000 students in two districts. In these positions, I have worked with countless teachers and administrators to improve the quality of education for students. Yet, I can write on half a page, or even less, the research ideas that I have found really useful and implementable in schools.

It is not because I have not encountered valuable and important ideas in the research I have read or heard at conferences, such as the ideas and insights in the work we reviewed at the cultural diversity conference at Stanford. My experience has led me to understand why we practitioners do not know how or choose not to apply the good research that seems to be quite abundant in recent years. Consequently, although I am hopeful about the usefulness of the Stanford conference, I am not optimistic.

Before I comment on the chapters we were asked to read, I would like to advance my views as to why practitioners do not apply the research that many academics feel they should. Perhaps most important is the fact that researchers often make incorrect assumptions—about how their work is disseminated, about the needs of practitioners, and about the experiences and perspectives of those in schools. All of these factors greatly reduce the probability of good research findings being implemented. For example, it seems that researchers and academics believe that research conducted and discussed at academic levels, and disseminated at conferences (attended mostly by people like themselves), is somehow communicated to practitioners who will have the ability to pull variations of the research together, organize it, and apply it. The reality is that those of us in the field tend not to read research because it is not in a form we can use. Even if it were, I'm not sure we would know how to apply it.

Furthermore, we cannot assume that personnel in institutions such as state colleges and federally funded educational laboratories (people frequently charged with disseminating information to practitioners) have the confidence and competence to do so. Too often, research emanating from these sources is filtered and loaded with the biases of the institutions, or worse yet, distorted, because people do not understand the intent of the scholars who conducted the original work. A case in point is the research on effective schools. After state college professors and consultants were through, the school effectiveness findings were hardly recognizable. Each disseminator had a different version of what they were and how the conditions for effective schools should be developed.

It is my feeling that researchers and academics must make explicit their philosophical bases, their points of view, and the ideologies behind their work. Further, it is imperative that findings in one study be considered in relationship to those in others—be they supportive or contradictory—in order to enable discussion, thought, decisions, and application by practitioners.

Researchers also frequently assume that we practitioners take research at face value. We don't. We are aware that ideologies and philosophies often drive research agendas as well as interpretations of data. Even if we agree with the points of view that underlie research, we become suspicious if they are not explicated.

Early in my career, I knew a number of superintendents and principals who were fired (this was in the early 1970s) when they implemented university research that promoted ideas such as flexible scheduling, elective programs, and so on. In these instances, researchers dealt directly with superintendents and principals (this is still frequently the case) and "sold" these ideas without allowing practitioners to hear the innovations weighed, evaluated, criticized, and commented upon by other academics or educators. Although I realize that the school people were not blameless, such was the stature of the "academic" that practitioners were flattered by their attention and offers to work collaboratively. They bought, so to speak, a pig in a poke. One of these ideas, flexible scheduling, did more to discredit or have school principals dismissed than any other idea I can remember. But still things have not changed. For example, in Oakland, we continue to be subjected to a wide variety of entrepreneurial efforts by academics. Many attempt to sell ideas and convince principals (they have learned to bypass the district office) to implement them or to help them with their experiments. In a school district that is desperate for programs and innovations that will help students, often our principals are easy sales.

My contention is not that researchers should be held accountable for the research that they do or the recommendations that they make, nor do I intend to blame them or want them to suffer consequences because their recommendations don't work. Rather, I propose a level of dialogue between researchers and practitioners that puts on the table all the points of view of any particular innovation, that is, the underlying assumptions, philosophies, ideologies, and results of evaluations of any pilots that may have been conducted. At this time, I am not aware of any formal mechanisms in place for this to occur. Consequently, educational practitioners are vulnerable to the salesmanship of researchers. As a result, many of us take an attitude of skepticism and suspicion—not unlike the attitude we would take toward anyone attempting to sell their wares.

I think that natural scientists, and sometimes social scientists, do a better job of linking research to practice than we do in education. For example, engineers, medical doctors, and even psychiatrists seem not only to have a much more direct line to research, but also less difficulty in applying it than do educators. In these fields, there appears to be a level of communication that fosters the translation and organization of research in such a way that it is coherent and applicable. Perhaps we would do well to study how this is done.

I have conducted research projects at Stanford, as Director of the Institute for Effective School Leadership, and at other times throughout my career. Further, I have a strong sympathy for the potential of research. I know how much knowledge has been developed that we are *not* utilizing in the schools, as desperate as we are to help students learn. Without assistance, it is very possible for practitioners to adapt bad ideas or, at the least, to make dangerous leaps from research to practice. For example, as I read the Spindlers' chapter, I could see how easy it might be for someone to conclude that American schools should become more German.

Again, I am not arguing for the control or limiting of research in any way. I profoundly believe in the need for researchers to have complete freedom. I am saying, however, that we need to make connections between research and practice in such a way that it is accessible and sensible to those in the field. In the absence of this connection, we will continue to do mindless, even destructive things to students. I urge the writers of the essays for this conference to go beyond their research and to become involved in helping all of us think about how their work can best be brought to the schools.

Turning to the essays we were asked to read for this conference, I'll begin by saying that I read them from several perspectives, which I will disclose so that you can see my biases, the points of view from which I read the papers, and the experiences upon which I base some of my comments.

One perspective is that of a practitioner—most recently as a superintendent. Another is that of someone who is familiar with the research in education. Not only am I an avid reader of current research, I have also consistently worked with researchers, and have directed and carried out research projects myself. The third perspective is derived from my views about culture. Although not necessarily "politically correct," they are my honest views. Let me elaborate this perhaps controversial perspective further.

I believe that all cultures have strengths as well as weaknesses—in other words, any one culture is likely to be highly developed in some areas and not in others. Recently, some researchers have tried to promote the view that cultures have neither strengths nor weaknesses, advantages nor disadvantages, but rather, they are simply different. I don't agree. I believe there are aspects of any culture that can be damaging to the individual, depending upon the individual's predisposition, personal desires, and aspirations. Moreover, I think that for the practical purpose of living in the U.S., there are some features of other cultures that are out of place, that must be examined carefully and changed if necessary. For example, I have read recently that a father tried to sell his daughter in this country. Now, while this might be culturally acceptable somewhere else in the world, it is not acceptable here—nor should it be. Further, growing up in a Mexican-American family, I am only too aware of the intense socialization of male children toward machismo and I know that later in life this orientation can have terrible effects on women, families, and relationships generally.

It seems to me that we have been asked to accept that cultures should be held inviolate—that they should be preserved and passed on in the form that they exist. Although it is my belief that we must work diligently to preserve the rich cultural variety that currently exists in our schools, I think we must also identify those aspects of culture (including elements of white, mainstream culture) that are harmful to individuals and families and that limit and restrict people's relationships with each other. The Spindlers' ideas of cultural therapy, therefore, make sense.

The last point of view from which I read the essays is based on my own personal convictions about the nature of children and young people. I profoundly believe that all students can learn, although I know that there is a great deal of evidence that would suggest otherwise, for example, low test scores, high dropout rates of some minority students, and so on. Further, I know that children learn in different ways and at different rates, and that they thrive under some conditions and not others. Most important, they can learn a great deal more than we now expect them to in school.

It was from these perspectives, then, that I read each of the chapters in this book and pondered on how useful I found them, how applicable were their ideas, and how much they resonated with my own experience. I will comment on those I found particularly relevant to my own work in Oakland.

I found the chapter written by the Spindlers the deepest and most integrated. It contained a number of important and useful concepts—the major one being cultural therapy. Cultural therapy appeals to me because it is consistent with my belief that all cultures have strengths and weaknesses—features that can both strengthen and debilitate the individual. Let me illustrate. I know of Mexican families that have immigrated to the U.S. wherein the wife begins to take an active interest in schools and other community activities. I have seen such women learn quickly about the American system and develop personally through reading and dialogue with others. In many cases, their husbands have demanded that they stop working and learning because they feel that their wives are becoming too independent, thus slipping from their control and in some cases, developing beyond them in personal ways. I have had such women come to me and ask what they should do. They want desperately to escape the cultural dictate—bound up in ideas of machismo—that constrains them. In the context of this democratic society, these women have a right to aspire to what they want to be and it is indeed their husbands who badly need cultural therapy.

The Spindlers' chapter affirmed something that I have believed for a long time, and that is that the cultural assumptions upon which our educational system is based contribute to the aimlessness of American education. The comparison of the German and American classrooms illustrates American teachers' emphasis on socializing children to conform (to white, mainstream values and behaviors). I too have witnessed teachers' frequent emphasis on conformity—often in lieu of or at the expense of a strong academic program. I find this emphasis particularly harmful and destructive to culturally different, poor children. First, because teachers' attempts to socialize children away from their home culture creates conflicts and stresses that are damaging, and second, because such an emphasis takes away from the teaching of skills and content that will help children acquire the level of education that they deserve.

I also found the Spindlers' distinction between the enduring self and the situated self clarifying. It made me realize how often we confuse the two and in so doing make the mistake of thinking that we are meeting children's needs simply by improving academic achievement. In fact, we may be working against our goals when we focus on the acquisition of instrumental competencies without at the same time paying attention to nurturing the enduring self.

Also of importance is the Spindlers' discussion of the different responses of Native Americans to the imposition of the dominant culture. The first response is the orientation of people to reconnect with the traditions and language of their past by distancing themselves from the environment of the dominant culture. In so doing, they deride any member of the group that does not adopt their ways or exhibits sympathy with "the other." The second response is to withdraw from the ways of both the traditional and the dominant groups. Existing in a cultural limbo, these people often pursue self-destructive lives. The third response comes from people whose orientation is toward assimilation. Some define their original ways as backward and futile, whereas others combine elements from both cultures. Finally, there are those who develop what the Spindlers describe as bicultural skills and abilities, thus allowing them to function in both cultures—in a sense, building a bridge between the two. I believe that these categories could be useful in explaining the borders described in the Phelan, Davidson, and Yu chapter—perhaps more so than the ones they presently use (e.g., psychosocial, socioeconomic, and so on). Indeed the Spindlers' point, that people's adaptation strategies reflect their attempts to preserve self-esteem, is critical as we consider students' varying responses to school.

The chapter by Cindy Pease-Alvarez and Kenji Hakuta draws our attention to the fact that educators' efforts to preserve children's home language can be an important means of sustaining and nourishing the enduring self. Unfortunately, government policies that promote bilingual education as transitional (rather than a program to build bilingual competencies) are in direct opposition to the important findings reported in this work. However, given the political climate and the long history of debate surrounding bilingual education in this country it may be better, at this point in time, to consider alternative means of assisting children in maintaining their home language, that is, making language a part of the regular school curriculum. In fact, this is exactly what we are doing in Oakland, where we will begin to offer Chinese, Vietnamese, Spanish, and other foreign language classes as a separate strand from bilingual education. Beginning in the primary grades and continuing through the secondary level, all children and youth will be able to continue to develop their home language as an academic enterprise, while other students will have an opportunity to learn these languages too. Although Pease-Alvarez and Hakuta point out the worth of helping children maintain their home language, they fail to discuss the important role that foreign language classes might play. Sustained dialogue with practitioners might well lead to a broader range of practical solutions.

There are other important questions that this chapter raises. For example, why do children choose the language that they use and why is their first language so frequently lost? Although the Pease-Alvarez and Hakuta chapter appears to blame the schools, I believe, based on my own experiences and also on what I observe, that there are other reasons as well. It seems to me that there is a powerful tendency for children and adolescents who find themselves in a new environment to want to become a part of it. In many cases, young people want to belong to their school community too strongly not to speak English, even at the sacrifice of their home language. At the same time, the maintenance of the home language is extremely important. It is clear to me that practitioners and researchers must begin to engage in a dialogue about the best way to help students maintain their home language, and make the transition to English in a way that satisfies their need to belong.

The chapter by the Suarez-Orozcos discusses differences between immigrants and U.S.-born minorities with respect to their motivations to succeed. The factors cited by the Suarez-Orozcos as being necessary to sustain motivation and family unity through generations resonates strongly with my own experience. I know of Mexican-American families who have been able to foster motivation in their children despite grinding poverty. Further, their children's children are also motivated. As a child of early immigrants, I have been able to follow many of these immigrants over 50 years. Those families that sustained motivation taught pride of self and the importance of instrumental competencies—in the Spindlers' words, they nurtured both the enduring and the situational selves. I do believe that the Suarez-Orozcos diminished the importance of the development of the instrumental self. My mother and our lifelong friends espoused both.

Concha Delgado-Gaitan's chapter strongly advocates an empowerment approach to community involvement and her vivid description of the accomplishments of Hispanic parents in Carpenteria, California is particularly noteworthy. I too believe that parents should be empowered. However, I disagree with Delgado-Gaitan if she implies that this level of involvement is always necessary, or even a condition for children's successes in school. It is important to remember that there are many parents who never set foot in schools, but whose children, nevertheless, excel. Further, it is certainly likely that some parents actually prefer a different style of involvement than those in Carpenteria. Asian parents, for example, are often in this category. It is also my own experience (in a Mexican-American community) that virtually everyone I knew growing up rarely saw or expected to see parents involved directly with schools. What is common between the parents I knew and those I see today whose children are actively engaged in schools and learning is that they have firm control over their children's behavior and level of effort in school. Although I don't want to diminish the potential of programs like the one in Carpenteria, I simply don't expect or think it is feasible for all parents to be involved at the levels Delgado-Gaitan describes. There are too many conditions today, such as long commutes, a need for both parents to work, and a range of other constraints that make participatory involvement impossible. I lean towards building on the strengths that parents have and generating multiple approaches (not just those that match white middle-class styles) to foster home-school partnerships. Different cultural groups have different modes by which they instill values and maintain motivation in their children.

The Multiple Worlds chapter by Phelan, Davidson, and Yu has direct policy and practical implications. It is clear to me that the concepts outlined by these authors could form the basis for analyses and assessment of the nature of relationships and interactions between students and between students and schools. This material makes an original and important contribution by helping us to understand the nature of borders that students encounter as well as the various adaptation strategies they use. I would encourage the authors to consider incorporating aspects of the Spindlers' theoretical framework and, at least, making reference to the similarities between the various types of responses of Native Americans to the dominant culture and the student adaptation types. The Spindlers' concepts of the enduring and situated selves seem to me to have particular relevance to the model of Phelan and her colleagues—particularly with respect to understanding the nature and causes of borders that arise.

As is, however, the chapter material has clear and strong implications for practice (e.g., the training of counselors, parent education, and most obviously teacher education and curriculum). For example, teachers, counselors, and even parents could be encouraged to use the Multiple Worlds framework to more accurately assess students' needs and identify the types of difficulties they may be having. Further, I believe that the questions and issues presented in this chapter could easily be translated into curriculum content and policies. If, in fact, it is liberating for people to understand themselves and the patterns that characterize their own behaviors as well as those things in their environments that constrain and enable them, then this work could be the basis for the development of a very liberating and consequently motivating curriculum. Obviously, there are also important implications for school climate—specifically, the importance of structuring activities in schools so that interactions between students are increased and designed to bring about the reduction of borders between student groups. This chapter reminded me once again how institutionally insensitive and ignorant school systems and districts can be of the needs of children and the struggles they go through.

I have discussed reasons why I think we practitioners do not utilize research as much as we probably should and have referred to the biases and perspectives from which I have read and commented on the various chapters in this book. Finally, I have made remarks on each of the chapters, judging them primarily on how useful I find them, as a practitioner, in terms of their implications for my school district.

The discussions at the Stanford conference were fruitful, enlightening and, best of all, fun. The forum of the conference represents the kind of dialogue for which I argue throughout my remarks. I want to thank Dr. Patricia Phelan and her colleagues at Stanford, as well as Dr. Harry Handler for his skillful facilitation of our group and for his humor. I felt privileged to participate in a conference with such a distinguished group of researchers and educators. I came away from this conference even more convinced than I had been that academics and practitioners must come together for the betterment of schools. At the same time, I feel we are still a long way from reaching the level of communication that I would like to see. Although this conference was certainly a step in the right direction, it is painfully clear to me that practitioners speak a different language than academics. Whereas I believe that we practitioners know far more than we are able to articulate about how schools can be improved, I am also aware that researchers can provide us with concepts and language to better express what we know. We will certainly all become better educated if we commit ourselves to more ventures such as the very rich discussion at the Stanford conference.

LAURIE OLSEN

When I approach reading research about schooling, and shaping my own research agenda, I do so grounded in a particular view of the realities of teaching and learning in this particular time and place. Here in California, we are in the midst of a major demographic revolution in which immigrants literally from all over the world are joining our already diverse population to form what may well be the most ethnically, racially, linguistically, and culturally diverse society that has ever tried to coexist. In the past decade, our state has grown more than twice as fast as the rest of the nation, mostly due to the thrusts of immigration. The enrollment of students who come from homes in which languages other than English are spoken has grown four times faster than the rest of the student population. With almost a hundred language groups, hundreds of cultural groups, dozens of national groups, and a rainbow of races represented in the schools, the issues of culture, language, and race are undeniably at the center of the new dilemmas and challenges of teaching and learning. Our schools have been shaped by a long history in the U.S. of struggles between patterns of exclusion of nonwhite racial groups from education and citizenship and forces for inclusion and educational and political access. Our own contemporary version of that struggle is far from resolved, and issues of educational equity, racial inclusion, and cultural responsiveness thus seem to me to be a central tension and key challenge of this era.

I am motivated in my own work primarily by a tremendous urgency stemming from a sense that we are at a historical crossroads in our societal dealings with race and racism, and in our responses educationally and politically to cultural and linguistic diversity. I view our society as immersed in a broad political struggle over diversity, and daily microincidents within schools and classrooms in which that struggle is being played out.

This working conference, sponsored by the Center for Research on the Context of Secondary School Teaching on "Cultural Diversity: Implications for Schools and Learning" is exciting to me first of all because it creates visibility and a forum for serious discourse about diversity and schooling, and second, because it pulls together a combination of practitioners, researchers, and policy makers to consider the problem and the role of research on these issues. My participation in this forum, and the lenses through which I read the research articles is informed in several ways. I consider myself a researcher although I did not come to this working conference in that role and have never produced research in a university or speaking to or from an academic discourse. And, although I have been a high school history teacher and work a great deal with teachers in schools, I am not really currently a practitioner. In fact, in this working conference designed to bring together policy makers, practitioners, and researchers, I find myself first of all puzzled about which category I have been assigned, and further concerned about the nature of these divisions. Knowledge development, in my view, encompasses all of these roles and more. I am a researcher, a provider of support and technical assistance to schools, a parent and an advocate, working toward a vision of schools and of a society that is equitable, fair, and wonderfully enriched by our diversity. When I read research, it is from all of these perspectives, and it is fundamentally as a pragmatist. All kinds of research are of interest to me, but my ultimate concern is how useful this research may be in addressing the major dilemmas and problematics of education and equity. My measures of utility are related to a series of concerns.

To look at issues of culture, language, or race at this time and place in history is to also be looking at relationships of power, dominance, and hegemony. The cultural, racial, and linguistic diversity that increasingly characterizes our schools is not simply a pluralistic relationship of different but equal groups, but is also deeply embedded in historical relationships of inequality and the current conditions of inequity. Not to raise these power relationships as part of research that is examining cultural diversity is both to impoverish the research itself by missing an important facet of the phenomenon and to contribute to a damaging silencing of the dynamics of inequality. I seek, therefore, research that describes and speaks to those dynamics of the perpetuation, creation, and contestation of inequality, and which furthers the creation of theory with explanatory power to provide new understanding of those relationships.

I am concerned, frankly, with the parameters of how the discourse has been framed as a discourse about culture. To what extent does naming it a dialogue about culture mask and avoid talking about relationships of race or class? To what extent does research about culture provide a lens for understanding issues of inequity?

This is not just a problem in shaping research questions and in conducting and analyzing research findings. It is also a challenge to the writing of research. Most academically produced research is directed to an academic discourse in both the language in which it is written and in the choice of how to frame a research question. Yet there is another discourse into which the research may be inserted. Any research on matters of cultural diversity at this time in history is occurring in a highly politicized macrosocietal context. The knowledge that flows from the university has a weight of official legitimacy and falls directly into a politicized arena where it is picked up and used in that political discourse. Recognizing this, researchers need to ask, "What are the dimensions of the political debate into which this will drop? How will this piece of research be useful and/or used in that debate? How can I make my findings and analysis clearly speak to that debate?" It becomes incumbent on the writers, then, to consider the dimensions of that political discourse and to speak clearly and directly to it.

The Cindy Pease-Alvarez and Kenji Hakuta chapter, "Perspectives on Language Maintenance and Shift in Mexican-Origin Students" focuses on the important element of attitudes and choice in language learning and use. The current political discourse over language policy and rights in education focuses primarily on the development of language proficiency, not on the issue of language use. Pease-Alvarez and Hakuta thus offer to the debate new concerns related to language identity, affiliation, and loyalty. Their work thus both provides a mechanism for reshaping an aspect of the public discourse over language rights and policy, and also provides an important close-up look at how dynamics of language attitudes play out in several educational contexts. Their chapter, however, is unavoidably falling into a policy context that is deadlocked over the appropriate role of schools in providing and developing bilingual skills. Given the broad and politically charged public discourse over language programs, one has to ask how the material will be understood and used. The problem then is severalfold. First, because the chapter asserts that home-language proficiency occurs as a result of parental use, the authors need to be clear in answering the following questions that flow from the policy debate: Is the level of proficiency resulting from parental use sufficient for literate use of the language? If not, is the value of the mother tongue to be interpreted only in terms of conversational value in family relationships as compared to possession of bilingual skills of a proficiency enabling academic usage? If a child's language affiliation, proficiency, and use are factors primarily of his or her parents' language use, does this then imply that what schools do is largely irrelevant in shaping the development, proficiency, and literacy of a child's native tongue? To not speak directly to these questions only contributes to the confusion in the policy debate.

A second concern is related to my perspective that in the midst of very dramatic and swift demographic changes and turmoil, teaching and learning (in individual schools and classrooms) involves a range of different and very context-specific challenges. Whereas one teacher may, for example, be working with multiple-language groups of recently arrived immigrants from a variety of different nations, classes, and cultures, another teacher may be teaching a class comprised 98% of U.S.-born African-American students. Whereas one may be in a community that has been richly diverse for decades; another may be in a community context that is confronting issues of cultural and racial difference for the first time. The dynamics of cultural diversity are fundamentally shaped by the specific context in which they occur and are created. Research conducted in one context may or may not be applicable to another. This makes it essential that the context specifications of any research on the issues of race, culture, and language in schools be made very clear, and the assumptions about the applicability clearly discussed.

Here is an example of how this concern entered into my reading of the papers presented at the working conference on Cultural Diversity. George and Louise Spindler's "The Processes of Culture and Person:

Cultural Therapy and Culturally Diverse Schools" takes the experience of an anthropologist in the field and equates it with the experiences of marginalization of an ethnic minority or lower-class child in relationship to a middle-class school environment.

> The ethnographers . . . were doing what persons coming into a new cultural situation must do if they wish on the one hand to "get along" and learn and at the same time keep their identity. These are the problems, as we see it, of the ethnic minority student or the lower class student in a middle class school environment. . . . For example, we feel permanently marginalized in our society. . . . This is a situation peculiar to the field ethnographer, perhaps, and yet the feeling dogs us that the child from a minority group in a mainstream dominated school must have many of the same kinds of feelings. They enter marginalized and their marginalization is reinforced. This is exactly parallel to what happened to us. . . . What may be most important here is that we learned how to make situational adaptations without destroying our enduring selves. Perhaps this is what many minority students with strong ethnic backgrounds must do.

The notion of cultural therapy, a wonderful approach in which a third party assists people from different cultures to become ethnographers in looking at each other and thus at their own culture, is simply asserted as being therefore equally applicable to both situations. This raises a host of questions for me, however, due to the very different power relationships between the cultural groups in each of these contexts. Before asserting a single intervention for both situations, I would want the Spindlers to explore the following questions: "What is the relationship between the cultures? How might the power relationships in the ethnographic context and the classroom context be different? What implications might those differences have for designing and applying an intervention strategy from one context to the other?" White middle-class teachers live in a dominant culture in which most of their experience is taken as the norm. The problem of helping them to recognize culture from that position in which the norm is simply taken for granted, diffused into the realm of the "normal," seems undoubtedly to me to be a very different problem than helping a child from a cultural, racial, or linguistic group that is subordinated to recognize and articulate notions of "culture." The process may be different, the issues of formulating and articulating cultural understandings may well be embedded in the power relationships and therefore be experienced differently, and the appropriate intervention would then be quite different as well.

A third concern I bring to reading research is knowledge of the tremendous hunger of practitioners in the field for research that can provide new directions, feed new innovations, and prompt new pedagogy and practice in schools. It has been my experience in working with teachers and community groups that the challenge of creating schools that work for the culturally, linguistically, racially diverse communities that now comprise so much of California is largely overwhelming. Many feel that old approaches no longer work and find themselves engaged in quests for new solutions, materials, pedagogies, and approaches. But they often do so in isolation, with little access to each other or to the research. I spend much of my time on the telephone letting one teacher know what another has discovered, informing one administrator of a program another school has just designed, passing along the word about recent research reports that speak to a particular dilemma. The hunger for information, for research, for involvement in networks of ideas, and support to meet the challenges of diversity is undeniable. But practitioners desperate for assistance, with little time to search the research literature, simply pick up what seems applicable—often unable to assess its appropriateness. An article written about research in one context may be applied wholesale to a completely different context. The basic assumptions of one research study may go wholly unexamined, and the findings accepted completely regardless of the "match" in assumptions and context. This simply underscores, I think, what I have already said about the importance of articulating assumptions, clarifying contexts, and spelling out the implications of research.

Research becomes a part of the repertoire of practice when those engaged in practice know about and can understand the research, and when the research fits some question, some conundrum, which the practitioner is facing. There are, clearly, problems in all three of these steps. Regardless of how useful a piece of research may be, the serendipitous nature of research dissemination means that key pieces of research may or may not ever be found by practitioners. The usefulness of research is then intimately connected to the *mechanisms* of dissemination. I would encourage the authors of the chapters in this book and other researchers working on the centrally important issues of language, culture, class, and racial diversity to write for and publish in the journals and media of practitioners, to provide workshops and seminars at the professional association meetings to which practitioners flock in great numbers seeking ideas, research, and stimulation for their practice. It strikes me as a tremendous waste that of the hundreds of papers delivered each year at AERA, few ever are presented at meetings such as the National Association for Bilingual Education, the National Council for the Social Studies, or other practitioner meetings.

The last concern I raise is over who drives the research agenda and from where the questions emanate that shape research studies. From my perspective, there must be a major knowledge-development effort in this nation if we are to create schools that can be responsive to and appropriate for the rich diversity of our communities. Further, knowledge-development efforts must speak to the daily dilemmas of practitioners in the field, acknowledge the historical and current inequality in racial and cultural relations, consider the political dimensions of the public dialogue about the role of schools at this time in history, speak to the tremendous complexity of contexts, and be based upon much closer and less bureaucratically divided relationships among practitioners, academic researchers, and policy makers. And an important element of this effort would be continued efforts, modeled on the Cultural Diversity Working Conference, to bring together groups of people who are situated differently within the educational system to consider together specific findings of research studies and the more general role of research in forging new responses to the challenges of our time.

ARLANDO SMITH

I appreciated being included in this conference because rarely, if ever, does research and theory merge with practice. In education, practitioners are studied, examined, and to some extent, dictated to, while seldom being included in the process of developing solutions. Sometimes I am of the notion that we are at a point in education where we need to throw it all out and start over. But what is going to take its place? This is a question of major significance. Where does the leadership come from? The fact that people keep researching education is an indication, I believe, that we can do better. Determining what is better must include the practitioners and consumers—administrators, teachers, and students—if the research is to have any value.

As I prepared to be a part of this project, I was confronted by one of the major dilemmas of educators—the fact that education has been researched and reresearched. The institution of education affords researchers the ideal institution to assess. Unfortunately, it is assessed as a monolithic entity rather than the polylithic institution that it is. Inherent in this is the assumption that there is something wrong. Rarely is educational research done from a perspective of what is right. Research on the strengths of public education, using the standpoint of building upon the strengths of the foundation from which an action plan can be developed, is uncommon. The prevailing thesis is mired in a "fix it" psychological mentality. This is why asking an active practitioner to review the research and discuss its effects prior to implementation makes the Stanford Conference Project unique.

"Now that we've done the research, what can we do with the data?" This is a natural question that is a consequence of the plethora of educational research that exists. This was the question I asked myself frequently as I reviewed the research. Because so much research is so far removed from the day-to-day operations of a school, more often than not, I viewed this as an opportunity to connect, firsthand, the theoretical with the realities of my life as a principal. Each day I deal with 1600 students, and over 70 teachers (any 15 of whom will be upset because there are one or two more students in the class than contractual agreements allow). Because the University Model of education has not often dealt effectively with practical, day-to-day functions, I attempted to ascertain from the research and the conference what was relevant to me and, I hope, other principals.

"Students' Multiple Worlds: Navigating the Borders of Family, Peer, and School Culture," by Phelan, Davidson, and Yu affirms what we have assumed for some time, that a holistic approach is most effective when addressing the needs of students. Also reinforced is the research of self-fulfilling prophecies and "Pygmalion In The Classroom." Students who have congruent worlds and make smooth transitions have strong, cohesive families. This is what our society values and these are the students who are valued by teachers. Thus, teachers are more comfortable with these students.

"In classrooms where students flourish, teachers know the students well, are attuned to their needs, and show personal concern for their lives." This is not new. As educators, what it does tell us is what it takes to make students successful if we are willing to put our personal prejudices aside for the good of the student. We should take the Hypocritic oath, in contrast to the Hippocratic oath. As educators, what do we lose by encouraging each student to excel at higher levels, even when we might feel otherwise? The research has shown, time and again, that this approach is effective. The value of the research of Phelan and her colleagues is that it was the only one of the chapters in this book that deals directly with the fact that the key ingredient in any class has to be the teacher. Their research makes the link between teacher attitude and student achievement and acceptance in the school environment.

So much can be derived from this work if researchers are willing to face the critical issues that confront us as educators head-on. The issues of race and teacher attitude are two such issues that must be realistically confronted. Students who describe borders as impenetrable say that classroom and school climate features do not support their needs. "In fact, they frequently describe instances of insensitivity or hostility from *teachers* and other students which threaten their personal integrity or devalue their background circumstances. . . ." Race is an obvious factor in students' achievement. This is sometimes a self-imposed barrier, but the teacher's attitude can make a tremendous difference—if the teacher is willing to accept the challenge. As I talk to students of all races, cultures, and academic levels, the theme that resounds repeatedly is, "I know those people don't like me." "I know that *teacher* doesn't like me." We must deal with people's perceptions of what is actually going on in schools. Schools are very Eurocentric. Even middle-class African-American and Hispanic teachers tend to exhibit the exact characteristics of their white counterparts. Students are judged and labeled the same way, thus adding class to the issue of race.

Parents are not without culpability. Yet, what the research on multiple worlds and borders concludes is that ". . . students must acquire skills and strategies to work comfortably and successfully in divergent social settings and with people different than themselves." This demonstrates the need to focus on teacher attitude. Teacher attitude is a central indicator of the climate a school will have. Teachers must overcome their fear of students, the very people with whom they are supposed to relate and connect. If this is effectively addressed, teachers will view students as "people" rather than "kids."

What we teachers intend to convey should be a prime focus of any research. This was the value of the research done by George and Louise Spindler on cultural therapy. Though "the students learn a great deal from each other that teachers don't control," they acknowledge that there are ". . . many teachers, perhaps all teachers, who have very strong biases that are quite unmovable because they are integrated with their own sense of identity and self . . ." They continue by stating, "Children with various sociocultural backgrounds attend schools predicated on mainstream, largely middle-class, and largely white Anglo-Saxon Northern European Protestant cultural assumptions. Such children acquire deficits in self-esteem when they fail to master essential instrumentalities in this context. This self-esteem is damaged not only by actual failure but by negative perceptions and low expectations of these children by teachers and other students." As an active practitioner, this information is valuable to me. However, it is not the information that is going to motivate those of whom that speaks to be different because of the exorbitant amount of denial we face in education. None of us will ever admit to denying our problems. How do we utilize this information to engage those who would be guilty? This is a major drawback of most research. I had hoped to be made privy to the framework to make this happen. There was none.

In California, and other states in the Southwest, the research by Carola and Marcelo Suarez-Orozco is especially deserving of extensive review. The imperative understanding is that we must do more in terms of recognizing the differences betweem Hispanic cultures, and not lump all Hispanics together. If we refrain from doing this for Hispanics, viewing racial and ethnic groups as monolithic, the value of our research is compromised. Then, and only then, when this understanding is gathered and accepted, can we help families through transitions, as their research suggested.

The research of the Suarez-Orozcos lends itself beautifully to addressing the structural needs of Mexican-American families. There are certain characteristics that are indigenous to certain groups. If we are to effectively work with these groups, we must first recognize these characteristics. The body of research highlights the need for extensive cultural awareness in *all* teacher education programs, and for requirements for continual, mandatory training and retraining after the attainment of credentials and tenure.

What happens, more frequently than not, is that we assume that everyone who teaches our children has the best interest of the child and the institution at heart. The fact of the matter is that this is not the case.

For me, a paramount problem with all of the research here (and elsewhere) is that it seems disconnected—each study is not tied to the others. Because each study is done in isolation there is not an integration of reality. As relevant as each individual work may be, the conclusions are narrow and are therefore of limited value to a school administrator because 1) schools are not monoliths, and 2) contrary to popular belief, everyone working in a school does not agree on the most effective approach to schooling. Research that continues to treat education, as well as various racial and ethnic groups, as monolithic will have a very narrow influence in the whole scheme of things.

Further, it is my feeling that research conducted without the input of practitioners satisfies the research bureaucracy, but does little else. All of the research presented here is extremely valuable. The case-study approach is solid methodology. What it will invariably lead to, however, is more questions and very few long-term answers.

REFERENCES

Cuban, L. (1992). Managing dilemmas while building professional communities. *Educational Researcher, 21*(1), 4–11.

Kaplan, A. (1964). *The conduct of inquiry–Methodology for behavioral science.* San Francisco: Chandler.

Olsen, L. (1988). *Crossing the schoolhouse border: Immigrant students and the California public schools.* San Francisco: California Tomorrow.

Phelan, P., & Davidson, A. L. Looking across Borders: A Group Investigation of Family, Peers, and School World as Cultural Therapy. In George and Louise Spindler (Eds.), *Cultural Therapy and Culturally Diverse Schools.* (Forthcoming)

About the Contributors

Concha Delgado-Gaitan received her Ph.D. from Stanford University. She is currently Associate Professor in the Division of Education, University of California, Davis. Her fields of research include anthropology of education; in particular, ethnographic research in the areas of family and school relationships, and sociocultural adjustment in immigrant families and communities. She is author of *Literacy for Empowerment: The Role of Parents in Children's Education* and *Crossing Cultural Borders: Education for Immigrant Families in America* (co-authored with H. Trueba). Among her numerous articles are: "School Matters in the Mexican American Home: Socializing Children to Education," *American Educational Research Journal*, 1992, 29(3) and "Involving Parents in the Schools: A Process of Empowerment," *American Journal of Education*, 1991, 100(1).

Kenji Hakuta received his Ph.D. in Experimental Psychology from Harvard University. He is currently a developmental psycholinguist who conducts research on bilingualism and language acquisition. His research themes include first- and second-language acquisition, the relationship between bilingualism and cognitive development, transfer of skills across language in bilinguals, translation skills in bilingual children, and language maintenance and loss in bilingual communities. Much of his research is conducted in school settings, often in collaboration with teachers and school administrators. His languages of primary interest are English, Japanese, and Spanish. He has been on the faculty at Yale University and the University of California at Santa Cruz. He is currently Professor of Education at Stanford University. Hakuta was a Fellow at the Center of Advanced Study in the Behavioral Sciences. His major publications include *Mirror of Language: The Debate on Bilingualism* and over 60 articles and edited books. He has served on various grants, publication, and policy review committees, and he is Chair of the Board of Trustees at the Center for Applied Linguistics in Washington, D.C.

Harry Handler is currently an Adjunct Professor and Assistant Dean, School Relations, U.C.L.A. Graduate School of Education. Prior to joining the Faculty at U.C.L.A., he was Superintendent, Los Angeles Unified School District from 1981–1987. He earned his Ph.D. in Educational Psychology at the University of Southern California. His research interests include the management of large urban districts, the politics of the reform movement, site-based management, and assessment of student performance.

Don Hill is the Director of the Professional Development Center (Stanford Schools/Collaborative), a partnership formed by Stanford University and a small number of school districts to create more effective connections between education research and practice. Before establishing the Center in 1988, he served as a social studies teacher at Aragon High School for 27 years, where he chaired a department that earned national recognition for effective teaching of higher-order thinking skills. He has served in many educational roles including: San Mateo Elementary School Board (9 years), Early Childhood Committee of the National Council of the Social Studies, Governing Board of Stanford Teacher Education Program, Consultant Bay Area Writing Project, Advisory Board of the Center for Research on the Context of Secondary School Teaching, and Director of the Service Learning 2000 Project. Don was educated at Wesleyan University (AB), Harvard Law School, Harvard Graduate School of Education (MAT), and London University.

Ann Locke Davidson is post-doctoral fellow at the Learning Research and Development Center at the University of Pittsburgh in Pennsylvania. She received her M.A. in Anthropology and her Ph.D. in Curriculum & Teacher Education from Stanford University in 1992. Her research interests center on the connections between curriculum, culture, and the construction of identity in relation to schooling. She recently completed her dissertation, which focused on connections between school and classroom processes and students' construction of their ethnic identity in relation to schooling. Davidson is the co-author (with Patricia Phelan and Hanh Cao Yu) of several articles and is currently working on a book with Phelan and Yu that focuses on students' family, peer, and school worlds.

Richard P. Mesa is currently the Superintendent of the Oakland Unified School District in California, which has a student enrollment of 52,000. His primary emphasis is on restructuring the school system and on developing long-term educational and fiscal programs to meet both the changing needs of students and the growing statewide budget problems. He has served as a superintendent in California for 12 years, beginning his career as a high school English teacher, and progressively working in a variety of top-level school administrative positions. He earned his B.A. in English and Physical Education from San Jose State University and his M.A. in Counseling and Guidance from Stanford University. In addition, he has done extensive graduate work toward a Ph.D. at Stanford University. His work at the university level includes 3 years as executive director of a nationwide urban and rural school leadership development project and teaching at Stanford, Santa Clara, San Jose State, and West Virginia universities. He has also served as Chief Deputy to Bill Honig, Superintendent of Public Instruction for the State of California. He has the unique experience of having taught and been an administrator at university, state department and public school levels.

Laurie Olsen is currently the Executive Director of California Tomorrow, a nonprofit organization committed to making racial and ethnic diversity work in California and to building a society that is fair and open for everyone. She also directs California Tomorrow's Education for a Diverse Society Project and is past Director of the Immigrant Students Project. In those capacities she has authored numerous policy, research, and advocacy reports and articles, among them: *Crossing the Schoolhouse Border: Immigrant Students and the California Schools, Bridges: Promising Programs for Immigrant Education,* and *Embracing Diversity: Teacher's Voices in California Schools.* In addition, Ms. Olsen is a sought after speaker and consultant to policymakers, practitioners, and advocates on issues related to immigrant education and the impact of changing demographics on schools. Ms. Olsen is the immediate Chair of the National Coalition of Advocates for Students. Her academic background includes both graduate work in anthropology and an M.A. in Teaching. She worked as a high school teacher in Vermont prior to joining the staff of the Clearinghouse on Women's Studies at the Feminist Press. Her work there included curriculum development, teacher training, and editing materials related to sex-role stereotyping and sex discrimination in education. For the past 15 years, Ms. Olsen has conducted social and policy research and has authored close to 20 publications on issues related to at-risk youth and public education and youth involvement. She also produced a national award-winning documentary video entitled, "Voices from the Classroom." For 3 years she served as Executive Director of Citizens Policy Center/Open Road. Ms. Olsen resides in Oakland, California with her husband and two sons. She is currently enrolled in the Ph.D. program in Social and Cultural Studies in Education at the University of California at Berkeley.

Lucinda Pease-Alvarez received her Ph.D. in Education from Stanford University. She has worked with language minority students as a teacher and researcher, and taught in bilingual and ESL programs at both the primary and secondary levels. As a researcher/teacher, she has collaborated with classroom teachers to develop and investigate ways of enhancing the language and literacy development of language minority students. As a teacher, she has taught courses on literacy development and first- and second-language acquisition. She is currently Assistant Professor of Education at the University of California, Santa Cruz. Dr. Pease-Alvarez's research interests are varied. She has investigated children's uses of oral and written language in home, school, and community settings. In addition, she has documented the pedagogical perspectives and practices of exemplary teachers who work with multiethnic populations. Her most recent research focuses on the role a variety of social factors play in language maintenance and loss in bilingual communities. She is a recent recipient of a National Academy of Education Spencer Fellowship.

Patricia Phelan is Associate Professor of Education at the University of Washington at Bothell. Dr. Phelan received her M.A. in Anthropology (1978) and her Ph.D. in Anthropology of Education from Stanford University in 1981. Since that time she has been a faculty member at the Medical Anthropology Program at the University of California at San Francisco and at Stanford University. This book and a number of articles co-authored with Ann Locke Davidson and Hanh Cao Yu result from Dr. Phelan's work as a Senior Research Scholar at the Center for Research on the Context of Secondary School Teaching at Stanford University from 1989 to 1992. Dr. Phelan's research interests include the relationship between students' contexts and experiences and their engagement in educational settings, school and classroom features that impact culturally diverse student populations, and mental health issues of children and youth.

Reba Page studied history at Washington University (B.A.), history and literature at Johns Hopkins University (M.L.A.), and curriculum and educational policy studies at the University of Wisconsin at Madison (Ph.D.). She taught high school English, history, and special education classes for about a decade. She now teaches and writes about curriculum theory, interpretive research methods, and the sociocultural foundations of education at the University of California at Riverside. She is the author of *Lower-Track Classrooms: A Curricular and Cultural Perspective* (New York: Teachers College Press), U.S. editor of the *Journal of Curriculum Studies*, and, with Linda Valli, co-editor of *Curriculum Differentiation: Interpretive Studies in U.S. Secondary Schools* (Albany: SUNY Press). She plans next to be schooled in science education.

Arlando Smith currently serves as principal at Gunderson High School in the San Jose Unified School District in San Jose, California. He is a product of urban schools, having received his elementary and secondary education in Los Angeles Unified School District. He attended California State University at Fullerton as both an undergraduate and graduate student. He has extensive experience working in public schools, where he has taught and coached students while serving in other capacities such as department chairman and in curriculum development. His vision for schools has been shaped by his observations while attending schools, speaking and listening to parents and other educators, listening carefully to what students want in school, and researching how students learn and the best possible environment for learning to take place. The most essential part of Mr. Smith's vision is that we keep our focus on the fact that schools are human institutions populated by people of all ages from all walks of life. With this in mind, he feels we should be driven by human needs, concerns, and agendas when we talk about schools. His view is that only when we see schools through the imperfect eyes of a human being do we begin to develop schools that are patient, tolerant, understanding, and flexible. Simultaneously, human beings must be driven to reach higher, improve, and work to be the best we can possibly be.

George Spindler came to Stanford University in 1950 as a member of an interdisciplinary research team doing case studies of teachers, administrators, and schools in the San Francisco Bay region. He stayed in a joint appointment in Anthropology and Education and although he took early retirement in 1978, he has maintained an active role in both the Department of Anthropology and the School of Education. He received his M.S. from the University of Wisconsin at Madison, and his Ph.D. from the University of California at Los Angeles. Both degrees were interdisciplinary, in cultural anthropology, sociology, and psychology. His research and publications have ranged broadly over the military, American culture, cultural transmission, Native-American cultures, Germany, comparative studies of schools in Germany and the U.S., and psychological aspects of personal adaptation to cultural change and urbanization. He and Louise Spindler have collaborated on most of their research and publications. Their latest book-length publication is *The American Cultural Dialogue and Its Transmission* (1990). Volume 17, 1992, of *The Psychoanalytic Study of Society* is dedicated to reviews of their work and original articles related to their work.

Louise Spindler is a pioneer in the study of male-female differences in adaptation to cultural change and has published extensively both alone and with George Spindler. She received her M.A. and her Ph.D. (1956) at Stanford University. She holds a lectureship in Anthropology and Education at Stanford. She developed an autobiographical and case approach in her field research with the Menominee Indians of Wisconsin; the Blood Indians of Alberta, Canada; the Mistassini Cree of Quebec; and in Germany and Wisconsin, in schools in adaptation to changing cultures and modernization. Her most recent publication on gender differences in adaptation to sociocultural change is "Male and Female in Four Changing Cultures," in *Personality and the Cultural Construction of Society* (1990), edited by D. Jordan and M. Swartz. She is author of the widely used textbook, *Cultural Change and Modernization* (1984). With George Spindler she co-edits the well-known *Case Studies in Cultural Anthropology*.

Carola E. Suarez-Orozco, Ph.D. candidate, has been educated at the University of California at Berkeley and the California School of Professional Psychology at San Diego. She has also completed a Clinical Internship in Psychology in the Department of Psychiatry at the University of California at San Diego. Ms. Suarez-Orozco is currently writing her Ph.D. dissertation on Familism in Mexican, Mexican-immigrant, Mexican-American, and non-Hispanic whites. She is also co-author of a book on the cultural psychology of Latino youths (with Marcelo M. Suarez-Orozco). Her publications have appeared in English, Spanish, and French. Most recently, Carola has been invited to enroll in the doctoral program in Immigrant Psychology at the Ecole des Hautes Etudes in Sciences Sociales in Paris.

Marcelo M. Suarez-Orozco is a Fellow at the Center for Advanced Study in the Behavioral Sciences at Stanford and Associate Professor of Anthropology at the University of California at San Diego. Marcelo Suarez-Orozco was educated in public schools in Latin America and at the University of California at Berkeley. He has taught at the University of California at Santa Cruz, the University of California at Santa Barbara, and the Catholic University of Leuven in Belgium. His essays have appeared in journals and books published in the U.S., Europe, and Latin America. He is author of *Central American Refugees and U.S. High Schools: A Psychosocial Study of Motivation and Achievement* (Stanford University Press, 1989); *Status Inequality: The Self in Culture* with George A. De Vos (Sage Publications, 1990), and *Antropología psicoanalítica* (Barcelona: Hogar del Libro).

Henry T. Trueba, Dean of the School of Education at the University of Wisconsin at Madison, was born in Mexico City and arrived in the U.S. in 1961, where he took an M.A. in Theology from the Jesuit Woodstock College, an M.A. in Anthropology from Stanford, and a Ph.D. in Anthropology from the University of Pittsburgh. He worked among the Mayan Indians of Chiapas, and the Nahuat Indians of Puebla, in Mexico. He served as editor of the *Anthropology and Education Quarterly* (1988–1991) and on editorial boards of many other professional journals. Among the many honors and awards he has received are the following: Distinguished Scholarship Award for Research on Linguistic Minorities from the American Educational Research Association (1986), Outstanding Hispanic Education Award from the American Educational Research Association (1987), Special Award for Distinguished Research on Bilingual Education from the National Association for Bilingual Education (1990), and, finally, he was made a member of the Wisconsin Academy of Sciences, Arts, and Letters in Madison, Wisconsin (1991). Some of his recent books include the following: *Raising Silent Voices: Educating Linguistic Minorities for the 21st Century* (Harper & Row) and co-edited (with G. and L. Spindler) *What do Anthropologists Have to Say about Dropouts?* (Falmer Press). In 1990, he co-authored (with L. Jacobs and E. Kirton) *Cultural Conflict and Adaptation: The Case of the Hmong Children in American Society* (Falmer Press). In 1991, he co-authored (with C. Delgado-Gaitan) *Crossing Cultural Borders: Education for Immigrant Families in America* (Falmer Press). He has currently in press (to be published by Falmer Press) three additional volumes: *Myth or Reality: Adaptative Strategies of Asian Americans in California* (co-authored with L. Cheng and K. Ima), *Language, Culture and the Teaching of Spanish for Spanish-Speaking: Towards an Integration of Theory and Practice* (with B. Merino and F. Samaniego), and *Healing Multicultural America: Mexican Immigrants Rise to Power in Rural California* (with Rodriquez, Zou, and Cintron). He has also published many journal articles and book chapters related to the role of language and culture in the acquisition of knowledge.

Hanh Cao Yu, a Vietnamese immigrant, is a doctoral candidate at the Stanford University School of Education in Administration and Policy Analysis. Currently, she is engaged in her dissertation which focuses on the ways in which Vietnamese immigrant student culture interacts with high school culture in response to specific school programs and policies. This work is an extension of an earlier collaboration with Patricia Phelan and Ann Locke Davidson. Ms. Yu received her Bachelor of Science in Business Administration at the University of Southern California and has co-authored several articles with Phelan and Davidson on family, peer, and school factors which impact ethnically diverse youth in school and classroom settings.

INDEX

Brown, C. G., 155
Buckley, T., 125

California
Assembly Bill 322 and, 145–146
demographic revolution in, 233–234, 238
Senate Bill 997 and, 155
Cao, H. T., 5, 140, 224–225
Carpinteria, Calif., 19–20, 147–154, 231–232
Carter, T. P., 133
Cazden, C., 14
Chang, H. N., 155
Chicano Student Organization (MECHA), 153
Chung, C. H., 23n
Cider, M., 54
Clark, R., 128, 131
Clark, R. M., 54
Clasen, D. R., 54
Clement, D., 54
Cochran, M., 141–142, 146–147
Cohen, D. K., 12, 23n
Cole, M., 23n
Coleman, J. S., 54
Collier, John, Jr., 49n
Collier, Malcolm, 49n
Comer, J. P., 141
Comite de Padres Latinos/Committee for Latino Parents (COPLA), 147–154
Communities, 20, 205–206, 218, 236, 238.
See also specific communities
of bilingual children, 89, 92–94, 97–104
curriculum and, 167, 174–175, 180–181
in Eastside study, 92–94, 97–98
family-school relationships and, 139–142, 144, 147–49, 156, 206
Hispanic cultural psychology and, 133
language and, 205, 208
and Multiple Worlds study, 65–67, 69–70
Conant, James B., 12–13
Cook-Gumperz, J., 205
Cortes, D., 110–111, 116
Crawford, J., 98
Cremin, Lawrence A., 8–9, 12, 142–143
Cross-cultural comparative reflective interviewing (CCCRI), 30–36
Cuban, L., 216–217
Cuban Americans, 18, 108–110, 116, 131

Cubberly, Ellwood P., 12
Cultural diversity
conflict and, 195–211
demographics of, 1
history of, 1–2, 8–16
interactional difficulties in classroom generated by, 17
prevalence of, 1
relationship between democratic society and, 211
as source of strength and richness, 22
Cultural pluralism ideals, 9–10, 13–16
Cultural therapy, 17, 21, 28–30, 36, 44–46, 197, 206, 212n, 228–229, 237, 241
adaptations and, 48
advocacy and, 211
definitions of, 28–29, 48, 203
essential features of, 48–49
focus of, 29
goals of, 29
how it can help, 203–204
premises embedded in, 204
and relationship between self and instrumental competence, 45–46
in Remstal, 44
Culture
definition of, 201
neutrality of, 228
processes of, 27–28
Cummins, J., 99, 149, 211
Curriculum, 64, 217, 230
active reading and creativity in, 186–188
adaptive, 163, 167–168, 176, 179–180
ambiguities in, 168–173
big picture of, 162–165
bilingualism and, 99–100
as commonsensical, 180, 182, 185–186, 191–192
and conceptions of cultural diversity, 4, 11
and differences in organizational milieux, 173–176
Hispanic cultural psychology and, 135
inconsistencies in, 169–171
intertwining of culture and, 163
order in, 171–173
patient practice in, 184
question-making formula in, 187–188
read-and-recall innovation in, 176–177
reverse images and, 182–189